C000175746

STORIES FROM LANGLEY

STORIES FROM LANGLEY

A Glimpse inside the CIA

Edited and with an introduction by **Edward Mickolus**

Potomac Books

An imprint of the University of Nebraska Press

© 2014 by the Board of Regents of the University of Nebraska

Disclaimer: CIA's Publications Review Board has reviewed the manuscript for this book to assist the authors in eliminating classified information, and poses no security objection to its publication. This review, however, should not be construed as an official release of information, confirmation of its accuracy, or an endorsement of the authors' views.

All rights reserved. Potomac Books is an imprint of the University of Nebraska Press.
Manufactured in the United States of America.

Library of Congress Cataloging-in-Publication Data

Stories from Langley: a glimpse inside the CIA / edited and with an introduction by Edward Mickolus.
pages   cm
ISBN 978-1-61234-688-5 (cloth: alk. paper)—
ISBN 978-1-61234-689-2 (pdf)
1. United States. Central Intelligence Agency—Officials and employees—Biography—Anecdotes. 2. United States. Central Intelligence Agency—History—Anecdotes. 3. Intelligence officers—United States—Biography—Anecdotes. 4. Spies—United States—Biography—Anecdotes. 5. Intelligence service—United States—Anecdotes. I. Mickolus, Edward F., editor of compilation.
JK468.I6S755 2014
327.12730092'2—dc23
2014020677

Set in Lyon by L. Auten.

CONTENTS

A Hero's Story

A Word from Our Predecessors

And from the Next Generation

INTRODUCTION

D uring the three years in the mid-2000s during which I served as a recruiter for the Central Intelligence Agency, I was often asked by would-be applicants, "Okay, I sort of get what I'd be doing. But what would I have to show for a career?" The answer for those considering a life in the National Clandestine Service (NCS), one of the four directorates of the CIA, was easy: just read the memoirs of such heroes as Allen Dulles, Richard Helms, William Colby, Gary Schroen, Richard Holm, Duane Clarridge, David Phillips, James Olson, Floyd Paseman, and countless others. In those pages, aspiring operations officers, collection management officers, staff operations officers, and targeters could learn of the multitude of experiences available to those who collect secret intelligence overseas, conduct counterintelligence investigations, and run covert action programs. But there was no easy answer for those considering a career as an analyst, support officer, tech officer, or a myriad of other roles critical to the Directorate of Support (DS) or the Directorate of Science and Technology (DS&T). There have been a handful of books about how to run the Directorate of Intelligence (DI), most notably by former Deputy Director of Intelligence R. Jack Smith and former Secretary of Defense Robert Gates (himself a former DDI), but nothing on what a more typical career looks like.

I could tell them about my career, which included serving in analytical, operational, management, and staff positions in all four directorates of the Central Intelligence Agency for thirty-three years and involving high-profile, complex, and diverse functions and disciplines. My work included being the CIA's first full-time analyst on international terrorism; analyzing African political, economic, social, military, and leadership issues; writing political-psychological assessments of world leaders; traveling to a score of countries in Europe, Latin America, Africa, Asia, and the Middle East; managing collection, counterintelligence, and covert action programs against terrorists, drug traffickers, weapons prolifera-tors, and hostile espionage services; lauding the achievements of America's silent heroes in the internal newsletter; designing major cross-directorate programs and CIA-wide events; testify-ing on the Hill; and recruiting, mentoring, and teaching scores of the CIA's next generation of leaders. While this sounds like a wide-ranging career, it's not uncommon at the agency. But how could I get potential applicants to understand that? It didn't seem enough simply asking them to take my word for it.

I raised this issue with a lunch partner, a brilliant twenty-four-year-old chemist already on the fast track in the DI. She suggested that while no current analyst would have the time or inclination to write a three-hundred-page manuscript—who wants to keep writing more after a hard day of putting together President's Daily Briefs?—I might be able to ask friends from my generation to con-tribute a few pages. She, in turn, could poll her newly arriving friends about what they are experiencing—things such as level of responsibility even at a comparatively tender age, depth of train-ing, and so on. Getting their input would make the collection more relevant to today's Generation Y members looking for something challenging and worthy of their abilities.

So I sent out the following note via several agency and intelli-gence community listservs and newsletters:

Your Help is Needed on DI-DS Mini-Memoirs Book Projects

I've frequently been asked while recruiting for the Agency "What's it like to work there? What will I do?" When these issues are raised by would-be NCS officers, I can easily point them to a truckload of DO memoirs. But there's nothing comparable to that for the DI or

DS-DA. There are some excellent how-to-do-analysis books (e.g., Heuer; Bruce & George; Westerfield's *Studies in Intelligence* compilation), but no true memoirs (Gates's *From the Shadows* is more on how to be a DCI rather than what he did as an analyst). There are some from the DS, but those few do not give the reader an appreciation of the breadth of opportunities available in the Directorate, much less the Agency and the Intelligence Community as a whole. Alas, few of us have the time to write a 300-page memoir. But many of us have great war stories that can be told on the unclassified level for, say, 5–10 pages. (So I've discovered in putting together the separate Agency humor book. Thanks to everyone who has contributed and for those who haven't—there's still time!) So a currently serving analyst and I are compiling a collection of circa 25-30 mini-memoirs that will serve as a book that would-be DI analysts can read before applying. I'm separately compiling the same type of book for would-be Support officers. Contributors don't have to have had a career solely or even preponderantly in one of those Directorates. We're just looking for short essays that can cover such things as:

1. the coolest thing you ever did as a member of the Directorate

2. the breadth of jobs you held in your Agency career that involved DI and/or DS skills

3. positions you held or experiences you had that were radically different from what you expected based on your first DI and/or DS position, but that used the skills you had and/or developed within the Agency

I've asked the current Directors of Intelligence and Support, respectively, for introductions (and, perhaps, their mini-memoirs as well). Several publishing houses have expressed interest in these projects.

So, here's the formal plea to you. You have had a great career, and have great experiences that you can share. Could you provide a 5-10 page piece by September 30, 2009 (the end of the fiscal year has a nice ring to it)? I'd be delighted to have you participate in one or both of these projects . . .

The response was heartening. Many former and current officers came forward to praise the idea, still others to suggest colleagues who had great stories, and a few others who actually wrote something. Contributors came from all levels of the agency. Some had served as leaders of the Directorates of Intelligence and Support, some at even more senior levels of the agency. Others had toiled in several other agency directorates and other federal agencies. Still others were internationally renowned experts in their substantive fields. Some had invented pathbreaking methods of analysis. Others had shown rare personal and physical courage under extreme stress. Still others were at the beginning or middle of their careers, wondering how their experiences would one day stack up to those described herein.

This has been a labor of love for the many contributors to this edition. Many who had left the agency decades earlier wrote back to offer their memories and best wishes for those who might follow in their footsteps. Many had to beg off because they remained under cover—yes, some analysts, techs, and support team members are covert—or the topics on which they wrote still remain too sensitive to talk about in public. Others modestly wondered whether their stories were compelling enough to merit inclusion (they were).

You hold in your hands the final result of our work. It has been written, as is most everything else in the agency, by a committee of individuals working together on what they love. One particularly moving note read: "I cannot thank you enough for giving me this opportunity . . . having reflected back on my career more than a decade after it ended made me fully realize how very blessed I was, and it will be wonderful, once you have security clearance for all our pieces, to be able to share it with family and friends." This is a place where people truly love to work, and it shows in their writing.

In addition to the contributors, I'd like to thank the many agency officers, those currently serving as well as alumni, who provided leads to authors, ideas for articles, and overall best wishes. Alas, cover and personal security considerations prevent me from naming them, but they know who they are, and the country will always be in their debt.

My answer to the applicants? Look around at all of the opportunities you have in the public and private sector. But at the end of your career, would anyone want to read your memoirs? Thanks for reading those contained in this book.

ABBREVIATIONS

ACIS	Arms Control Intelligence Staff
ADCI	Associate Director of Central Intelligence
AIS	Agency Information Staff
CAP	Career Analyst Program
CD	Clearance Division
CEQ	Council on Environmental Quality
CIA	Central Intelligence Agency
CIO	Central Imagery Office
CIRA	Central Intelligence Retirees' Association
CO	Commanding Officer
COMIREX	Committee on Imagery Requirements and Exploitation
COS	Chief of Station
CSI	Center for the Study of Intelligence
CT	Career Trainee; or Career Training Program
CTC	Counterterrorist Center (separate from the NCTC)
DA	Directorate of Administration
DAO	Defense Attaché Office
DCI	Director of Central Intelligence
DDI	Deputy Director of Intelligence
DEFSMAC	Defense Special Missile and Astronautics Center
DI	Directorate of Intelligence
DIA	Defense Intelligence Agency
DNI	Director of National Intelligence
DO	Directorate of Operations
DP	Directorate of Plans
DS	Directorate of Support

DS&T	Directorate of Science and Technology
ERAC	Environment and Resource Analysis Center
FBIS	Foreign Broadcast Information Service
FE	Far East Division
FMSAC	Foreign Missile and Space Analysis Center
FRUS	Foreign Relations of the United States (series title)
G2	Dirección General de Inteligencia (the state intelligence agency of Cuba)
GIS	Geographic Information Systems
GOSPLAN	Soviet Economic Planning Committee
HRP	Historical Review Panel
ICBM	Intercontinental Ballistic Missile
IG	Inspector General
INF	Intermediate-Range Nuclear Forces
IRBM	Intermediate-Range Ballistic Missile
JCS	Joint Chiefs of Staff
JOTP	Junior Officer Training Program
KGB	USSR intelligence organization (1954–91)
LAMM	Land Armaments and Manpower Model
LIMS	Logistics Integrated Management System
MST	Mobile Search Team
NATO	North Atlantic Treaty Organization
NCS	National Clandestine Service
NCTC	National Counterterrorism Center
NGA	National Geospatial-Intelligence Agency
NIC	National Intelligence Council
NIE	National Intelligence Estimates
NIMA	National Imagery and Mapping Agency
NPC	Nonproliferation Center
NPIC	National Photographic Interpretation Center
NSA	National Security Agency
NSC	National Security Council
OB	Order of Battle
OCG	Office of General Counsel
OCI	Office of Current Intelligence

ODCI	Office of the Director of Central Intelligence
OER	Office of Economic Research
OGI	Office of Global Issues
OIA	Office of Imagery Analysis
OIG	Office of Inspector General
OIM	Office of Information Management
OIS	Office of Intelligence Support
OMS	Office of Medical Services
ONI	Office of Naval Intelligence
OPA	Office of Public Affairs
OPEC	Organization of the Petroleum Exporting Countries
OREA	Office of Russian and Eurasian Affairs
ORR	Office of Research and Reports
OSD/NA	Office of the Secretary of Defense/Net Assessment
OSI	Office of Scientific Intelligence
OSR	Office of Strategic Research
OSS	Office of Strategic Services
OSSB	Overseas Security Support Branch
PCS	Permanent Change of Station
PDB	President's Daily Brief
RI	Records Integration
SACEUR	Supreme Allied Commander Europe
SAD	Special Activities Division
SAFE	Support to the Analysts' File Environment
SALT	Strategic Arms Limitations Talks
SCIF	Sensitive Compartmented Information Facility
SDI	Strategic Defense Initiative
SIO	Senior Intelligence Officer
SIS	Senior Intelligence Service
SOVA	Office of Soviet Analysis
START	Strategic Arms Reduction Treaty
TDY	Temporary Duty Assignments
TF	Theater Forces
TO&E	Table of Organization and Equipment
TSD	Technical Services Division

UNSCOM	United Nations Special Commission
USAID	U.S. Agency for International Development
USSOCOM	U.S. Special Operations Command
USSS	U.S. Secret Service
WINPAC	Office of Weapons Intelligence, Nonproliferation, and Arms Control
WMD	Weapons of Mass Destruction

STORIES FROM LANGLEY

ONE

Speaking Truth to Power

CIA Intelligence Analysts

Getting In

Why Join the Directorate of Intelligence?

Careers in Intelligence Analysis

VOLKO F. RUHNKE

The public retrospectives over the past several years on the failure to warn of the September 11, 2001, terrorist attacks and the mistaken assessments of Saddam Hussein's weapons of mass destruction programs have put the tradecraft of the intelligence analyst under the microscope. The examinations of pre–September 11 analysis spoke of the importance of analysts "connecting the dots" and guarding against "failures of imagination" while the Iraq weapons of mass destruction (WMD) postmortem seemed to warn against straining too hard to imagine connections between dots that do not really connect at all. So what have we learned that all can agree on? First, we know that U.S. (and allied) intelligence analysis clearly could have been more competent. There is no doubt that analysis failed in these cases, with serious consequences. Thus, secondly, intelligence analysis is worth the investment to make it better.

How has it been improved? We have moved resources, reorganized, and strengthened connections across the intelligence community—as the country has done in response to past intelligence failures. But will those rearrangements be decisive? What is the element on which success or failure hangs?

I assert that the answer is, in a word, talent. Will the intelligence community attract to its ranks the talent it needs to succeed? For intelligence analysis, that talent includes the ability to think strategically: the dynamic kind of analysis that realizes that what you are studying is studying you back—and reacting!

This kind of analysis includes the tenacity to squeeze the most understanding you can out of fragmentary information; unlike a commercial venture, intelligence analysis cannot invest in just the most profitable areas but must work on even the toughest and least rewarding problems when national security or the national interest demand it. Even when intelligence collectors are not finding much information, or the information is ambiguous, the intelligence analyst remains on the hook to make a call, to be as helpful and unambiguous as possible.

This kind of analysis also includes the knack for asking the right questions. As policy consumers have told us, a good analyst answers their questions, but a great analyst answers the questions that they should have asked but did not. Classic intelligence analysis divides into policy support (answering the questions coming in the door, no matter how tough) and strategic warning (looking ahead at those difficulties or opportunities not yet on the policymakers' radar).

Finally, this kind of analysis includes the disposition to walk the fine line between policy relevance and policy prescription.

The Ministry of Bad News

One of my favorite professors in the Master of Science in Foreign Service (MSFS) program at Georgetown—who had had a long career in foreign affairs and was serving in a senior policy post downtown at the time—told our seminar the following story. Working in an embassy, he had become close to the host country's president. One day on the golf course, the president asked his opinion of the makeup of his cabinet. The professor responded that he was impressed with how the organization of the cabinet included ministers covering all relevant issues of national policy and was filled with intelligent individuals. There was only one position in the cabinet missing, said the professor to the president: a minister of bad news.

My professor was commenting on the age-old tendency in government (and other enterprises, for that matter) of those individuals in charge of an area of endeavor to tell their boss that things are going fine. Policymakers tend to be optimistic about their own policies—how else could they sell them to an interagency principals committee? So it is not a bad idea to have someone who is truly an expert watching the policy-relevant issues for anything that may be headed off the rails, and whose job it is to bring such information forward. Intelligence analysts—policy-neutral experts on policy-relevant matters—often find themselves playing that role.

So what kind of mindset toward international affairs might make you someone who would *thrive* in that role? Do you believe you can offer the right answers to today's controversial foreign or national security policy questions? Or are you not so sure but fascinated by the strengths and weaknesses of the opposing positions? Well, if it is the former, intelligence analysis might not actually be the best career for you.

If the latter, I am with you. As a new MSFS student in 1984, I experienced something that I called "intellectual vertigo"—I had just arrived from an undergraduate program in international relations elsewhere that, I was soon to realize, had spoon-fed me from only one end of the political spectrum. There I was in Washington with professors who had served in administrations from one side or the other, in power and out of power, challenging me to test the opposite case. In the MSFS program I learned that I might not have the right answer. And so I dedicated myself not to pushing one side of the policy argument but to elevating the level of policy debate, and I found the right career. The most useful posture for the intelligence analyst is as the policymaker's referent, adviser, and coach but—though often a deliverer of bad news— never a critic or a cheerleader.

Follow Your Bliss

Naturally, the success of U.S. intelligence analysis will depend not only on mindset, knack, or raw analytic talent but also on substantive expertise. Effective intelligence analysis often requires getting under the skin of an adversary. So immersion in one's topic is at least a huge plus, if not essential.

7

Such immersion requires the investment of time, typically before one's career even begins. An MSFS student once asked me: What topics should I invest in? What expertise is the intelligence community looking for? My first answer probably was unsurprising in ticking off the areas of key U.S. national security and foreign policy concerns: terrorism, the Middle East, WMD, China, and so on. Sure, the community has a hiring focus on such topics. You could probably further refine the complete list as well as I could.

But what may surprise some is that analytic offices are looking for and hiring expertise well off that beaten track. Global coverage remains an important objective, and, as I write, most of the CIA's regionally and functionally organized analytic offices are interviewing and hiring. My own group seeks Middle East and terrorism specialists, but it seeks in its recruiting to leaven that expertise with a diversity of perspectives. And, in any event, the Middle East–based terrorist threats we follow are global in nature, as are our counterterrorist partnerships, so a mix of global expertise is needed.

My second answer to the MSFS student was to follow her bliss—to get deep into the international affairs topic that really grabbed her, whether it was Iranian diplomacy, South American economies, or new European institutions. Her best chance of impressing an interviewer would be to show the depth of her investment as proof not only of her expertise but also her passion for the topic. Analytic managers know that it is such passion—and not pay incentives—that at the end of the day fuels excellence in intelligence analysis, so her interviewers would be looking for this passion in her.

In addition, although the intelligence community recognizes the criticality of and nurtures substantive depth in its analysts, for better or worse it must also be ready to shift its analytic resources in reaction to world events and its consumers' interests. The imperative for any analytic directorate to be both deep and agile means that opportunities for substantive mobility for individual careerists will remain legion. I began my career working on Soviet military issues (the "big fight" of the day) and am now helping to lead analysis of terrorism, and I am not atypical.

Analytic managers know that they frequently will have to ask experts on one topic to "read in" on others, so the demonstrated ability to dig not only *deeply* but also *quickly* is a sought-after skill. If you are interviewing for a job as an intelligence analyst, show your energy for research and your creativity in finding the reliable source. Again, the intelligence community works on many questions whose answers are not only obscure but also on which adversaries are actively working to thwart the search.

The Broader President's Daily Briefing

I will not go into the advantages or disadvantages of analytic careers in this or that agency here. Most if not all agencies are building up their analytic services in response to an integrated approach to the threat of terrorism and the mandate—for example, from the WMD Commission, to ensure that senior policymakers receive intelligence analysis from all agencies that have expertise and views relevant to a given issue. Toward those objectives, the career opportunities for analysts are becoming broader across agencies, and the ability to move among analytic services is growing.

The creation of a director of national intelligence (DNI) and the National Counterterrorism Center (NCTC) are cases in point. The Office of the Director of National Intelligence is encouraging and adding incentives for joint or "purple" tours—meaning service outside one's own agency, particularly in organizations such as the NCTC that integrate work across the intelligence community and thus rely principally on analysts on detail from elsewhere. The NCTC is in the process of standing up its own career service as well and presents an excellent opportunity to help shape a new enterprise in the war on terror as that enterprise gets rolling.

In the past, each agency's analysts served their own dedicated customer sets almost exclusively—the CIA, the president, the Department of Defense, the Defense Intelligence Agency, and so on. Today, many agencies write for the President's Daily Briefing, which means not only that a broader group of intelligence analysts can reach the most senior audiences but also that their work must "meet threshold"—that is, pass through the same fine-toothed quality control process managed under the Office of the Director of National Intelligence to ensure that the analytic tradecraft is sound and the material is of sufficient import.

How does such quality control work mechanically? In the intelligence analytic profession, we put a great deal of sweat, blood, and tears into a process of coordination and review. Coordination is the lateral check on an individual analyst's work: every other analyst in an agency—and, increasingly, in the entire intelligence community or in outside institutions as well—with some substantive stake in an article or paper gets a chance to weigh in on it. That way, we have milked the tension among analytic perspectives for value and done what we can to provide a 360-degree look at any topic. Review is the vertical check; managers, editors, and others up the line act as reader advocates to ensure that the product stands up and hits the mark.

At the end of this process, an individual's work becomes a product of the corporate agency or the intelligence community and bears that agency's imprimatur—though possibly at the expense of an individual's pride of authorship. It is a process that can be grueling over months and years, especially when that passion for substance is engaged, when the nature of the mission means that critical issues are at stake in any coordination skirmish, and when there are deadlines to be met. We call it collaboration, but it is not for everyone.

We do it because the mission leaves our analysis, our writing, and our briefing little room for ambiguity, shortcuts, or errors. We are writing for the busiest people in the world, who are reading and already conversant with our source materials, and who are keenly focused on the questions we are addressing because lives and billions of dollars are at stake. U.S. intelligence analysis has never been error free, but it might be enlightening to compare the community's attention to coordination and review to quality control processes in, say, today's news media.

For this reason, if you interview for a position in intelligence analysis, you will notice the interviewer's interest in hearing about your ability to collaborate, to work effectively even with difficult people and even when the pressure is on. The interviewer also is likely to be interested in how hard you have worked to improve your writing and oral presentation skills. He or she will be listening for clarity of thought, economy of words, and precision of language.

Intelligence Analysis and the Global War on Terrorism

Along with the broadened opportunity for the career analyst to support policymaking at its most senior level, intelligence analysis in the global war on terrorism affords a greater role for the analyst than ever before in supporting not only policy but also operations. The old model of analyst-operations interaction in the intelligence community was dominated by the separation of the disciplines, and it limited analysts principally to providing their operations counterparts with collection requirements and feedback on reporting. Intelligence analysis today is shifting to a new model in which the operator—intelligence or military—is becoming as important a consumer as the policymaker, and the analyst is becoming a key asset for the development and support of operations.

Resource Listings of the Central Intelligence Agency

The Central Intelligence Agency was created in 1947 with the signing of the National Security Act by President Harry S Truman. The act also created a director of central intelligence (DCI) to serve as head of the U.S. intelligence community, act as the principal adviser to the president for intelligence matters related to national security, and serve as head of the CIA. The Intelligence Reform and Terrorism Prevention Act of 2004 amended the National Security Act to provide for a director of national intelligence who would assume some of the roles formerly fulfilled by the director of central intelligence, with a separate director of the CIA.

The director of the CIA serves as the head of the CIA and reports to the director of national intelligence. The CIA director's responsibilities include: (1) collecting intelligence through human sources and by other appropriate means, except that he shall have no police, subpoena, or law enforcement powers or internal security functions; (2) correlating and evaluating intelligence related to the national security and providing appropriate dissemination of such intelligence; (3) providing overall direction for and coordination of the collection of national intelligence outside the United States through human sources by elements of the intelligence community authorized to undertake such collection and, in coordination with other departments, agencies, or elements of the U.S. government that are authorized to undertake such collection, ensuring that the most effective use is made of resources and that appropriate account is taken of the risks to the United States and those involved in such collection; and (4) performing such other functions and duties related to intelligence affecting the national security as the president or the DNI may direct. The function of the CIA is to assist its director in carrying out these responsibilities.

To accomplish its mission, the CIA engages in research, development, and the deployment of high-leverage technology for intelligence purposes. As a separate agency, the CIA serves as an independent source of analysis on topics of concern and also works closely with the other organizations in the intelligence community to ensure that the intelligence consumer—whether a Washington policymaker or battlefield commander—receives the best intelligence possible. By emphasizing adaptability in its approach to intelligence collection, the CIA can tailor its support to key intelligence consumers and help them meet their needs as they face the issues of the post–Cold War world.

The CIA offers global employment opportunities in seeking a diversity of people for the important job of keeping America safe. These include Clandestine Service officers to be on the front line of human intelligence, as well as individuals skilled in science, engineering, technology, analysis, foreign languages, and administration for positions in the United States and overseas. Several career paths are available at the CIA.

Analysts are skilled subject matter experts who study and evaluate information from many sources. Information flows in from around the world, including satellite surveillance, foreign newspapers and broadcasts, and human contacts. This information varies widely in reliability, and often it is conflicting or incomplete. The analyst's role is to develop meaningful and usable intelligence assessments from all those sources. Often this is like putting together the pieces of a puzzle, received at different times from different places, to form a picture that is complete enough to comprehend—even when some pieces are still missing. An intelligence analyst pulls together relevant information from all available sources and then analyzes it to produce timely and objective assessments, free of any political bias. This finished intelligence product, which may be in the form of a written report or oral briefing, could very well appear on the desks of the president and his key senior advisers. Each morning, the DNI delivers the President's Daily Briefing, an extremely sensitive intelligence document containing short assessments of current worldwide developments as well as anticipated events that will require the president's attention in the future. The assessment content represents a team effort by analysts across the community.

The National Clandestine Service (NCS) is the frontline source of clandestine information on critical international developments, from terrorism and WMD to military and political issues. The mission requires NCS officers to live and work overseas, making a true commitment to the CIA. This is more than just a job—it is a way of life that challenges the deepest resources of personal intelligence, self-reliance, and responsibility. Operations officers work with collection management officers to determine what kind of assets to seek and what information is needed. Living under cover, many operations officers almost must work at a "day" job, a necessary challenge that is part of their clandestine role. Staff operations officers contribute to the NCS mission primarily from the CIA's Washington-area headquarters, providing fast-paced research and case management in support of colleagues overseas. This includes monitoring counterintelligence issues and providing support needed to deal with foreign contacts in the field. Staff operations officers must be knowledgeable on both operational tradecraft and international issues in order to enhance their interaction with field-based officers.

The NCS has a program for recent college graduates, the Professional Trainee Program, after which trainees may be considered for the Clandestine Service Training Program. The CIA also has a comprehensive program to foster the acquisition and maintenance of foreign language skills. The Central Intelligence Language Institute uses native speakers and the latest instructional technology to teach sixteen languages. All employees who attain tested levels of language expertise through full-time training, part-time classes, or self-study are eligible for monetary incentives. (For a description of each proficiency level, go to www.govtilr.org and consult the "Unabridged Version of the Interagency Language Roundtable Scale.") New employees who already possess excellent language skills may be eligible for a significant hiring bonus. The CIA has two language incentive systems: the Corporate Language Hiring Bonus Program—under which new employees can earn up to thirty-five thousand dollars in hiring bonuses for superior language skills—and the Corporate Language Program.

The CIA also hires qualified scientists, engineers, and technology specialists, as well as support staff for a range of positions. The Graduate Studies Program may also be of special interest. The program looks for bright graduate students who are focusing on international affairs, languages, economics, geography, cartography, physical sciences, and engineering. Other majors may be accepted on a case-by-case basis. Students selected for this program should be entering either their first or second year of graduate studies following this assignment. Selected students will become acquainted with the work of professional intelligence analysts through active participation in CIA projects with the potential to have selected pieces of their work disseminated throughout the intelligence community. The program allows the CIA to assess students' skills and knowledge as they relate to permanent employment opportunities.

Applicants for positions must be U.S. citizens. The CIA Recruitment and Retention Center does not accept résumés, nor can it return phone calls, emails, or other forms of communication, from U.S. citizens living outside the United States. The CIA recommends submitting your résumé online in response to a specific position. The online résumé submission link is found at the bottom of each position listed on the employment site. Multiple online submissions for a position are unnecessary and slow the processing of your application. If you are contacted about a position, be prepared to undergo a thorough background investigation examining your life history, character, trustworthiness, reliability, and soundness of judgment. The CIA also examines your freedom from conflicting allegiances, potential to be coerced, and willingness and ability to abide by regulations governing the use, handling, and protection of sensitive information. The CIA uses the polygraph to check the veracity of this information. The hiring process also includes a thorough mental and physical medical examination in relation to performing essential job functions. More information about jobs at the CIA is available at www.cia.gov/careers, where you may also submit your résumé online.

The Best Speech I Ever Gave, the Best Thing I Ever Wrote

MARTIN PETERSEN

I have given hundreds of speeches in my career, and I have probably written thousands of reports, memos, and items of intelligence. Hardly unusual. Some were clearly better than others, and many probably sank without a trace. Again, hardly unusual. Of all the documents I produced in over thirty years, I am most proud of two. The first is an address I gave about thirty-five times and always in the same place—in the lobby of the Original Headquarters Building with the newest class of the Sherman Kent School standing on the seal and facing the atrium. I wrote the second document in response to a request from then-DCI George Tenet to accompany his Strategic Intent initiative, and it will not be reproduced here. But together these two works sum up everything I believe about the CIA and the remarkable men and women who do the mission.

Charge to New Analysts

Good morning. I am Marty Petersen. I have held a number of positions in the Directorate of Intelligence (DI) over the years but what I really am is an intelligence analyst, one with almost thirty years' experience now. And you, you are the newest class of the Career Analyst Program. Welcome. I want to take a few minutes to tell you why you are standing where you are, why your education in intelligence starts here.

Look to your left. That is a statue of General William Donovan, to whom we trace our modern roots. The star on the wall represents all the officers of the Office of Strategic Services (OSS) who gave their lives in service to the nation. The book beneath the star lists their names.

Now look to your right. There are eighty-four stars on that wall—more than one for every year of our existence. Those stars commemorate the men and women of this agency who gave their lives in service to our nation. There are analysts on that wall. And those men and women walked through the same doors you walked through and strode across the seal on which you now stand.

There are many markers in many buildings in Washington commemorating many good men and women. But this building, this organization, is different. We labor in the shadows, and even in death many of our colleagues remain unknown, not only to the public, but to all save their families and a few fellow officers.

Your class starts in this place because you are a link to all those that have gone before and will come after. The Career Analyst Program is more about mission, values, and culture than it is about skills. It is about why we exist and the standards we hold ourselves to and that you will be expected to hold yourselves to as well. You have joined a very select group of men and women, and in the weeks ahead you will come to appreciate how unique that group is.

[Holding up copy of President's Daily Brief] This is what the building is all about. It does not look like much. The first few times you read it, you may not be impressed. It looks simple. And it is—if we do it right. But everything here—the case officers in the field, the analysts at their desks, the support people and the clerical people, the collection gadgets—is geared to produce this slim document fifty-two weeks a year for the most important and powerful man in the world and for about a dozen of his closest advisers.

The DI mission—your mission—is to make the complex intelligible: not simple, intelligible. To make our guy smarter than their guy, whether it is across a mahogany conference table or across a battlefield. And you will do that by explaining in this document and others the forces at work on any issue, the other fellow's perspective, and the risks and opportunities in it for the United States.

One of the people I worked with when I started used to say that if he could do anything for a new person it would be to take them to Nevada to see an A-bomb test. Not me. I'd take you to Honolulu where I went to grad school. We'd get lunch at a little seaside café I know. While you are munching your teriyaki burger, I'd have you face the water, and I'd tell you to look to your right at the notch in the mountains. I'd say that is Kolekole Pass, where on December 7, 1941, Japanese zeroes streamed through, passed in front of where we are now, and attacked Ford Island to your left, where the Arizona memorial now sits and which to this day gives up bits and pieces of the sailors and marines still trapped inside. And I'd tell you that that is what happens to a nation that has all the pieces of the puzzle but does not have a Directorate of Intelligence to put them together.

Sadly, sadly, after September eleventh I have to take you to a second island, to ground zero at the tip of Manhattan for a different lesson: someday—God forbid—your very best may not be good enough. If that happens, then you have to steel yourself, critique your own performance, draw the right lessons, and rededicate yourself to the mission, even as the waves of criticism—the merited and unmerited—break over you. We do not have the option of quitting our post, or walking away, or answering back. We serve in silence.

I believe there are those in the world who would do us harm, take our liberty, our livelihood, imperil our children and our families. We are on guard—all of us—as much as the cop on the beat or the soldier at his post. Only we stand it in the dark places of the world. Places where the United States often does not want to be seen, where people the United States does not want to be seen with, hold power. The Central Intelligence Agency is the eyes and ears of the nation, and the Directorate of Intelligence is the voice of the CIA.

I believe knowledge is power, that good policy is rooted in superior knowledge. I believe this agency is often the critical source of that knowledge. I also believe that the United States is a force for good in the world, but how effective we are depends as much on our knowledge as it does on our raw power and intentions.

What we do—what you will be expected to do—is terribly difficult and terribly important. That was true in 1766 when Washington wrote that "there is nothing more necessary than good intelligence to frustrate a designing enemy, and nothing requires greater pains to obtain," and it is, if anything, truer today because the enemies are even more designing, to use Washington's term, and even more powerful. When we get it wrong, American lives can be lost. If we are right but ineffective in getting our message across, the consequences can be the same as getting it wrong.

The language of business is much in vogue, but we are not a business; we are a profession, a profession which you now join—a profession with its own ethics and standards. Part of it is DI tradecraft, about which you will hear much and learn much. But it is more than that. We are a secret intelligence organization in a democracy, and we often work the gray areas—an organization charted by our government to break the laws of other governments. This puts a heavy obligation on us to be honest and ethical in all our dealings with one another, with the consumers of our services, and with the people of the United States.

DI culture emphasizes respect for ideas and people, and for expertise at all levels and in all the professions represented in our directorate: analytical, technical, support, clerical, and managerial. All of us have a shared responsibility in maintaining DI tradecraft and standards. The demands on us all are great. Hours can be long. Flexibility is essential to success here. There is a sense of service and sacrifice and patriotism, although it is not talked about much.

There will be late dinners and missed events in the course of your career. There will be times when it will be hard to read a newspaper or watch the news, perhaps because what they have to say is incorrect, sometimes because what they have to say is too true. These things take a toll on you and on your family.

But there are rewards, too, and none greater than the knowledge that what you do matters. The work is important. You will make a difference. I have seen it time and time again over the course of my career. Time and again the men and women in this building have pointed the way, and in doing so they have made the world a little better, a little safer.

And as you go through your career, I hope you will recall standing in this room on this day. And I hope you come to appreciate the spirit of service, sacrifice, and patriotism that imbues this antechamber and is exercised in the belief captured on the wall behind you: that one pillar of our democracy is a commitment to truth.

Take a moment. Look around with new eyes.

Briefing the President

3

Working with Words and Enjoying the View

JOHN HOLLISTER HEDLEY

What do you do for recreation? What really appeals? If you discover that words and ideas actually are recreational for you, more so than golf or bridge or any other pastime could ever be, then the Directorate of Intelligence of the Central Intelligence Agency might be the place for you. You might be as incredibly lucky as I have been, to be absorbed in a career that—while demanding—does not seem like work at all. And if you find deadlines to be exhilarating, you can be in clover!

It took me a while to find this out about myself, to recognize that working with words and ideas and like-minded people was, professionally, not merely what I did best. It was who I am.

The CIA was not the career I had foreseen. The CIA's offer caught me by surprise, and I came without connections or what I might have considered requisite East Coast credentials. I did not go to a Philips Andover. Never gave a thought to an Ivy League school. (I would later learn that although some do, most don't, and that's not what matters most.) Instead I worked my way through Coffeyville, Kansas, Community Junior College in the 1950s, earning money as a member of the Teamsters' Union, unloading cans from railroad boxcars in one-hundred-degree heat.

For gas money I played trumpet in a dance band and a Dixieland band. In high school I had been a butcher's helper and on Saturday nights corrected freshly inked galley proofs for our town's Sunday newspaper. I spent a year at the University of Kansas, waiting tables in a fraternity, then volunteered for the draft and served two years as an enlisted man in the army. Sent to Berlin as a combat infantryman, I answered an ad in the weekly newspaper of Berlin Command, submitted a writing sample, and was chosen to be one of the newspaper's three editors.

After the army it was back to Kansas to complete an undergraduate degree in journalism. Lacking other plans or career prospects, a master's degree seemed in store. Instead I fell in love, became engaged, and got married in a span of six months. (This is a timeline I did not recommend to my own daughters, of course! That said, celebrating our fiftieth wedding anniversary by renewing our vows testifies to the fact that it worked for my wife and me.)

Marriage took me to Tulsa, Oklahoma, and the University of Tulsa, where my wife completed her degree and I worked in the public relations office writing newspaper stories about the university. From there I became public relations director in the national headquarters of the U.S. Jaycees. But academic interests (and the GI Bill) drew me to a master's degree in history and political science through night classes at Tulsa, and then to doctoral study in political science at the University of Missouri. Earning a PhD there stamped me as a consummate Midwesterner, where in fact I have spent very little of my adult life.

After returning to Tulsa as a college professor, a call came from the CIA. Out of curiosity I had sought out a visiting CIA personnel guy my last year at Missouri. Invited to Washington for interviews I took the opportunity both to gain insight into the CIA and to spin off for some dissertation research. When the agency later called with an offer, I already had signed a contract to teach the following year so I turned them down.

Exactly a year later, a second call came out of the blue repeating the offer. Someone back there evidently liked my mix of credentials: a PhD academic credential emphasizing international relations and comparative government, experience in journalism, overseas time—in Berlin, no less—and military experience. I liked the idea of being immersed in as much information as could be acquired about what was going on in the world. If I said no a second time, there might not be a third offer. So, with an amazingly supportive wife, a toddler, a dachshund, and as much of our possessions as we could cram into our car, I came east on a two-year leave of absence. That was forty-four years ago.

For more than four decades the essence of my CIA adventure has been writing—and rewriting. Reading and reporting. Exchanging ideas and putting ideas into words. Thinking and synthesizing. Writing, editing, the use of words—these are always central to the ultimate objective of informing policy. I was assigned to the Office of Current Intelligence and was enthralled from the beginning. My analytic account included Soviet policy toward Berlin, the bellwether of the Cold War and a city where I had lived and which I had come to love. I could not imagine a better place to begin. And the secretive, classified culture of the CIA struck me not as confining but liberating. As a young professor I had worked into the wee hours most nights on the next day's (or that day's) lectures. Not being able to take work home felt like being on vacation!

Something else that has always appealed to me is the variety of experiences the agency offers. Among other things the CIA gave me regular opportunities at one time and another to work throughout the night, to stay at work well past a reasonable dinner hour, and to come into the office before dawn! But in the process I discovered that working with words can get you around. The agency has seen to it that I revisited Berlin but also got acquainted with Bangkok. I have been to Bali, Belgrade, and Brussels. I have traveled to Morocco and Manila; Munich, Mexico City, and Melbourne; Tokyo and Tel Aviv. I have seen Seoul, Singapore, and Sumatra, the Netherlands and New Zealand. Several times I have been blessed with visits to London, my all-time favorite.

After helping launch and edit a classified newspaper version of the CIA's National Intelligence Daily, I served overseas. Returning to headquarters I became head of the Intelligence Directorate's substantive intelligence exchanges with key allies. I was invited to edit and be a briefer for the most sensitive and selective current-intelligence publication—the President's Daily Brief (the PDB)—and to oversee its production as chief of the Current Support Group.

Before my retirement the agency gave me a salary for starting up a newspaper (the agency's internal *What's News at CIA*, originally published only on paper), for being a college professor again (as CIA Officer in Residence at Georgetown University), and for reading books (as chairman of the Publications Review Board).

The sheer abundance of memories from such widely varying assignments makes it hard to pick a particular work experience to describe. In my mind's eye I still can see the old city in Jerusalem, terraced rice paddies in Bali, minarets in Rabat, and floating villages on the Mekong. But a morning in Washington may say it best. It was the kind of glorious morning that can grace one of Washington's elusive but spectacular spring days. The vice president of the United States hailed me as I walked into his office. "John, it's just too nice out to work in here; let's go outside!" We stepped through French doors onto a small, secluded seating area where two chairs were tucked atop the marvelously ornate old Executive Office Building.

We sat there, George Herbert Walker Bush and I, each with a copy of the president's PDB in our lap. For a time we simply basked in the day, enjoying the breathtaking, close-up view of the White House and the greenness of the sun-splashed lawn stretching from the portico toward the Washington Monument. The cloudless sky was a deep blue, the air balmy. A waiter appeared with fresh-squeezed orange juice and steaming hot coffee and silently disappeared. The vice president and I enjoyed a quiet spell savoring it all, before we began to read and talk.

This of course came early in the day. Next would come a dash back to CIA Headquarters for the crowded feedback meeting. How was the PDB received? Where was the focus? What were the questions? That would be followed by a production meeting. Between those two gatherings in a packed conference room, I would be in the office of Director of Central Intelligence Bill Casey, recounting the morning's briefings. Soon the flood of analysts' words would begin again. It would be another afternoon of choosing candidates for tomorrow's PDB edition, cutting the size of almost every offering to make it shorter, simpler, clearer, more readable. Then into rush hour traffic for more than twenty miles to a different world. How was your day? How was school? Drive the carpool to swim-team practice or help coach soccer. PTA or a vestry meeting. Relax with Johnny Carson. How did it get to be midnight? It's late, but life is good.

Not forgotten was the magic of the moments that morning in the room of the Old Executive Office Building, and the realization that came with it. Here's this kid from a little town in Kansas, sitting with the vice president of the United States, just the two of us, overlooking the White House, chatting about what is going on in the world, and thinking, This is my job. I get paid to do this. It's still hard to believe.

4

Never Boring, Often Meaningful, and Almost Fun

HENRY APPELBAUM

When I graduated from college in 1962, my future was uncertain. A career in law was an obvious option; I had been accepted by several of the nation's top law schools, but during my undergraduate years I had gradually become disenchanted with the prospect of a career in law. I had spent a summer in Spain with the Experiment in International Living. International affairs increasingly captured my interest, but I had not yet made up my mind as to what avenue I should pursue. Diplomacy? Intelligence? Private Industry? Academia? I decided that I wasn't ready to make a firm commitment in any of these directions and I needed some time to think about each of them.

First I had to do military service, so I enlisted and spent six months on active duty at Fort Dix, New Jersey. Military service was eye-opening. Among my fellow six-monthers was a wide assortment of people. I got to know people from many backgrounds, with different ways of looking at the world.

While I was in the army I decided to pursue my interest in foreign affairs by applying to master's degree programs in international public administration. In late summer 1963 I began graduate studies in an innovative program at the Maxwell School of Syracuse University. Our studies began with a semester on campus, followed by a year in India, and concluded with a final semester at Syracuse. I found the teaching at Maxwell to be, on balance, superior to what I had I experienced as an undergraduate at Harvard. The professors were mostly young and energetic. The first semester was marked by the tragic assassination of President Kennedy on 22 November. On a happier note, I met my future wife, Amy, a graduate student in public administration.

My work in India had two components. I did some research under the auspices of the Maxwell School on the China-India war of 1962, and I had an internship of sorts in the U.S. embassy in New Delhi. While the formal program proved valuable in my eventual service in the State Department and CIA, what really affected me personally were my daily experiences in that fascinating country. I was struck not only by the extremes of poverty that people somehow survived, but also by the sheer numbers of people seemingly crammed into every inch of space—even in rural areas—each with his or her own individual story. Amy and I were married in June of 1964 at the home of my Syracuse faculty adviser in New Delhi and we traveled around India and later in Southeast and East Asia.

In 1965, after receiving my master's degree, I accepted a position in New York City in a major bank. This financial institution trained me in Japanese banking, language, and culture, with the intent of stationing me in Japan. At the same time, I continued to pursue a career in the government. I was accepted into the Central Intelligence Agency and the Department of State. I chose diplomacy over intelligence and banking and joined State in 1966.

For six months, before my date of entry into the State Department, I worked in Senator Robert Kennedy's New York office as a staff member. During this brief but very intense experience, I had many interactions with members of the Kennedy family. I did everything from handling personal crises of ordinary citizens who came in off the streets, to overseeing the office interns, to chauffeuring Ethel Kennedy and her children around town. Once, while chauffeuring Senator Kennedy around New York City, I made my one and only attempt to offer him a serious policy recommendation: I urged him to come out against the Vietnam War. The senator had heard it all before and his nonresponse to my somewhat sophomoric remarks consisted of fiddling with the radio dial in search of something more interesting to listen to. He eventually did come out against the war, but not, I suspect, because of anything I said.

In the State Department, my first—and, as it turned out, my only—foreign post was Montevideo, Uruguay, from 1967 to 1969. First-tour officers in those days were usually assigned to rotate through several sections of the embassy. Highlights for me included a stint as acting labor attaché and several months as special assistant to the ambassador, for whom, among other things, I wrote a speech on the then-dismal state of the Uruguayan economy and what needed to be done about it. Our second child was born in Montevideo, a charming if somewhat rundown city.

I received strong kudos from the heads of each section in which I worked. As a result, I snagged a plum position upon my return to Washington as special assistant to the assistant secretary of state for Latin America. Yet I had mixed feelings about the whether the Foreign Service was the best place for me. In the State Department, I had to actively advocate for the official policy of the day, regardless of my own views. Among the key policy issues of the late 1960s was the Vietnam War, which was anathema to me. In 1971, I made the switch to the Central Intelligence Agency.

Life in the CIA

Surprisingly, intelligence work actually provided me more freedom from political pressure than did diplomacy. My fellow intelligence analysts and I were required to provide objective information and analysis that was not skewed by any partisan agenda. An added plus was that the CIA provided opportunities to work in international affairs without having to constantly uproot my family every several years.

The CIA had two major wings, the Directorate of Intelligence (DI), which was responsible for analyzing intelligence information, and the Directorate of Operations (DO), later called the National Clandestine Service, which carried out the kinds of sensitive actions for which the CIA is best known. I was invited to join the agency as a prospective operations officer, but in training it became apparent that I was much better suited for analysis. My previous experience in India led to a decision by the DI to pull me from training early and put me to work immediately, heading the overnight shift of a task force dealing with the Indo-Pakistani War of 1970-71 (which resulted in the founding of the country of Bangladesh). For my work on this task force I received some special recognition, including a modest pay raise. As far as anyone could remember, it was unprecedented for someone still in the probationary two-year trial period to receive such an award.

My next assignment was to be the sole DI analyst working on the then-obscure, low-priority countries of Afghanistan, Bangladesh, and Sri Lanka. The CIA sent me on a three-week trip to visit the countries I was analyzing. I had the opportunity to travel through the immense mountains of southern Afghanistan and over the fabled Khyber Pass to Pakistan.

In 1973 the CIA lent me to the Nixon White House to serve on the National Security Council (NSC) staff—the fiefdom of Henry Kissinger—focusing mainly on the Indian subcontinent and as a backup person on the Middle East. As it happened, I ended up working as much on the Middle East as on South Asia because the Middle East was of much higher priority to the administration. The October 1973 Arab-Israeli War broke out at a time when the main NSC staff specialists on the Middle East happened to be absent, leaving me responsible for analyzing it. In 1974 I was sent to six countries in the Middle East on Air Force Two as an adviser to the advance team for Nixon's final presidential trip abroad. The other people on the trip had little experience or expertise on the region. On our short flights between each stop, I wrote an extremely well-received brief on the current situation in the country we were about to visit. Importantly, it included information on appropriate etiquette and boundaries of acceptable behavior.

My time on the White House staff was both exhilarating and exhausting. The Nixon administration was collapsing. I was in the audience when President Nixon resigned. After Nixon fell, I was relieved to return to the CIA.

I became an editor of various CIA classified and unclassified publications geared toward specific audiences inside and outside the intelligence community. In 1978 I began a two-year stint as an editor of what is arguably the agency's highest-priority publication, the President's Daily Brief (PDB). I then went on to supervise a group of analysts working on Africa and then a group working on part of South America. I took an orientation trip through Central Africa in 1982.

In 1983 I was chosen to be one of two CIA representatives to the American Political Science Association's Congressional Fellowship Program. The CIA's public participation was aimed at improving relations between the legislative branch and the CIA. The heart of that program involved working in congressional offices. I spent a half year each in the offices of Senator Paul Tsongas (D-MA) and Representative Robert Torricelli (D-NJ), both of whom became immersed in foreign affairs through their committee assignments and were eager to have someone with my expertise on their staffs. In Tsongas's office I worked mainly on Central American issues. For Torricelli I worked on a wide range of national security problems, including arms sales and broader international relations, particularly with regard to Latin America.

I returned to the CIA and briefly headed up one of the units that analyzed intelligence on South America. That was the last time I would focus exclusively on one region.

In 1985 I was assigned to the PDB staff as an editor and briefer. This small elite staff was responsible for preparing and hand-delivering the PDB—the CIA's early-morning substantive intelligence report to the president—and orally briefing him on late-breaking events and other developments. In the case of Presidents Reagan and Carter, we did not personally present the PDB. We would brief the national security adviser, and he would incorporate our material into his briefing of the president.

When George H. W. Bush became president in 1989, he was already enthusiastic about the PDB. He had received the publication and the supplementary briefing daily when he was vice president. He had also headed up the CIA in the mid-1970s. Unlike his predecessors, he preferred to be briefed directly by us. He liked to hear from midlevel officials with direct involvement in the analytical process. He had extensive experience in foreign affairs at the senior level. As a result, I often learned as much, if not more, from him as he learned from us. He restricted access to the PDB to a small circle including only the president, vice president, chairman of the Joint Chiefs of Staff, a few cabinet-level advisers with national security responsibilities, and their top aides.

President Bush knew many of the people on whom we reported. In the middle of the briefing, President Bush would sometimes scribble out a personal note to someone mentioned in the PDB. The session was occasionally interrupted by a telephone ringing in his desk drawer. He would open the drawer and answer the phone, and it would be a world leader such as Nelson Mandela, François Mitterrand, or Mikhail Gorbachev. He also regaled us with jokes, anecdotes, and funny accents and urged us to "crank up the CIA humor machine" in our briefs.

In 1987 I was named deputy chief of the PDB staff. My responsibilities expanded to include a range of day-to-day management duties. As deputy chief I had to do even more writing, editing, and rewriting of others' work, often late at night. Every other morning, I got up before 3:00 a.m. and arrived at work around 4:00 a.m. in order to read in on the latest developments and be briefed by the overnight watch staff. The previous night, I would have worked until at least 9:00 p.m. or later. I regularly worked twelve-hour weekdays in addition to several hours each on Saturdays and Sundays.

Several of the recipients of the PDB had some unique characteristics. National Security Adviser and later Defense Secretary Frank Carlucci was typically our first briefing in the morning. He was ready to go at 5:30 a.m., and had we not gotten there in time he would not have waited. Secretary of State George Schultz did not pull his punches. If he disagreed with something, he let us know. He seemed to like our graphics, charts, and economic data. But if we slid him a report that did not interest him, he would slide it back across the desk to us without a word. Schultz was the only one who had us travel with him on domestic trips.

National Security Adviser Brent Scowcroft attended all our presidential briefings during the first Bush administration. He often had his eyes closed, which became a standing joke with the president. But if President Bush asked a question and I didn't happen to know the answer, Scowcroft's eyes would snap open and he would answer the question himself. It was clear that he had been paying close attention all along and he invariably knew what he was talking about. I often briefed Colin Powell on Saturdays after his morning run. He would speed-read the whole PDB, flipping rapidly through the pages, and when he came to a part that he questioned, he would come to a screeching halt and challenge me on it.

Vice President Al Gore was one of our most engaged and responsive recipients, as was his top aide for foreign and defense affairs, Leon Fuerth. Fuerth gave rise to a growth industry at the CIA, namely the production of one-page papers on issues raised by the PDB. Specialists would usually prepare these papers within twenty-four hours and we would edit and deliver them along with the next day's PDB.

Inauguration Day 1993 was one of the most memorable days of my CIA career. That morning, I briefed Senator Gore at his home at about 7:00 a.m. Our briefing was interrupted, and as Gore was hustling off to a preinauguration event, he told me to catch up with him in the afternoon. Then I went to the White House to give President Bush and his national security adviser their last briefing. By this time a snowstorm was raging. DC police were blocking access to the White House, so I had to trudge through the snow. While I was sitting in the Oval Office, Bush was cleaning out his desk. He threw a drawer full of presidential souvenirs in my direction. I then went back to the CIA in the snow to get new updates and finally caught up with the newly inaugurated vice president in midafternoon in a crowded hotel suite downtown. I waited for a couple of hours in the middle of a room full of young aides who were excitedly getting dressed for the inaugural balls. Eventually, Mrs. Gore escorted me to an empty room and offered me coffee or tea. The new vice president came in, exhausted, and sprawled across the bed. Nonetheless he asked me to pick up where I had left off.

In 1994, after nine years on the PDB, my immediate superior, Charles Peters (the long-time chief of the PDB staff), and I were called in by a senior official and were told that while we were doing a great job, it was time to pass this plum assignment on to someone else. We had already been in these jobs far longer than had usually been the case. Agency leaders wanted to make the transition while the PDB was going well. It was also clear that they wanted more diversity on the PDB briefing team. Peters retired from the agency shortly thereafter. From 1994 to 1996 I worked as an analyst on classified material within the DO.

By that time, I had been diagnosed with a mild case of Parkinson's disease. I felt that it was time to leave because the disease was slowly but inexorably progressing. I also did not want to deprive more junior people from job opportunities within the agency by staying too long. I formally retired from the CIA in 1996, only to be hired back immediately on a year-by-year contract.

After my retirement party on a Friday, I returned the following Monday to work at the CIA's Center for the Study of Intelligence (CSI). The center had been recently established to promote classified and unclassified scholarship on the agency, including critical appraisals of agency history. I was in charge of a number of publications, mostly unclassified, including two long ground-breaking monographs by veteran intelligence professionals that I edited. One of these books, *Sharing Secrets with Lawmakers: Congress as a User of Intelligence*, by L. Britt Snider, broke new ground on the subject of the CIA's interaction with Congress. *The CIA and the Vietnam Policymakers: Three Episodes*, by Harold P. Ford, amassed extensive evidence proving that senior officials in the Kennedy and Johnson administrations disregarded important aspects of the CIA's pessimistic assessments of the Vietnam War.

For three years while I was at the CSI, I was editor of *Studies in Intelligence*, a venerable publication that dated back to the early years of the CIA and published articles directed primarily toward the intelligence community. *Studies in Intelligence* covered various aspects of historical, operational, doctrinal, and theoretical aspects of intelligence. I worked on both classified and unclassified editions. I was also involved with large public conferences cosponsored by the CSI that brought together people from government, business, academia, and the press to examine historical events such the Rosenbergs' trial, the U-2 program, the ending of the Cold War, and the role of Congress in foreign policy. In 2004 I retired for the second and final time.

Final Reflections

I've thought a lot about my career, and I realized that my main professional objective over those years was nothing more than to work on substantive matters that were interesting and meaningful to me and to others involved in the acquisition, analysis, and use of intelligence. I preferred to work behind the scenes as an intelligence analyst rather than in the public eye as a diplomat. Although I held several low- to midlevel supervisory posts during my career and was rated an able and sensitive manager, I preferred to focus as much as possible on substance. I sought assignments that would broaden my knowledge on an expanding array of nations, regions, and global problems such as terrorism, wars and weaponry, nuclear proliferation, narcotics trafficking, the economy, and counterespionage. I was especially interested in what makes a particular country or region culturally unique and how that shapes its politics and place in the world.

My career thus advanced more along a horizontal axis than a vertical one; I was not particularly interested in rising in the chain of command—in climbing the greasy pole—but rather in expanding my areas of substantive expertise. Thus, I was well-placed to take advantage of exciting opportunities, such as working in Congress, on the National Security Council, and the PDB. I benefitted from the wide variety of job possibilities offered within a single federal agency. I always took pleasure in mentoring junior analysts; I particularly enjoyed helping them become better intelligence analysts and better writers.

I was fortunate to have the opportunity to interact with extremely capable national leaders and unsung heroes across the political spectrum. Among the people I particularly admired were Harold Saunders, my superior at the National Security Council, who epitomized grace, professionalism, and generosity of spirit, as well as the widely respected Brent Scowcroft, Colin Powell, and Paul Tsongas.

5

Briefing Presidential Candidates

JOHN HELGERSON

Editor's Note: John Helgerson's pioneering *Getting to Know the President: CIA Briefings of Presidential Candidates, 1952–1992* (Washington DC: Center for the Study of Intelligence, Central Intelligence Agency, 1996) served as the basis for this presentation to the Central Intelligence Retirees' Association

Thank you very much for the introduction. I thank you, Betsy, and indeed all of you for inviting me to speak today. I have talked with CIRA (Central Intelligence Retirees' Association) occasionally over the years, but I was astonished to find that the last time was more than six years ago, in October of 2002.

Betsy has wisely given me some guidelines about how long I should plan to speak and take questions. This brought to mind a story about George Bernard Shaw, the British author who found himself arranging a literary colloquium. Shaw told one of the speakers that he would have twenty minutes. Shocked, this man of letters responded, "How can I possibly tell the group everything I know on this subject in twenty minutes?" Shaw replied, "I suggest you speak very slowly."

In my case, Betsy has not recommended that I speak slowly, or rapidly, but she did suggest a focus—namely, the subject of presidential transitions and what our agency has done to facilitate them over the years. I would like to discuss in some detail a couple of the early transitions and then a couple of the most recent ones. With just some quick anecdotes about several of the others along the way, we'll leave some time for questions and answers.

I will be happy to elaborate on any of the transitions that I discussed in detail in my book.

When I reflect on this subject I do it in terms of lessons learned—that is, what did we go through in supporting a given presidential transition and how—specifically—does that instruct us regarding how to do it better next time? I developed the interest and familiarity with this subject because I was asked to go to Little Rock to brief president-elect Bill Clinton. I did that for two and one-half months. When I was informed I was to do this, I thought I would look in the file and see what we had done previously that would shed some light on what I ought to do. You would not be surprised to hear that there was no file. After that experience, I resolved to document what I had done, including what we had done over the years.

Here is a lessons-learned tip right up front in case you want to predict the outcome of the next election: all candidates who decline to be briefed by our agency lose the election. You are doubtless wondering who could say no to such an offer, but in fact there were three. George McGovern, Walter Mondale, and Barry Goldwater were the three candidates who declined to be briefed and in every case they lost. I will leave it to you to figure out if there is some cause and effect there or if there might also have been other reasons for their defeat.

Let me start at the beginning, which for our agency was with Harry Truman. When Truman came into office, he found himself surprisingly uninformed about some very important things. For example, Secretary of War Stimson appeared in the new president's office twelve days after he had been sworn in to brief Truman on the Manhattan Project. Truman himself wrote in his memoirs, "There were so many things I did not know when I became president." Acting on this concern, he took it upon himself in the summer of 1952 to ask our director, Walter B. Smith, to make arrangements to provide intelligence briefings to Dwight Eisenhower and Adlai Stevenson while they were still candidates.

In fact, Truman went further than that, personally inviting

Eisenhower and Stevenson to lunch at the White House, where they would be briefed on world developments. Truman was powerfully offended when Eisenhower, declining the invitation, said he thought he should be briefed "only on those matters concerning which information could be made available to the American public." I found in the Eisenhower Library a handwritten note that Truman sent Eisenhower in response, saying, "Partisan politics should stop at the boundaries of the United States. I am extremely sorry that you have allowed a bunch of screwballs to come between us. You have made a bad mistake and I am hoping it won't injure this great republic. There has never been one like it and I want to see it continue regardless of the man who occupies the most important position in the history of the world. May God guide you and give you light."

Of importance to our story, Eisenhower wrote a letter to "Beetle" Smith, observing, "The past two days my whole headquarters has been in a little bit of a steaming stew over an incident in which, according to the papers, you were at least briefly involved. It was the meeting that Governor Stevenson had with the president and the cabinet. According to reports reaching here you were brought in to brief the governor on the world situation. To the political mind, it looked like the outgoing administration was canvassing all its resources in order to support Stevenson's election." Well, you know the relationship between Beetle Smith and Eisenhower. Smith had been Eisenhower's chief of staff in Europe, and he was powerfully disappointed and offended by Eisenhower's letter. To make matters worse, the newspapers made a big issue of the tension between Eisenhower and Truman.

Despite the tense and public early exchanges between the outgoing president and Eisenhower, in the end the latter agreed to receive intelligence briefings if they were done by midlevel agency officers. Eisenhower did not want to have senior officials or the director involved in briefings prior to the election. He received four such briefings before Election Day.

If I were to draw any one lesson from the agency's first involvement in briefing candidates it would be that when these briefings are being arranged or delivered, it should be done in a very low-key manner to keep politics out of it and permit a dispassionate discussion of the real issues.

I suspect you are getting a little nervous that I am going to go on at this length about every transition. I promise not to do that. But I do want to say a few things about the Kennedy transition, because the election of 1960 was the one that was the most political of all, with regard to our agency. Our director at the time was Allen Dulles. Dulles had made clear to senior agency managers, perhaps including some of you, that he personally wanted to handle transition matters with the incoming administration. Dulles briefed Kennedy on two occasions before the election. On one occasion in midsummer he traveled to Hyannis Port, and on a second occasion he briefed Kennedy at his home in Georgetown in September.

We all remember the four televised debates during the 1960 campaign. Unfortunately for our agency, John Kennedy had paid attention at hearings of the Senate Foreign Relations Committee. In the televised debates Kennedy cited Allen Dulles to the effect that Soviet economic growth was outpacing that of the United States. And he cited intelligence assessments related to the alleged bomber gap and missile gap. None of this helped us, particularly with Richard Nixon, who felt himself put on the defensive because of Kennedy's use of CIA material.

Kennedy's staff was worried that he had come across in the debates as soft on China because of his unwillingness to declare that he would defend Quemoy and Matsu, the offshore islands controlled by Taiwan. To avoid a similar situation related to the Cuba issue, one of Kennedy's aides, Richard Goodwin, on the night before the final debate issued a preemptive statement on Cuba. This statement, issued in Kennedy's name even though he had not seen it, said, "We must attempt to strengthen the non-Batista, democratic, anti-Castro forces in exile and in Cuba itself, who offer eventual hope of overthrowing Castro."

In Nixon's view, this statement by Kennedy put Nixon in an awkward spot. He felt he needed to attack Kennedy's position on backing anti-Castro forces even though he, Nixon, had knowledge of and supported the budding CIA covert action program to deal with Cuba. For his part, Kennedy to this point had received no briefings on the program. Nevertheless, Nixon, in the wake of this experience, suspected the CIA of briefing Kennedy earlier and in more detail than was ever the case. Ten days after the election in November, our former director of plans, Dick Bissell, traveled with the director to Palm Beach, Florida, to the Kennedy home and briefed Kennedy on an array of issues, including Cuba. But even then the briefing was at a general level.

Those of you who are familiar with this period probably have read various books on what became the Bay of Pigs operation. Almost all of them quote from the famous book by Arthur Schlesinger called *A Thousand Days*. Schlesinger begins one of his chapters, the one on the Bay of Pigs, by saying this: "On November 29 [keep in mind that this is during the transition after the election, but before Kennedy is sworn in], twelve days after he had heard about the Cuban project [that is, when Bissell had gone to Florida] the president-elect had received from Allen Dulles a detailed briefing on the CIA's new military conception. Kennedy listened with attention, then told Dulles to carry the work forward." This passage, which in effect holds Kennedy responsible for approving the Bay of Pigs planning, is found in almost every book on the subject.

In studying this transition period, I became aware that our director's schedule would not have made this briefing possible. And indeed it's a briefing that never occurred. In writing his book, Schlesinger had misunderstood a fundamental point. He had obviously seen government documents indicating that the president had approved the Cuba program on that date. But, critically, on the twenty-ninth of November 1960, the president was not John Kennedy; rather, it was still Dwight Eisenhower. During the transition, Kennedy never did receive a briefing on the detailed military plan for the Bay of Pigs. He was briefed on the whole operation only after his inauguration in early 1961. This episode makes clear how important it is to reflect carefully on what one tells, or does not tell, a candidate or president-elect during the transition period. When the time came that Kennedy was finally briefed on the program in a revealing and useful way, it was only a very short time before the operation unfolded.

The first lesson to come from our experience during the transition following the 1960 election was to pray that the CIA stays out of presidential debates on TV. In the election just held (November 2008) we were lucky. The world economy was collapsing, with the result that no mention was made of the CIA in the debates. A second, more important lesson from the transition is that the director himself should not monopolize the briefings and contacts. Allen Dulles, for all his wisdom and charm, came across as condescending to the younger Kennedy. Clearly the intelligence community would be better served by selecting slightly less senior briefers, depoliticizing the whole undertaking.

To make good on my promise to more quickly jump through some intervening history, let me mention that if there is a lesson from the transition to President Lyndon Johnson, it is that one should not ignore the vice president. As vice president, Johnson had been receiving almost no tailored or direct intelligence support. The day after Kennedy's death, John McCone tried to rectify this situation by starting daily briefings. At a time when the influential Dick Cheney has been our vice president, the widely publicized Sarah Palin aspired to the vice presidency, and the irrepressible Joe Biden is vice president, it is hard to believe that we ever ignored vice presidents. On several occasions in our history we have done so, however, and it has come back to bite us.

Nixon was so disaffected by his impressions of the agency growing out of the earlier loss to Kennedy that he did not want any CIA briefings during the transition period before his inauguration. But there is an invaluable lesson to be learned from the transition to Nixon nevertheless. We are nothing if not resourceful. While we had no access to Nixon at his transition headquarters at the Pierre

Hotel in New York, our representatives who had been positioned in the city did have daily access to Lawrence Eagleburger and regularly, but not every day, to his boss, Henry Kissinger, who in early December had been named national security adviser. Kissinger came to have a very good impression of our agency and our responsiveness, based on the many tailored intelligence assessments we prepared for him and Eagleburger. This clearly helped Dick Helms get off to a good start with Kissinger.

Kissinger wrote in his memoir *White House Years*: "It is to the director that the assistant first turns to learn the facts in a crisis, and for analysis of events. And since decisions can turn on the perception of the consequences of action, the CIA assessment can almost amount to a policy recommendation." Concerning Helms personally, Kissinger wrote, "Disciplined, meticulously fair, and discreet, Helms performed his duties with a total objectivity essential to an effective intelligence service. I never knew him to misuse his intelligence or his power. He never forgot that his integrity guaranteed his effectiveness, that his best weapon with presidents was a reputation for reliability. The CIA input was an important element of every policy deliberation."

Kissinger very much appreciated the work that our agency had done for him during the transition. The lesson from this transition is to recruit the staff even if you cannot get to the president.

The transition to Gerald Ford was another case in which the lesson was to maintain a good relationship with the vice president. Bill Colby saw Watergate closing in on President Nixon. As a result, he invited Ford to visit our agency and then began a process of providing him daily briefings. This, by Ford's own account, paved the way for a very good relationship once Ford came into office.

The transition to Jimmy Carter in 1976 was an interesting one because of Carter's seemingly insatiable interest in the substantive material. He was the only candidate who ever asked for briefings before he was even nominated. Interestingly, he was given such a briefing, a step the agency has taken on only that one occasion. After he was nominated, Carter received a succession of long briefings, all-day affairs in Plains, sitting in his family room twirling a globe, as if to point to a country and want to talk about it. The agency's national intelligence officers and various DI officers spent hours with Carter during this period. At the direction of the White House, CIA director George H. W. Bush attended most of these briefings.

The lesson from the Carter transition was to understand the president. This one liked a lot of detail and long briefings. Give it to him. Adjust the product and the briefings to the individual receiving them. The other lesson derives from a matter we have not yet discussed. Director Bush elected to give Jimmy Carter a fairly comprehensive briefing on covert action programs and some sensitive collection programs prior to his being sworn in but after he was elected. This backfired. Carter was not taken with many of these programs and cancelled a couple of them very quickly after his inauguration. The lesson seems to be that it is best not to hit a new president cold with such programs. It is better to brief them when there is a substantive reason, an occasion when one can demonstrate the payoff as well as the technique itself.

The transition to Ronald Reagan was the first in which the agency had senior officers on the scene to provide daily briefings as well as the PDB. In contrast, Carter had asked that a courier provide him the PDB, which he then read, or did not. With Reagan, we knew what he was reading and heard his comments and questions. You will remember Dixon Davis and Dick Kerr, who were in California meeting with Reagan nearly every day. The obvious lesson here is that if you can arrange it, there is great payoff to the daily contact.

The transition to Bush 41 in 1988 was, for the CIA, the smoothest transition of all, because Bush had been vice president and CIA director. Mention of George H. W. Bush gives me reason to note his invaluable contribution to the whole history of support to new presidents during periods of transition. Let's remind ourselves of his various contributions. As director, Bush briefed Carter. As vice president–elect, he ensured that Reagan received the briefings. As president-elect, Bush continued to receive the same briefings he had received as vice president. As president, he arranged for president-elect Bill Clinton to be briefed. As the father of George W., he underscored the value of the CIA briefings to his son when he became president. Rounding out the legacy, Bush 43 did a masterful job ensuring a good transition, including intelligence support to President Barack Obama. Simply put, George Herbert Walker Bush was largely responsible for the success of our support of presidents-elect in half a dozen or more transitions. Without him, can we keep this train on track in the future? We owe it to him.

Concerning my own service in Little Rock with Bill Clinton, let me say, for your amusement, that the highlight occurred in the first two minutes of the first briefing. The lead item in the PDB that day was about Somalia. Prior to the briefing, I had been killing time in the reception room of the governor's mansion by reading the CIA World Factbook entries on the countries addressed in the PDB. After some introductory pleasantries, the president-elect picked up the PDB and started reading the first piece. He then looked up and asked, "John, what's the population of Somalia anyway?" To his clear surprise, I promptly and authoritatively responded 12.24 million (or whatever it was at the time). He seemed impressed at our command of the facts. I thought I should leap up and spike the book.

One thing we learned in that transition is the value of technology. Although we operated out of improvised offices in a Comfort Inn motel, we had a big phone line installed and were able to produce imagery, graphics, handouts, and all else that we needed. In fact, we put together a PDB that was literally indistinguishable from the one that was published at headquarters and given to the president. And with the secure communications we were able to provide immediate answers to classified questions. This had a big impact.

The notable thing about the election of Bush 43, of course, is that it was not resolved for a full month beyond the election. Interestingly, however, a week before the legal resolution, President Clinton approved briefings of Bush, Cheney, Card, and Rice. He clearly knew how it was going to come out. On this occasion, our current director of intelligence (DI), Michael Morrell, was the briefer. He briefed the president-elect in Crawford and elsewhere prior to inauguration, and then stayed with him as the briefer after the inauguration. This is something we should have been doing over the years. The continuity of briefings from the same agency officer before and after the inauguration goes a long way toward solidifying and maintaining our access to the new president. This was a valuable lesson.

In a way, we are still in the transition to President Obama. This time, the DNI rather than the CIA director was in charge. I was flattered that the DNI and our own director read the account of our historical experience that I had published a decade earlier. They had a number of questions about what had worked and not worked. Clearly, we are learning from experience.

The DNI and a number of others briefed the president-elect in Chicago before the election. It would not surprise anyone or violate any confidence if I were to say that those briefings centered heavily on topics of current interest. When election night came, intelligence briefing teams were prepositioned in Chicago, Phoenix, Wilmington, and Wasilla. We were prepared for whatever happened.

After the election, Chicago continued to be the center of the action for a while. Now that President Obama is in the White House, he is briefed and reads the PDB, just as you have seen described in the newspapers. A lawyer himself, the president reads carefully and asks a number of questions. Some of these can be answered on the spot; others that involve more complicated issues involve preparing memos for later delivery.

Admiral Blair looks at the PDB very carefully the night before, as some but not all of the directors have done over the years. And he's normally there with the president for the briefing in the morning. This group would be interested to know that even with the DNI in charge, the great majority of the items in the PDB are still written by CIA analysts. A number of very strong pieces by other agencies' personnel appear, but day in and day out it is still pretty much a CIA operation.

Our agency has been the primary player in supporting nearly a dozen presidential transitions. Looking at the span of time since Harry Truman, I think it is safe to say that the process did not work as well for the first few transitions as it has more recently. Since the midseventies, for example, presidents-elect have for the most part agreed to daily briefings by CIA officers, as well as agreeing to receive the PDB itself. This goes a long way toward enabling us to provide tailored support and timely follow-up. As we establish these relationships, we need to be flexible. Every president is different, and we must play by their rules concerning such things as level of generality, format of the book, and time of delivering the briefings.

Overall, we have had two aims in our efforts to brief newly elected presidents. One is to get them up to speed on world events; the second is to establish a lasting relationship for continued briefings once they are in the White House. In general, we have done better at the first than with the second, but the multiyear trend is in the right direction. Most important at the moment, we have a solid relationship with President Obama—one based on fifty years of experience and strengthening every day.

Let me stop now and take your questions. I am mindful that many of you were involved in the events I have described and I would welcome your comments. Thank you very much.

AUDIENCE MEMBER: John, you discussed the participation of the director and the DNI in these briefings. I gather that in some of them the director is actually doing the briefing, where in others the director is a participant and then takes part in whatever dialog takes place. Can you assess positive and negative aspects of that? That is to say, is that a good idea? I have my own opinion, but I'd be interested in your view of it.

SPEAKER: I trust everyone heard the question. My view is that it's a very good idea to have a director or DNI do the first of the briefings—a kind of an overview of the world, if you will, with each candidate. I think that makes sense because it underscores the importance of our business, and directors have a gravitas the rest of us do not. But my view is that after the first briefing it is wiser for directors to bow out in terms of taking the lead or doing the talking. Whether they sit in or not in the Oval Office has advantages and disadvantages. But I think in the briefings of candidates and presidents-elect it is best to have people who are obviously nonpolitical and whose motives with regard to their job are not suspect. Stick with the substantive experts, albeit at a fairly senior level.

New presidents come into the job knowing some substantive foreign affairs issues very well, for one reason or another, and then there are other areas about which they know little or nothing. It is somehow a lot easier to uncritically absorb a useful briefing if you're hearing it from an expert. In such circumstances, where no recordings are being made and the discussions go on in a nonpolitical environment, even presidents tend to relax and engage in a useful exchange.

I came to know the interests of George H. W. Bush better than any other president because I was the DDI (deputy director of intelligence) during the four years he was president. Some of the things he would share with his briefer were so candid that you wondered what he could possibly have been thinking. Bush later explained to me that he would do this because you (CIA) are the only people in the government whose confidence he knew he could trust. It is touching, really, but that's what happens in many of these sessions.

Other questions?

AUDIENCE MEMBER: There is always talk about shortening the transition period after the presidential election. What would that do, from the point of view of intelligence support? Would it help to have a shorter transition period? Or would it make it tougher?

SPEAKER: Interesting question—were the transition period shorter, would it help or hurt? I have to confess that I've never really thought about that, because I don't think there is any likelihood it will happen. For us in intelligence, I think it wouldn't make a big difference. The one thing that clearly is to our advantage in the current system is that by and large nobody else shows up, with the notable exception of the Secret Service. They provide absolutely indispensable service in many respects. I was dumbfounded, in Little Rock, when the staff of the president-elect would ask me things like how we get secure communications, or a safe, or security clearances. I found myself being an intermediary for any number of other purposes. Striking, really, but they were grateful that we were there from day one. The transition gives us a chance to develop a relationship, an opportunity we would not have if we used the British system where, following the election, one person immediately walks out the door of 10 Downing Street while the successor walks in. To repeat what I said earlier, we have two motives in this whole process—one is to inform the president-elect on the world situation; the other is to establish the relationship. I'd hate to see that lost and I think this otherwise unwieldy long period works to our advantage in that respect. As far as the substance goes, I don't think it would make much difference.

AUDIENCE MEMBER: What I just heard is that our main name is still that of integrity. Namely, in doing what we do, during the transition process, when nobody else is there to help, we do the right thing. Which is one of the big parts of the definition of integrity: we are there, and we do it well. Thank you very much; I appreciate hearing that. I hear so little of it with regard to the rest of our government.

AUDIENCE MEMBER: John, if you can entertain a question related to the inspector general (IG) rather than to your presentation here today. What do you see coming down the road? We see Nicholson recruiting his son, apparently; we have allegations against a chief of station for rape, and other continuing problems. Do you see the IG office function or mission changing and anything we can do to support along the periphery there?

SPEAKER: Wayne, that's a profound question that doesn't lend itself to an easy answer. Fundamentally, with human nature being what it is and with us being involved in the espionage business, there will be a continuing need for the offices of Inspector General, Security, and Counterintelligence, and our basic missions will remain unchanged. The positive side, of which I am aware because I stay in touch with my counterpart IGs from throughout the U.S. government, is that we have fewer of almost all kinds of problems than one finds in other big agencies or the private sector. Our careful hiring does pay off. But people still get into trouble and do ill-advised and occasionally illegal things. The problems are never going to go away completely.

Like the rest of the agency, we in the IG office don't get a lot of publicity for the vast bulk of our work, which is audits, inspections, reviews, and, indeed, investigations, which results in the highlighting of best practices and promoting good management, economy, and efficiency. We try to distill lessons learned even from the gravest problems in order to prevent recurrence and promote the mission. To use a dramatic case, we had a situation a couple of years ago where an officer embezzled more than $350,000 from one of our locations. That individual is in prison now. But my concern was more with vulnerabilities in the processes, which enabled the criminal to do that. Fortunately, managers in all appropriate components have taken actions to strengthen our information technology systems and to train those who supervise and handle funds to heighten fraud awareness.

Concerning some of the most controversial programs we have had to look at in recent years, such as those related to detentions and interrogations, our primary concern is to see that proper guid-ance is made known to agency officers so that they do not run afoul regulations, sometimes in uncharted territory. If agency low the legal guidance they are given, they need have t they'll be called to account or held responsible, even o badly wrong. In the time I have been inspector gen-ve never called anyone to account or suggested admin-r legal action because they did what they were told to nt to proper legal guidance.

Occasionally we have found that the agency has not received

legal guidance from the Department of Justice on key matters. The Office of Inspector General (OIG) does not make the law. Neither do we interpret the law; the Office of General Counsel (OGC) does that. We look to see if agency officers are following it. Regarding one key issue, there simply was no legal opinion. On that occasion, I brought this matter to the attention of our general counsel and director. I also raised the issue personally with appropriate senior officials of the National Security Council, White House Counsel's Office, Department of Justice, and discussed it personally with the vice president. The bottom line was that it was essential the agency be provided, by Justice, a relevant legal opinion to protect our officers by clarifying what they could and could not do. Other senior officers of the agency also made these points to their counterparts, and eventually a relevant legal opinion was produced.

Interestingly, one of the first actions our new president has taken, concerning the issues I am referring to, was to direct relevant agencies of the U.S. government not to rely on any of the legal opinions written by the Justice Department in the wake of 9/11. New opinions presumably will be written. Concerning a matter some of you have asked me about, I think personally that there is absolutely zero chance that anybody in our agency, presently or formerly, will be prosecuted for anything they did in good faith, consistent with one of the legal opinions that have since been withdrawn. I certainly could not countenance that and believe it would be fundamentally wrong. In the history of our involvement with these issues, only one individual has been prosecuted, and he was not at all a part of the formal program. He was not trained or authorized. Rather, he took it on himself, in a remote location in Afghanistan, to beat a detainee to get information, and the detainee died. This individual, an agency contractor, was investigated by the OIG and prosecuted in the Eastern District of North Carolina. He was convicted and is now in prison serving an eight-year sentence.

As a closing point, let me underscore again that in most of what the OIG does, we find components and programs running well and meeting the agency's mission. Across the board, the agency has been operating at a very high operational tempo ever since 9/11. Based on my work as IG, I am immensely proud of my agency colleagues. I know you're proud of the agency as well. Once you are in, you are always in. Thank you very much; it has been a pleasure to talk with you today.

Monitoring Soviet Military Capabilities

6

The Soviets Go on the LAMM

MICHAEL D. FLINT AND BOYD SUTTON

I n 1979–80, I—Michael Flint—worked in Soviet/Warsaw Pact Theater Command and Control and our branch was one of the first to start using an early version of SAFE (Support to the Analysts' File Environment). I used SAFE as an analysis tool, not just a search-and-retrieve system. One of the quick-reaction publications was on Soviet military readiness, which was sent to Henry Kissinger while it was still in draft.

In 1980 I worked on the Land Armaments and Manpower Model (LAMM), which provided unit-specific order-of-battle history (equipment, readiness, subordination, and location) for Soviet and Warsaw Pact forces (1960–2000). This was later extended. The data were used by the Pentagon to support long-range force planning.

In my view, this was the nadir of the old Office of Strategic Research (OSR) crowd's contribution to national security. During this period, we in the Theater Forces (TF) division were monitoring combat operations by Soviet forces in Afghanistan, monitoring ground forces in the southwestern USSR for indications of preparations for Soviet intervention in Iran (which may have required a U.S. military response), and conducting a major review to reassess Soviet ground forces readiness. The LAMM project was another major effort during this busy period that had us join forces with the Defense Intelligence Agency's (DIA) Ground Branch (where I had worked prior to moving to the CIA in 1975).

Ben Rutherford (the Gray Eminence) was chief of Theater Forces and supported the effort, although he was not sure we could make it work. Ben had long experience in theater-forces analysis and played a leading role in community efforts to produce National Intelligence Estimates on theater forces (NIE–11–14).

Boyd Sutton was chief of the Theater Forces Ground Branch and the originator of the idea to build a database of our equipment holdings for Soviet and Warsaw Pact ground forces to include projections so we could better support the Pentagon (especially the Office of the Secretary of Defense/Net Assessment, or OSD/NA). Boyd provided the management cover and coordination with other agencies that was so critical to success. One of Boyd's key management decisions was to organize the branch around the major functions we were performing. Boyd also made the decision early on to hire contractor support for analysis and data entry. The contract went to a contracting company, which provided us with retired U.S. Army officers that understood ground forces. The firm's help made a major contribution to our success. Finally, Boyd had a great relationship with his DIA counterpart, Lt. Col. Pete Meckle. Pete and Boyd worked together to ensure proper working relationships between the CIA and DIA; this allowed the end product to become a CIA-DIA coordinated database.

Andy Marshal (chief of OSD/NA) and his team were our primary customers and provided us a better understanding of U.S. force planning and the role our projections would play in OSD/NA's net assessment efforts. One of the key insights we learned from the OSD/NA was that U.S. force development was also linked to war campaign plans. When we studied Soviet force development we noted that this relationship also held true for them (our understanding of their war plans was another key ingredient to understanding equipment deliveries, and this also helped us to better understand Soviet operational level war plans. This highlighted another lesson: that cooperation and coordination with one's consumers helps to improve the intelligence product as well as improve its utility.) These were the days when U.S.-Soviet net assessments played a major role in military budget debates and U.S. force planning. One of the tools used created measures of effectiveness, in which a unit's equipment is given a firepower score reflecting quantity and quality, with newer equipment—WEI/WUVs (weapons effectiveness indicators and weighted unit values)—and other scoring systems, to include a scoring system devised by a contracting company. We included these firepower scores in our analytical tool, a hierarchical database. By using the scoring systems we were able to reflect the *impact* of modernization (both equipment deliveries and organizational changes). The OSD/NA also used scoring systems to compare U.S. and NATO modernization with that of the Warsaw Pact and to reflect combat power buildup in a mobilization and deployment scenario. This provides them with a very useful analytic tool.

Derk Swain devised this LAMM database to store unit-specific data and to manipulate that data by time (years), units, equipment, or firepower scores. He worked in real time to make the software meet our needs, one of the most productive software development efforts I ever saw. Derk and I often worked side by side to develop software techniques that improved data entry and data manipulation. In my view, Derk was the real hero of this effort and I will never forget his ability to immediately understand our needs and, within minutes, develop software routines we could use right away. Derk would then revise them as we worked to incorporate lessons learned. It may be useful to note here that software became an issue when sharing data. These were the days before Windows and Microsoft Office and the easy integration of data from various software sources. Derk used the agency's mainframe computer and a very powerful, but dated, set of code to allow data entry and data manipulation. We were able to achieve compatibility with the OSD/NA but had real difficulties getting compatible with anyone else. The teaching point here is to arrange for better coordination from the beginning to work out such problems.

Early on we discovered the Rosetta stone to Soviet equipment modernization, something that the intelligence community had never before been able to decipher. One of the original efforts was to devise a method of adding data to the database in an efficient manner (some had predicted it would take us many years to do so). Developing these procedures was my major contribution. In essence, we used knowledge of the Tables of Organization and Equipment (TO&E) of Soviet ground forces to devise small unit package codes. I had worked in the DIA as one of the contributors to the DIA Organization Guide, which provided a generic TO&E for types of units. One of my discoveries while there was that units in different parts of the USSR were equipped differently (geography and potential enemy threats within theaters of operations affected unit equipment holding). During the LAMM project we soon discovered that a unit's readiness also had an impact on equipment holdings (readier units had newer equipment, while low-readiness units were equipped with older equipment). We soon learned by comparing Soviet reports with other data sources that we could identify those units that would first get equipment for troop testing and those "leading edge" units to get first-production runs due to their readiness and war plan priorities. We also found that units getting new equipment transferred their older equipment to less-ready units (usually from the western to the far eastern sections of the USSR). As noted above, our discussions with the OSD/NA led us to be alert to such trends due to similar trends within U.S. ground forces.

One of our analytical techniques was to develop *data-capture sheets* organized by time (1960–80) and unit (for each of the combat regiments and independent battalions/companies within a division and for each nondivisional unit). After reviewing the unit-specific data and comparing it to trends for other, similar units within a specific region for a specific time frame, plus analysis of equipment related to organizational trends (as reflected in several years' worth of the DIA's Organizational Guide), we made *unit-specific assessments* (where we filled in any blanks in the data based upon our analysis). These assessment data were captured on a separate table from which we created *data-entry forms*. The data-entry forms enabled rapid data entry into the database, which reflected subordination, location, readiness, and equipment on a year-by-year basis for 1960–80. In effect, we created large, hard-copy, paper spreadsheets to capture and document raw intelligence and another set to document the assessment. Again, these were in the days before the powerful computing tools that analysts have access to today. I have often wondered how much more effective we could have been with such tools (I suspect we could have been at least twice as effective).

One of the more interesting aspects to me was the advantage a historical perspective gave to analysis. Part of the historical research included a week I spent in London reviewing old British intelligence files (I'm the only analyst I know that ever did this) in order to assess Soviet ground order of battle (OB) information for our start year of 1960. The year 1960 was arbitrarily chosen to provide us with historical data for evaluating and understanding trends in Soviet force development. I was able to chart British OB holdings from the post–World War II period up through 1960. One of the techniques we used during this effort was to provide a sense of continuity of units histories and to recognize that proper identification of units usually lagged the real event by several years (analysis and understanding of the raw intelligence took time before the true facts were uncovered). As we moved from 1960 to 1980 (the then-current year) we used DIA OBs and found the same problem with late identification of reality (sometimes proper identification lagged the real event by five years). As I had also worked in the DIA OB branch, I understood their data sources and analytical techniques and procedures. The "trick" I soon discovered was to use an historical perspective for looking at the data so that older data could be revised to reflect newer knowledge. Up to this time, all OB work was basically done without much consideration of previous history.

Once the period 1960–80 was entered into the database, we began to research Soviet writings for indications of future (1980–2000) force development goals and to research the database to calculate time intervals between equipment upgrades (for example, artillery generally was retained for longer period before modernization than were tanks). Learning these delay periods helped us predict when the next upgrade was due. A key and new part of the projections was to assess what we called "influencing factors." These included production rates for military equipment, the influence of trends in other forces (e.g., British artillery increase in the size of a battery to twenty-four tubes), and the effect of the Soviet economy (already in real trouble at this time). We thus had a rationale for unit-specific projections that had been reviewed by key intelligence community players and for use by key U.S. force planners. The net result was that the Pentagon was able to learn that not all Soviet divisions were equipped and manned to the same standards and that this could profoundly affect U.S. planning for military actions in different theaters. Previously, the rule of thumb was to use the OB and DIA Organizational Guide's TO&E. As the organizational guides were based on the very well equipped Soviet divisions in East Germany, a highly inflated estimate was derived from this process. Estimates of East European divisions were even more inflated as they never were able to catch up to Soviet organizational and equipment patterns.

TONY WILLIAMS ADDS: We briefed the army chief of staff for intelligence on the program (the army helped contribute to our success by sending us contractor funds). Later the army used extensive unit-specific data from LAMM for one of their force planning support publications (*Soviet Force Development*). OSD/NA used our data extensively in their net assessment work (later we provided NATO data as well so we had force trends on both sides) and it was the basis for a DI publication I wrote (*Soviet Ground Force Trends*). This publication was the first time a DI military-related publication talked about the negative effect the economic troubles in the USSR was having on Soviet forces. I don't remember any "Eureka" moments, but rather a gradual improvement in our understanding of Soviet (and later Warsaw Pact) ground forces (and later air and naval) across the intelligence community.

BOYD SUTTON NOTES: Mike is far too modest in describing the importance of his contribution. Mike *was* LAMM! Yes, I had the initial idea—the basic concept. Mike, who was and is still a good friend, and I spent many evenings and occasional weekends in my office scratching out our ideas on the blackboard. But the world is full of seemingly great ideas that turn out to be just too unwieldy—impractical to implement. When Mike came up with the idea of "small unit package codes" as a shortcut for data entry, he made the "impossible" possible. Mike's approach to coding data entry is where the "model" part of the Land Armaments and Manpower Model came from. He was rewarded with the largest cash award ever given to an OSR analyst for his brilliant ideas and hard work.

We should not, however, focus on the "fifteen seconds of fame" when looking at what analysts do. What turned me on (as an analyst and as a manager), and I think what turned Mike on, and what turned the LAMM team on, was knowing that we were working on something important, something leading edge that we felt would make a difference—that, and being part of a real team of people who worked together to produce a critical result. That's fun! It makes you want to get to work every day. It makes you go home at night feeling that you are doing something that matters with people who care and who have your back.

So what was the critical result, you ask? First, we were able for the *first* time to produce solid projections of how the Soviet Army was really organized and equipped and how and when that would change over the coming decade. Every Department of Defense program—indeed, the entire structure of the U.S. Army—is based in part on a realistic appreciation of what they might have to face. It's difficult to overstate the importance of having confidence in what's likely to be facing them in those "out" years (not just today, which is something you can't do very much about).

Before LAMM, projections were largely guesses without much direct evidence and long on assumptions. But we really understood how the Soviet system ticked. Doctoral work in a university is supposed to be a genuine contribution to the state of knowledge in the subject of focus. Most of the analysis I saw during my career—especially after the Office of Strategic Research (OSR), the Office of Economic Research (OER), and subject-specialty organization was abandoned in the DI—contributed *very* little knowledge to the fundamental understanding of anything at a systemic level. Most analysis is short-term, and based on rather limited information and shallow understanding at a systemic level. Literally every analyst and manager involved with LAMM was exceptionally proud to be part of an effort to produce PhD-quality work and genuinely increase understanding at a systemic level. *That* tends to turn on real analysts.

We briefed several directors of intelligence community elements—the director of central intelligence (the DCI, who at the time headed the intelligence community as well as ran the Central Intelligence Agency), the director of the Defense Intelligence Agency (DIA), the director of the National Security Agency (NSA), and more. One of the most fun opportunities was briefing Lt. Gen. William Odom, who was then assistant chief of staff for intelligence of the army. He was a smug, self-important, overbearing (and brilliant) so-and-so. I had friends on his staff who forewarned me that he was loaded for bear and was incapable of believing that any CIA analyst could possibly understand anything about any army, U.S. or Soviet. My DIA counterpart, Lt. Col. Pete Meckel, accompanied Mike and me. We went through what we had done, how we had done it, and what we were able to conclude as a result. He was dumbfounded. His staff said they were on board. I dealt with Bill Odom many times, and this was the only time I saw him subdued.

On another occasion, we briefed Gen. Glen Otis—who was then commander of the U.S. Army Training and Doctrine Command and had recently been commander of U.S. Army Europe. Again, Pete came along with Mike and me. We also briefed him on the conclusions of a joint CIA-DIA study on Soviet military readiness, informed in part by the LAMM work, as Mike described. I expected a blast from General Otis because our conclusions were sharply at odds with those of army intelligence. In fact, his intelligence chief was a personal friend of mine from my own army days and he'd given me a heads up. (There's another key point there for future analysts. Know your audience and keep up your networks.) After the briefing the room was silent for a moment. Then General Otis said, "That's the first time I've heard an intelligence briefing that makes sense." (I felt badly for my friend at that point.) He went on to explain how our conclusions gave him the ability—and gave other key army commanders the capability—to have more confidence in the plans they made for opposing Soviet forces in Europe.

Typical "threat estimates" more or less assumed—based on little direct evidence—that all Soviet units were unreasonably "ready" and well-trained. General Otis said that, as an experienced military commander, he and others like him knew that that wasn't right. They also knew that their own forces simply couldn't respond to that hyped threat. So they had to plan realistically for what they thought they could do and for what they thought was a more reasonable threat estimate—even if that wasn't the official estimate. He told us that worried him a lot. But the new estimates we now provided not only matched what he saw as "military common sense," but gave him greater confidence in the planning and training efforts of U.S. and NATO forces.

After I left the Theater Forces ground division's branch, I went to the National War College as a student for a year. Most of my military classmates were operators, not intelligence people. Many of them had been in key planning or command positions. Many told me that the new intelligence estimates (they had never heard of LAMM) had filtered down and created a lot of smiles. "Gee, those intelligence weenies finally got it right." One of those was Lt. Col. Wesley Clark, who later became Supreme Allied Commander Europe (SACEUR). His prior assignment had been as a special assistant to Gen. Bernie Rogers, who had been SACEUR at the time. He and I had many conversations about Soviet forces and the U.S. Army's capabilities. He confirmed a lot of what General Otis had told me. It is difficult to overstate the importance of what LAMM led to. But I doubt the National Security Council (NSC) has ever heard of it. So what?

65

That isn't as "sexy" as briefing the president or the NSC—just an army four-star—but it had real impact and, perhaps even more important, it increased General Otis's confidence in the intelligence he was getting. It's important to remember that for intelligence to matter, it has to be believed and acted on. What we (CIA and DIA working together) did with LAMM had a huge impact on the believability of analysis on the Soviet Army. That's *way* more important than fifteen minutes of face time with some big guys.

This point speaks to prospective analysts. The professional and friendly relationships an analyst develops are vital. Every analyst is (or should be) strongly encouraged to know counterparts, to build real relationships with other analysts in the intelligence community, with customers, and with select academics. Not only are such relationships vital to the job they are doing, but they could become important to the job they *will* be doing ten years or more down the road. In my experience, the DI talked a good game in that regard but seldom followed through. As late as 1997, when I did a specific study for DCI George Tenet, fewer than 10 percent of the analysts and branch chiefs I interviewed could even name their counterparts or customers, much less speak about a relationship with them. And the number was even lower about knowing "outside" experts. We should recruit extraverts, or at least those who are by nature somewhat gregarious. Loners, no matter how brilliant, will seldom have the network of relationships that grease the skids of the intelligence business. They should know that it's not all about sitting in an isolated cubicle, protecting secrets, and playing cards close to the vest. Knowing that getting out and about and building networks and relationships is important could encourage some prospective analysts—the right ones.

7

Making the World Safe through SAFE

MICHAEL D. FLINT

This is a story about how an old-time pencil-and-paper analyst was brought into the world of automation kicking and
screaming, but who was soon converted due to the power of
automation to aid analysis. In the mid-1970s there was very little
automation in the world of Directorate of Intelligence (DI) analysis. The Support to the Analysts' File Environment (SAFE) program was just beginning and the Office of Strategic Research (OSR)
Command Analysis Branch, led by Morgan Jones, was selected
to be one of the first DI branches to convert to this new computer
program. Jean Skillman was the SAFE manager who worked with
us to help us learn to use this new tool. She did an exceptional job
and should have received a "hero" award of some type. (A lesson
learned here is that the support mechanism is a key element of
successfully implementing a new tool.)

The SAFE system in those days consisted of two main components:

MAIL RETRIEVAL: In those early days, the branch received its
raw intelligence via computer printouts based on needs statements, known more formally as Boolean logic statements.
These needs statements were revised over time to select to those
countries and subjects for which an analyst was assigned (I had
Soviet/Warsaw Pact Theater Command and Control, for example; and Boyd Sutton had National Command Authorities as
his area of responsibility). During this period, Soviet unclassified military writings were focusing a lot on the Great Patri-

otic War (World War II in U.S. parlance). We soon saw that in their historical writings there was also a message about the evolving Soviet/Warsaw Pact command-and-control system. In essence, the Soviets were justifying their evolving modern command-and-control system based on lessons learned during World War II. We could correlate the unclassified history data with classified raw intelligence and make better interpretations of what was really happening.

DOCUMENT RETRIEVAL: In this phase, we would scan the printouts (usually about a hundred individual raw documents a day per analyst) recovered from the mail retrieval component and select those documents of interest for filing. We would attach a code sheet to the raw intelligence document selected and hand-enter codes we had devised for subjects of interest (e.g., 3235 was the code for general staff communications, so BR3235 would be a basic document on general staff communications) and country codes for countries of interest (e.g., URR for the USSR). An analyst assistant (ours was Mary Isabel, a real gem and wonderful lady) would type those codes into the SAFE document retrieval component and then microfiche the document and place the microfiche into a filing cabinet. We each had a book of the codes we had devised.

Because we as a branch were careful to fully code documents of interest for all subjects covered by the branch, we could combine subject and country codes to create fairly complicated subject codes for search and retrieval. Remember, at this time, SAFE could not do word-search document retrievals.

At first, I was not convinced that all of this work was worthwhile. But the coding process also had a bonus effect of helping me at least to remember more of what I read. Several months into the project we began to see the value of sorting through thousands of documents quickly to find those we needed for further analysis. SAFE document retrievals brought up all data relating to the question at hand, thus providing the analysts a broader view of the subject matter than they might otherwise have gotten from just reviewing their individual "shoe box" files. SAFE provided an analytical function beyond just document storage and retrieval.

It may be difficult for today's analysts to comprehend, but during the mid-1970s, there were no automated word-processing tools, so analysts used pen and paper to write out their documents. These handwritten notes would be typed by a secretary (Mary Anne Leggit was ours) and then the branch chief would review and make red-pencil suggestions. This resulted in many, many drafts, redrafts, and rewrites. Our branch chief, Morgan Jones, a frustrated editor, was a major pain as he red-lined almost everything. He once told us of stopping on the road to correct the wording of a road sign. I could believe it of him. Microsoft Word and Power Point would have been godsends in those days, but they would come much later. The bottom line was that preparing finished intelligence documents was a difficult and time-consuming process, especially when doing a report on a major subject area (what we called "basic intelligence," as opposed to the short-term current intelligence so common today). This process required retrieval of related documents (SAFE helped greatly here), analyses of the raw intelligence, making the intellectual leap between the facts gathered from a review of the raw intelligence to an interpretation of what the data meant for U.S. policy or conduct (no tools available), and then converting the findings into a consumer-oriented finished document (again, no tools available).

I used SAFE to help me write several finished intelligence products. Some were on Soviet/Warsaw Pact evolving command-and-control capabilities (of interest to other analysts and sometimes helpful for supporting collection operations). The basic research we did on staff procedures and communications units and facilities greatly helped us to understand the raw data we received. One of the key issues we faced at this time was the activation of Soviet/Warsaw Pact wartime major command headquarters (fronts, equivalent to U.S.-NATO army groups, and theaters of military operations, somewhat similar to a NATO theater command). Soviet World War II military history provided key information that was also bountiful at that time. (My experience has been that too often analysts fail to understand a target country's history and realize its use in current-era analysis.)

One of my finished intelligence reports was on Soviet airborne troops command and control. This subject was of interest to the National Security Council (NSC). Remember, during the October 1973 Arab-Israeli War, the possible intervention of Soviet airborne troops was of great concern to U.S. policymakers and the Department of Defense. The research we conducted on the activities and procedures of Soviet airborne troops also provided a window into the alert status and readiness preparations of these troops. Changes to U.S. procedures involving indication and warning resulted from this basic information. My interest in Soviet airborne troops dated back to the Arab-Israeli War. During that war I was still in DIA, assigned to the Pentagon to do current intelligence support of the Joint Chiefs of Staff. During the war we noticed that the Soviet airborne troops were placed on alert, and we were concerned that they might be used to intervene as the Israelis began to win and seemed to pose a threat for a drive on Damascus, Syria. After the war, I got to talk to some Israeli tankers (armor officers) who seemed more than confident they could have handled the airborne troops. (As a former U.S. Army armor officer with experience in Germany, I suspect their confidence was justified.)

The most notable "almost finished intelligence document" I can remember was on Soviet military readiness. We addressed this subject as a result of an NSC request we got one day. I just happened to be nearby when Morgan got the request and I immediately turned to SAFE to see if we had enough data to adequately address this subject. Finding a wealth of data coded in SAFE, we responded back to the NSC that we could accept the tasking. In a matter of days (rather than the weeks and months that preparing a basic, finished intelligence report usually took), I was able to prepare an initial draft report. I received a phone call from an

NSC staffer requesting its status and I let them know I had a first draft. It wasn't long thereafter that the NSC was requesting the draft and it was sent to them, bypassing the normal staffing, editing, and finished-publication procedures. The front office was not happy about this rapid response but they let it happen. Sometime later we got the draft back with a Blue Note (a personalized note from someone senior to the recipient) attached, signed by Henry Kissinger, thanking us for an on-target report. Without SAFE, we could not have responded so quickly or so well. The bottom line here is that basic research provides the intellectual foundation for meeting consumer intelligence needs quickly and that working with the consumer on their timelines is more important than a pretty publication that is fully vetted but too late to matter.

Transition from Analysis to Strategic Planning

From 1989 to 1995, I worked on strategic planning for future intelligence systems while assigned to the Committee on Imaging Requirements and Exploitation (COMIREX). The imagery community underwent several reincarnations, including as the Central Imagery Office (CIO), then the National Imagery and Mapping Agency (NIMA), and finally the National Geospatial-Intelligence Agency (NGA). So while my résumé looks like I was jumping between several organizations, it was just new clothes for the same model. With the creation of the NGA, I retired. Even after retirement, I continued to work on strategic planning for the development of informational needs for the future and using those needs (derived from analysts) to evaluate proposed future intelligence-support architectures (the physical hardware and operating concepts that would enable tasking, collection, processing, exploitation, and dissemination). Although many analysts I knew distrusted the engineers that proposed and developed hardware systems and the engineers were driven almost crazy by working with analysts—like me—putting the two disciplines together resulted in an improved understanding of what was needed as well as what was possible. There were often disagreements based upon the different cultures and agendas, it was one of the most interesting times in my career. I will always remember when one of the most politically savvy and diplomatic guys I ever worked with once threatened to punch out one of the engineers. Ah, those were good days!

8

Getting the Facts Right

TONY WILLIAMS

I n the mid-1970s U.S. policymakers and military leaders had a perspective on Soviet military leadership that caused them to misunderstand the process so badly that any serious understanding of likely Soviet actions and reactions in the national security realm was undermined. Much of this misapprehension was caused by the infamous "mirror imaging" about which one hears so much. In the Command Analysis Branch of the Office of Strategic Research (OSR), we were determined to get a real grasp on how Soviet national security decisions were made and executed at the national level. And we started with the assumption that everything we "knew" was wrong. (Now, of course, the Key Assumptions Check is part of the Directorate of Intelligence's analytical tradecraft. The work I am about to describe, conducted along with Boyd Sutton and Mike Flint, became the intellectual forerunner of this technique.) Boyd Sutton did some groundbreaking work on the Soviet National Command Authority, which was based on solid research and analysis. The key part of the effort after the research was to develop theories or models that accounted for the largest number of data points. This is a nontrivial issue, because it is all too common today for journalists to cherry pick the "evidence" and select that which supports their favorite theory, leaving the rest of the fruit to fall on the ground and rot. And in the end Boyd got it 100 percent correct.

His example led me to tackle the central military leadership organ—the Soviet General Staff. The effort took several years and got me entangled with various senior U.S. military and political leaders. The upshot of my research was to identify the General Staff as not only a planning organ, but an operational command organ at the national level as well. This was in direct contravention to the conventional wisdom in the Departments of State and Defense and in academia at the time. The U.S. Navy was especially irritated at my work because they saw in it a threat to their own autonomous operational authority in the contemporary U.S. system. (This was prior to the Goldwater-Nichols legislation, which mandated joint collaboration among the armed services.) Ultimately I was able to convince Admiral William Crowe of this, but not without some serious lifting by others, including both Boyd Sutton and Mike Flint.

Ironically, while the U.S. State Department's analysts were willing to accept the Soviet General Staff as an operational command organ, they were not willing to accept that it had any significant role in the five-year economic plans. Again, through some serious research, including my involvement in collection activities, I was able to demonstrate something that even I didn't expect at first. To wit, the Soviet General Staff not only participated in the five-year economic planning process, but also drove that process. Some of my historic research revealed the fact that the economic planning process at GOSPLAN (an acronym derived from Gosudarstvennyy Planovyy Komitet—the committee responsible for Soviet economic planning) was based on the General Staff's wartime mobilization planning process. This was because the original planners at GOSPLAN came from the Soviet General Staff (or, more accurately, from its predecessor the Workers and Peasants Red Army General Staff). Furthermore, I uncovered evidence that demonstrated conclusively that the General Staff had begun its five-year planning process one year before GOSPLAN began the overall state economic planning process, and GOSPLAN based its effort on the General Staff's work. This analysis had an unexpected side effect for our economic analysts. When I discovered that the General Staff had started its planning effort with the assumption that the current five-year plan would hit all its targets, and then did not adjust for failure, we were able to get a better handle on real inflation in the USSR. This was something with which the CIA had long struggled.

This work also had another interesting and unexpected result. When Minister of Defense Andrei Grechko died unexpectedly in 1976, there was considerable analytical thrashing in Washington and elsewhere over his potential successor. Another OSR analyst and I were the first to predict that Dmitriy Ustinov, the Party Secretary for Defense Economic Affairs, would be the next Soviet minister of defense. Some of the analysis we used was based on my work on the General Staff. Ustinov's close work with key General Staff elements in the years preceding Grechko's death, Ustinov's appearance in public ceremonies with senior General Staff officers in his Soviet military uniform, and other activities led us to conclude that Ustinov was a far more logical choice for the job than the other apparent candidates. For me, the fact that the CIA's military analysis office was the first to make this call spoke volumes to the efficacy of military analysis at a time in U.S. intellectual history when social and economic analysis had eclipsed military analysis in importance. Ultimately, through the judicious use of open and classified sources of information, including historical research, I was able to describe in detail the entire Soviet General Staff's structure and its major operations, including its role in economic planning and foreign military aid programs. This effort extended over about five years and resulted in numerous briefings and papers, including three papers in excess of one hundred pages. The point here is that truly valuable analysis requires both time and patient effort. But it can lead to the most unexpected results.

Another outcome of my work was to advance our understanding of how to use the Support to the Analysts' File Environment program (SAFE) as a variegated research tool. By allowing all analysts in the branch to add keywords to the file for a given document, a long and rich set of keywords was developed for each document in the branch SAFE file that exceeded what any one analyst would have ever conceived. When I returned to search the SAFE keyword data base, as I did regularly, that keyword list gave me additional insights into how various documents interrelated, and allowed me to engage in a rudimentary relational analysis activity before that term had come into regular usage, and before the tools to do real relational analysis existed. The point here is that one can almost always push any tool beyond the uses for which it was originally conceived with a little imagination, some cooperation with others, and a lot of hard work. It should also be noted that a branch that never exceeded a dozen analysts, over a period of about six to seven years, was able to create one of the most comprehensive files of military and defense information the CIA had ever had until the advent of modern computing capabilities in the 1980s. The Command Analysis Branch SAFE file came to exceed thousands of unique documents, each with dozens of keywords attached by the branch analysts.

Winning the Cold War

9

An Economist's Look at the Soviet Union, and Beyond

ROBERT E. LEGGETT

ollowing my years of study at Lehigh University, I applied for employment with the Central Intelligence Agency (CIA). I was hired as an analyst in the Office of Strategic Research (OSR). My first assignment was in a branch whose responsibility was to analyze military-economic issues on the former Soviet Union. With my academic work in hand, I found myself competing with Soviet specialists, most with advanced degrees. I gradually built my expertise until I became noted as a leading expert on the Soviet economy, especially in the area of investment policies. My career spanned three decades and included interesting assignments in and outside of the Directorate of Intelligence (DI)—that is, in several DI offices, on the National Intelligence Daily staff, in the Office of Congressional Affairs, in the Counternarcotics Center, on the National Intelligence Council (NIC) and in the Office of Information Management. In the process I was privileged to brief high-level officials from the executive and legislative branches of government, participate in Congressional briefings, and write analytic assessments on important issues—such as the Soviet economy, organized crime, counternarcotics, counterterrorism, the security of U.S. embassies—that went to high-level U.S. policymakers. I received numerous awards, including multiple Exceptional Performance Awards and a Certificate of Distinction awarded by then-DCI Robert Gates.

Career Path

My career began with an assignment in the Office of Strategic Research as a military-economic analyst. With the Cold War in process and no academic training in areas relating to the Soviet Union, I was immediately confronted with some daunting challenges. I was faced with meeting new people, moving to the Washington DC area with its traffic problems and tremendously high housing costs, and coping with being the new guy in a totally unknown profession. Most challenging of all was the need to learn how to be an analyst in the Directorate of Intelligence. To be successful in the DI, one needs to be a top analyst—that is, be able to research, analyze, and write well in the distinct DI style. An analyst also must be able to market his or her product and get it to the customer—high-level policymakers—in a timely way. Certainly one's ability to communicate, particularly in the form of briefings, can be one of the most challenging but also one of the most rewarding aspects of an analyst's career. Speaking before a congressional committee or an academic forum or speaking one-on-one to a member of Congress or to congressional staffers can be exhilarating. One of my assignments early on in my career was to address an academic seminar at American University on the state of the Soviet economy. I remember it well. I was as nervous as could be.

In any event, here I was in Washington DC, an analyst with the Central Intelligence Agency, striving to integrate myself into the culture of the DI and its daunting challenges—faced with mastering research and writing skills, learning how to communicate with policymakers, learning to be corporate in my approach to issues and problems, and generally learning the ropes. Except for a one-week introductory course welcoming one to the DI, there was no formal training available to help one navigate through these difficult waters. It was sink or swim.

My first assignment, given to me during my first year, was to attend the military subcommittee meetings at NATO in Brussels, Belgium. The subject matter of the meetings was to help write and then review in subcommittee a paper—one of a select number of assessments done by NATO each year—on the military and economic potential of the Soviet Union. I was responsible for representing the U.S. position at the military economic subcommittee meetings. It was a great opportunity to travel overseas, to represent the U.S. government and the agency, and to get my feet wet as an analyst.

For the next several years I worked as an analyst in the OSR following various issues related to the USSR. One issue I became involved in was to better understand the meaning of the "Defense Budget" published by the Kremlin each year in its statistical handbook, *Narodnoe Khozyaistvo*. The published Soviet data amounted to a modest 4 percent of its national income produced and accounted for only about 7 percent of its total state budget expenditures. Given the size of the Soviet military establishment at the time, this clearly appeared to be a misleading and inaccurate measure of what Moscow was spending on defense. But what did the number represent? That was the question that the intelligence community was trying to answer. The subject led to my first opportunity to publish in academic journals—a heady experience for any professional analyst. Indeed, one of the most satisfying aspects of my analytic career was the opportunity to publish both internally and externally in scholarly journals and books—an opportunity I took advantage of frequently. For example, in the October 1978 issue of the journal *Soviet Studies*, Sheldon Rabin and I discussed the question of the meaning of the Soviet-published "Defense Budget." We were unable to rule out a real basis for the official Soviet number. We provided, however, several alternative explanations for the published budget in the article. Our most plausible explanation was that the announced budget was an operating budget whose level was sometimes manipulated by the Soviet government for political purposes.

After some four years of working on Soviet military economic issues, I transferred to the Office of Economic Research (OER). Given my graduate degrees in economics and my strong interest in economic issues, it seemed like the right thing to do. For the next twenty years, with some breaks for assignments outside of the OER, I became a student of the Soviet economy. The issues addressed over the years varied widely. One such was an attempt to measure the rate of inflation in the Soviet machine-building sector. Industrial wholesale prices in the USSR were set at the time by the State Price Committee (Gosudarstvennii komitet tsen). Once set they were supposed to remain constant until changed by official reform or revision. Many Western experts believed, however, that Soviet enterprises escaped fixed prices by making cosmetic changes to established products in order to raise their prices—the so-called new-product-pricing phenomenon.

The question was how to verify that new-product-pricing was actually done and if so to measure the rate at which prices were being raised. The machine-building sector was studied because of its importance to the Soviet economy. The hedonic technique—the use of regression analysis to examine the connection between price change and quality improvements in machinery items—was used to test for the presence of this phenomenon and to determine what impact, if any, it had on machinery price levels over the period studied. The study and the results were published internally within the OER and in the June 1981 *Journal of Comparative Economics*. The study found that the new-product-pricing phenomenon did exist and that the price increases were "substantial for the items studied during 1967–1973."

I also analyzed the nature of the USSR's capital stock—that is, the plant and equipment used in its production process. A critical element in the Kremlin's intensive approach to modernization during the 1980s was the modernization of the capital stock in the country. A successful modernization program depended, in part, on speedier retirement of the USSR's aging plant and equipment. Soviet statistics were used often by analysts as indicators of the country's progress in its modernization effort. In the summer 1986 issue of the *Journal of Comparative Economic Studies*, Martin J. Kohn and I published "A Look at Soviet Capital Retirement Statistics: Unraveling Some Mysteries?" The results of the analysis, which was published internally as well, indicated that Soviet retirement statistics were not wrong or useless, although we urged caution in the use of the data. On balance, we found that

Soviet retirement rates were generally very low, suggesting that Moscow's efforts to modernize the economy were proceeding at an extremely slow pace.

A good deal of my subsequent analytic studies focused on Moscow's investment policies. These more macroeconomic studies of Moscow's investment decisions provided an important piece of the puzzle in understanding how the USSR's economy was performing. Indeed, I became looked upon by the policy and academic communities during the 1980s as the expert on Soviet investment policies. My investment studies during the 1980s were widely published internally as well as in various journals. For example, an article I wrote entitled "Soviet Investment Policy in the Eleventh Five-year Plan," was published in *Soviet Economy in the 1980s: Problems and Prospect* by the Joint Economic Committee of Congress. Another article, entitled, "Soviet Investment Policy: The Key to Gorbachev's Program for Revitalizing the Soviet Economy," was published by the Joint Economic Committee of Congress in *Gorbachev's Economic Plans*, November 23, 1987.

Midway through the 1980s I asked for and received an assignment in the Office of Congressional Affairs. This assignment, albeit short lived, was one of the most interesting and exciting assignments of my career. Interacting with members of Congress and various congressional committees was fascinating work. I threw myself into learning as much as I could about how Congress worked and how to best serve the DI in getting its analysis the widest exposure possible on Capitol Hill. Many working days were filled escorting analysts and high-level agency officials to the Hill. A number of unique experiences still stand out in my mind—such as arranging and attending a one-on-one briefing for Senators Ted Kennedy and Bill Bradley as well as escorting Deputy Director of Intelligence (DDI) Robert Gates to address one of the committees of Congress. One episode that stands out in particular occurred while I was attending a briefing at the Senate Select Committee on Intelligence in the classified SCIF (sensitive compartmented information facility) in the Hart Building. About halfway through the session, Senator John Glenn came into the briefing room and announced that the space shuttle Columbia had exploded and all the astronauts had perished. He then broke down crying, overcome by emotion.

The DDI asked that I return early from my congressional assignment to again work on analyzing the Soviet economy. I spent the second half of the 1980s analyzing the macroeconomic performance of the Soviet economy. As before, I published a large number of articles internally as well as in academic journals. I enjoyed immensely the work and the opportunities for travel and speaking before professional groups, congressional staffers, and academic seminars. Two articles were representative of the analysis I did: "Gorbachev's Reform Program: 'Radical' or More of the Same?" published in 1988 in a book edited by Susan J. Linz and William Moskoff entitled *Reorganization and Reform in the Soviet Economy*; and "The Soviet Union: An Economy in Transition and Its Prospects for Economic Growth," a chapter coauthored with Robert A. Kellogg, in a book edited by Ronald D. Liebowitz, in 1988, and entitled *Gorbachev's New Thinking*.

My analyses of the performance of the Soviet economy, as mentioned above, were a part of the agency's overall assessment of the USSR's economy during the period of the 1970s and 1980s. That analysis came under heavy criticism in the early 1990s after the fall of the Soviet empire. According to a case study published by the Kennedy School of Government: "In the wake of the 1991 collapse of the Soviet empire and the most dramatic realignment of geopolitical forces since World War II, the Central Intelligence Agency found itself fighting for its institutional life. At what should have been its moment of greatest glory—the demise of its prime ideological adversary—the CIA stood charged that it failed the mission for which it was founded: accurately assessing the political, economic, and military state of the Soviet Union."

The criticism by the media was harsh at times. Senator Daniel Patrick Moynihan opined, for example, in the *New York Times*, on May 19, 1991, that "for a quarter of a century, the CIA has been repeatedly wrong about the major political and economic questions entrusted to its analysis."

It is not my intention or place to defend the agency and its analysis. But I find the criticism difficult to understand. From my limited vantage point, it appears to me that the economic analysis that was done was accurate. It indicated that Soviet economic growth trended downward for several decades as the economy experienced repeated harvest failures, bottlenecks in industry, shortages of energy and labor, and chronically low productivity. The Soviet system of planning and management simply was too centralized and clumsy to manage effectively the increasingly complex and sophisticated economy. In addition, the perverse nature of the system of incentives discouraged innovation, technological change, and the efficient use of resources. I would agree with Robert Gates who said that "the body of information, analysis, and warning provided to policymakers was of extraordinarily high quality."

I left the DI as the Soviet empire was crumbling to take an assignment in an area that was totally foreign to me—the security of U.S. embassies abroad. It turned out to be a broadening assignment. I headed up a group that assessed for the State Department and intelligence community the threat to U.S. embassies abroad. I worked for the first time for an officer from the Directorate of Operations (DO). She was outstanding. She gave me a tremendous amount of responsibility and wide latitude to be creative. I stood up an analytical group to assess threats to U.S. embassies and designed publications that focused on analyzing such threats. It was a great experience to see an organization that I had built come to life and the publications I designed appear each month.

Following my work on U.S. embassies, I was given an assignment with a community focus in the Counternarcotics Center. My tour in the center involved writing and coordinating drafts of analytic assessments of numerous counternarcotics issues. These assessments involved writing a draft, convening the intelligence and law enforcement communities to review the draft, and publishing and distributing a final paper to policymakers. One such assignment involved the drafting of a National Intelligence Estimate that assessed the threat to the United States from various forms of narcotics and narcotics traffickers. One daunting step in the process of publishing the NIE was to defend it before the DCI and the representatives of the various community agencies.

While working in the Counternarcotics Center I witnessed an event that I found both shocking and surreal. Upon reporting to work one morning, everyone was summoned to a meeting with the director of the center. He informed a stunned group of officers that Aldrich Ames had been arrested for espionage. I was shocked, having never imagined that a trusted colleague would do such a thing. Ames had worked in the same complex as I did! It was a shock, to say the least.

My next assignment, as the deputy national intelligence officer for global and multilateral issues on the National Intelligence Council, was probably the most challenging of my career. The National Intelligence Council serves as the senior advisory group to the director of central intelligence. Its primary function at the time was to support the director by producing interagency reports and analyses, including National Intelligence Estimates (NIEs). The NIC also was and continues to be a focal point for the DNI for improving the intelligence community's responsiveness to policymakers' needs. The NIC traces its roots back over forty years to the Board of National Estimates, formed in 1950, and the national intelligence officer system, established in 1973.

As the deputy national intelligence officer I was responsible for managing, usually writing, NIEs on multiple subjects. Working for a national intelligence officer whose sole interest was humanitarian emergencies around the world, was challenging. She focused her energy almost exclusively on an NIE titled *Global Humanitarian Emergencies, 1997*. The paper focused on complex humanitarian emergencies—situations in which armed conflict, government repression, and/or natural disasters cause at least three hundred thousand civilians to depend on international humanitarian assistance.

I focused most of my efforts on writing NIEs on international organized crime and terrorism. One of the proudest achievements of my career was the management and writing of an NIE titled *The Foreign Terrorist Threat to the United States*. To the best of my knowledge, this NIE was the first document of its kind that correctly analyzed and assessed the seriousness of the threat from foreign terrorist groups to the American homeland. It predicted a major terrorist attack in this country within three years. The timing was incorrect, but the basic message was on target. If only policymakers and others that we briefed on the paper had paid more attention to it.

Having served two years on the NIC, I decided to make a major change in my career path and took an assignment in the Office of Information Management (OIM). This assignment, while not career enhancing, turned out to be rewarding. I interacted regularly with the State Department's historians in getting intelligence materials and documents on covert actions and other subjects declassified for the Foreign Relations of the United States (FRUS) series. The FRUS volumes go back almost to the time of the Lincoln presidency, and are an official accounting of the foreign relations of the United States. Getting material declassified for the series was a monumental task. Clearly the protection of sources and methods is critical to the viability of the intelligence, but in my view the agency officials assigned to monitor the release of documents went much too far in obstructing the release of these materials. As a consequence, a huge amount of resources went into the review and release of such materials—as much as was assigned to the agency's counterterrorism effort at the time, according to DCI George Tenet.

In the process of managing the release process, in addition to briefing the Historical Review Panel at the State Department, I established a high-level panel of officials from State, the CIA, and other agencies that met regularly to discuss the release of materials. I also managed for the DCI and the director of OIM a Historical Review Panel (HRP) of academic experts to advise the DCI on issues related to the release of historical intelligence documents. I believe I made a difference in getting materials out to the American public that should have been released, but it was not an easy task. The agency's review officials, especially the representative from the Directorate of Operations, fought me tooth and nail.

While at OIM, I managed a major project that led to the release of a large volume of documents and the convening of a major conference at Princeton University to assess the CIA's analysis of the Soviet Union from 1947 to 1991. The global contest between the United States and the Soviet Union dominated international relations for some forty-six years (1945–91). The issue I took on was to measure the degree to which U.S. policymakers read, understood, and acted upon the intelligence assessments they received from the CIA. To do this, I headed up an effort to have intelligence documents on the subject reviewed and released and to hold a retrospective conference on the subject with the Center of International Studies at Princeton University. In all, about 860 DI finished intelligence documents, encompassing some nineteen thousand pages, were released for the first time. Combining these materials with documents released previously, almost one hundred thousand pages of materials and over 3,500 documents were available to the conference participants. A description of the released materials is contained in a volume edited by Gerald K. Haines and Robert E. Leggett titled, *CIA's Analysis of the Soviet Union 1947–1991*.

The conference was held at Princeton in March 2001. Using the materials provided, leading U.S. intelligence analysts presented papers that assessed the agency's analytic record on the Soviet economy, Soviet politics and foreign policy, Soviet science and technology, and Soviet military intentions and capabilities. The papers and the record of the conference, including editorial comments, speeches, and concluding remarks can be found in *Watching the Bear: Essays on CIA's Analysis of the Soviet Union* edited by Gerald K. Haines and Robert E. Leggett.

After almost thirty years as an analyst for the Central Intelligence Agency, I retired in November 2001. I was privileged to serve the agency and my country during a period of considerable challenge and danger. I feel a sense of pride in being just a small part of a larger effort to confront and defeat the Soviet Union. The world changed with the remarkable events surrounding the demise of the USSR, unfortunately, however, not all for the better. But a new generation of analysts work in the DI on a new set of issues that in many ways may be more challenging than the ones we faced during the Cold War.

10

Two of the "Coolest" Things I Did Working for the CIA

ROBERT BLACKWELL

spent thirty enjoyable years as a Directorate of Intelligence (DI) analyst and supervisor. I had several assignments and many travel opportunities. Two experiences, in particular, stand out to me as especially memorable.

You Die, We Fly!

Leonid Brezhnev, head of the then USSR, died in November 1982. I was a branch chief in the DI's Soviet office and was a six-year veteran of the organization. President Reagan asked Vice President George H. W. Bush to attend the funeral in his place. Bush, at the time, was in Africa and he flew to Germany before going on to Moscow for the funeral. Bob Gates, then the executive officer for the DI, told me to take a document to put in the hands of the vice president. The document contained the agency's information on Yuri Andropov, Brezhnev's likely successor. I was excited about the opportunity and took a change of underwear just in case I could talk myself onto the plane and fly to Moscow. Luckily for me, my plan worked!

On the plane, it was pretty much all business. Vice President Bush was trying to get a handle on what was happening in the Soviet Union in a general sense. Never in a million years did I think a vice president of the United States would be listening to me talk about what I knew on the topic. It was a heady experience! He threw questions at me for several hours. He had his own people around him, but they didn't ask questions. Mrs. Bush also was on the plane. At one point, she asked me whether or not the Soviets believed in the afterlife. I told her they didn't believe in God and she said that it was a shame they didn't have the comfort of believing they would see their loved ones in the next life.

When we landed, I had to take the document to the embassy. I didn't get to go to the funeral, but we all watched it on TV. The funeral, a state event, seemed to go on forever. The procession included military vehicles, tanks, missiles, and long lines of goose-stepping soldiers. In those days, the Kremlin hierarchy stood on the top of Lenin's tomb and this alignment showed who had the most clout. We all watched closely to see who stood where. Andropov had the top position and was also the one who greeted Vice President Bush—itself a sign of power. We expected that he would be next in line. In addition, Andropov and Bush had something in common. Bush had been head of the CIA and Andropov was previously head of the KGB, the USSR's main intelligence organization.

Other U.S. officials later flew in for the funeral. Secretary of State George Schultz was there as well as Senator Howard Baker, from Tennessee. Other high-ranking officials that came included Indian premier Indira Gandhi. It was quite a powerful crowd. I stayed in Moscow less than three days. I came back on a plane with Howard Baker.

While Andropov led the Soviet Union for a while, we soon realized his health was not good. He died a little over a year after Brezhnev. This time, Bush asked me to accompany him. Not that long later, he did so again when Konstantin Chernenko, Andropov's successor, died. Bush commented that his motto was: "You die, we fly."

It was a fascinating experience because I was right in the middle of history being made in a country I had studied for most of my adult life. Bush later sent me a picture on the plane with him and others. He wrote: "You die, we fly, best wishes and warm regards from George Bush." The picture has a place of honor in my family room.

My Trip with Les Aspin in 1989

In 1989 I was the national intelligence officer (NIO) for the USSR in the agency. It was a great job—probably the best one I had in my career. At that time, Les Aspin was the chairman of the House Armed Services Committee. I knew one of his aides, who asked me to come along with them on a trip to the Soviet Union in August 1989. It was a wonderful opportunity.

In the 1980s the Soviet Union and the United States almost went to war. The KGB thought the United States might use nuclear weapons on their country. For a number of years, they had seen our fighter pilots flying all over the Soviet Union and they were worried. The United States had information that indicated the USSR might use weapons on us. Both sides seemed to have concluded that the other party was planning an attack on the other.

Mikhail Gorbachev came to power in 1985. His agenda was focused mostly on improving the Soviet Union's economy. He was less concerned about military issues. Ronald Reagan asked Gorbachev to visit the United States. Reagan hoped he could get Gorbachev to sign onto a Strategic Defense Initiative (SDI), an ambitious project that would construct a space-based antimissile system to deter either side from beginning a war with the other. This program was immediately dubbed "Star Wars." The Soviets did not like the Star Wars concept, but Reagan and Gorbachev had a decent enough relationship to continue the discussion.

Prior to Gorbachev's visit, Reagan asked to be briefed on the USSR. I was selected to brief him on what the Soviet Union was all about. Reagan didn't understand how the Soviet Union's economy worked. I planned what I was going to say and showed my outline to then DDI Bob Gates. Gates said my approach would not work with Reagan because he did not have extensive knowledge about the Soviet Union. Reagan liked stories and Gates said that I needed to tell him some stories he could grab onto in order to make the connections. So I told him a story. It was a story of two families—one landowner and one peasant. The landowner had everything anyone could want, a beautiful wife, clever and talented children, abundant fields, wealth, and so forth. The peasant lived in a hovel, barely surviving, and had an ugly wife with boorish children. One day a magical creature appeared before the peasant and said, "You are granted one wish. Say but the word and I will make you and your family like the landowner up on the hill. You will have wealth and eat well all your days. The peasant thought for a moment and then said, "No, I don't want that. I want you to make HIM like ME." Reagan liked the story—he had a glint in his eye when he heard it, and seemed to understand the implications of the Soviet view on life.

Reagan never gave up trying to convince Gorbachev to endorse Star Wars, but he was never successful. Gorbachev did, however, institute a policy of *glasnost* (openness), which called for more sharing of information between the United States and the USSR.

As part of this glasnost, Marshall Sergei Akhromeyev, a high-ranking Soviet military official, came to the United States in July 1988 as part of a reciprocal agreement in which Les Aspin would then tour the Soviet Union. Aspin took Akhromeyev around various military facilities and showed him what we had.

Akhromeyev toured a U.S. aircraft carrier off the coast of Norfolk, Virginia. The general had trouble believing that women were capable enough to work in this environment. He was flown around the country by a female pilot and had a difficult time understanding how pilots could land a plane on the deck of a "bobbing" sea. After General Akhromeyev viewed U.S. troops, he admitted to Aspin that the Soviet soldiers were not suited to perform these tasks and could not live up to the U.S. standards.

The following year, in August 1989, Akhromeyev returned the favor and took Les Aspin and several other officials, including me, to the Soviet Union. It took some work to get all of the things in place for the chairman to make the trip. Fourteen members of the House Armed Services Committee toured military installations in the Soviet Union along with five experts from the White House, the Defense Department, and private industry.

At the time we left, we expected a good reception from Akhromeyev and others because of glasnost. I think we got much more than we bargained for because, as it turned out, we got to go everywhere we wanted to go. Indeed, they didn't even ask us to give up our cameras or film.

At first, we flew to Germany to visit the Soviet Group of Forces there. They were very happy to see us and showed their wares in a mock war. The plane we were on was pretty well mixed with Russians and Americans. We became friends, to some extent. We flew to Moscow and then to various places. We went first to Kiev where they demonstrated Soviet weaponry. We then went to Yalta, Stalin's old "hang out" where I got to sit at his seat at the round table; it overlooked the Baltic Sea. It was a great view—no wonder Stalin loved the place. We stayed overnight at Yalta and then flew to Sevastopol in the Ukraine, the heart of the Soviet Navy. We got to walk all over one ship and found, to our surprise, a swimming pool three decks down.

Next we flew to Uzbekistan, where we stayed for a day or two. After we got to Uzbekistan, we flew to Almaty (Alma-ata), the capital of Kazakhstan. While we were there, we started to relax as we had been going pretty hard the first part of the trip—Aspin was a "hard driver," even for a congressman. Some of the guys went off and got a massage. The Soviets then took us outside of the city to an open-air arena where athletes were trained in the high altitude so they could function better in regular meets. We stayed there a few days and then we flew off to Baikonur, the heart of the Russian space program and Soviet nuclear missiles. I expected the Soviets would not let us take pictures there, but they didn't stop us.

There was a shrine to Yuri Gagarin, the first cosmonaut, in Baikonur. We found out that the Soviets had a space shuttle, but they only orbited it once without anyone in it and then it came down in Baikonur. In addition to the one space shuttle, we saw two others that had been built. They were never used as far as we know. Baikonur was the place where they built their own version of our Saturn V rocket. They even let us see that. We crawled around in it, and we could see anything we wanted to. In the "old days," this would never have happened.

We eventually came back to Moscow and went north to visit a nuclear missile silo. I don't remember what type of missile it was, but they were "at the ready" if need be. If they thought something was coming at them, they were ready to counterattack. That made all of us a little nervous.

Prior to the trip, I had gotten cameras from the National Photographic Interpretation Center (NPIC), as it was known then. I didn't think I would be allowed to take them because the other times I had been in Moscow, I wasn't allowed to snap a picture of *anything*, railroad bridges, whatever, let alone what you would find in Baikonur. On this trip, I took pictures freely, and I took hundreds of everything. It was wonderful.

After coming back, I briefed people about the trip and gave the pictures I had taken to NPIC and those who might be interested. There were hundreds of pictures—a huge cache of Soviet materiel.

The trip was important because the two armed services had not known much of what the other side did. After the two exchanges between Akhromeyev and Aspin, each side had a greater insight into the other's military systems. From my perspective, most of the people on both sides felt that we had learned a great deal.

11

A Cold War CIA Analyst Remembers

ANNE CAMPBELL GRUNER

t was 1978, the height of the Cold War, post-Vietnam, a time of the OPEC oil crisis and stagflation. Having attended the Edmund A. Walsh School of Foreign Service at Georgetown and passed the oral and written Foreign Service exams, I intended to enter the State Department as a Foreign Service officer after graduating with my Master of Arts in Law and Diplomacy from the Fletcher School at Tufts. That was not to be. President Jimmy Carter had cancelled two Foreign Service Officer classes due to budget cutbacks and it was unclear when there would be another class. Having been an intern in the CIA's Office of Strategic Research (OSR) the summer before, I had applied to the agency's Career Trainee (CT) Program as a backup to the Foreign Service. Thanks to Jimmy Carter, my backup plan became my primary plan.

The OSR, as it was known, was a bastion of former military officers and not considered a welcoming environment for female employees. I enjoyed my internship, however, and my summer project in OSR's Soviet theater branch on the effects of weather on the tactical air balance in Central Europe. The project became the basis of my master's thesis at Fletcher, entitled "The Modernization of Soviet Frontal Aviation and the Tactical Air Balance in Central Europe." My thesis was simple: while the Soviets had larger numbers of combat aircraft, the United States and NATO had *better* aircraft and thus quality offset quantity. NATO troops would thus fare okay in a war with the Warsaw Pact in Central Europe. In retrospect, that theme was the hallmark of the CIA's Cold War Soviet military analysis. Such analysis earned CIA the enmity, if not the grudging respect, of the Defense Intelligence Agency (DIA) and the Office of Naval Intelligence (ONI). The CIA's Soviet military estimates have been the topic of countless books, analyses, debates, and symposiums. After that fateful summer, that subject became my life for years to come.

After graduating from Fletcher, I entered the agency's CT Program, which was billed as an exclusive training program for high-quality recruits. At that time, the program was essentially a case officer training program for the Directorate of Operations (DO) with a few recruits in each class tagged for the Directorate of Intelligence (DI). Whatever my CT class might have lacked in judgment, it made up for in spirit. A surprising number of my DO-bound classmates were terminated early in their careers for various injudicious behaviors; but that is another tale. I had been told by agency shrinks that my psychological profile matched that of men going into the DO (there were no such profiles for women at that time). But I resisted entreaties to join the DO, preferring the presumptively more intellectual milieu of the DI. The Foreign Service finally offered me an appointment while I was still a trainee. Feeling I could not desert the trainee program, and perhaps because I was having fun, I turned down the Foreign Service, one of those fateful decisions that determines one's life.

After completing the CT Program, I was delighted to be assigned as a military analyst to the Soviet Strategic Forces Division in OSR. Although I had interned in the Theater Forces Division, strategic nuclear forces was my first love ever since I had learned how to calculate nuclear bomb blasts and overpressure on hand-held bomb calculators at the Fletcher School. Now, in the OSR I was going to be a Soviet "ICBM analyst." I would follow the large intercontinental nuclear missiles that could strike the United States. Unlike the Theater Forces Division, where analysts counted tanks and airplanes and there were few women, the Strategic Forces Division had quite a few women for its time. At a recent reunion of OSR colleagues, I met these women again and almost all of them have risen to senior positions.

I thus began my career as a "bean counter," following the deployment of the Soviet Union's fifth generation of strategic nuclear missiles. I painstakingly watched on satellite imagery as the silo paving blocks were rolled into place at missile sites in order to argue with the DIA about whether this or that missile was now operational. In actuality, the analytical issues were fierce and the National Intelligence Estimates (NIEs) intensely debated and footnoted. How many warheads could be deployed on an SS-18 ICBM? Was the SS-16 mobile ICBM secretly deployed at the test range? Today, these issues seem almost trivial to me, but at the time, I thought I was working on the most important issue in the world—nuclear war. My analysis of Soviet missile production—using a costing analytic mode ironically known as SCAM—suggested that Soviet missile production was going to begin declining in the relatively near future. This was heresy and surely I had made a mistake, management thought. This tidbit of analysis, however, fell into a broader picture being painted by a variety of Soviet military analysts in the mid-1980s that depicted an eventual decline in Soviet military forces and signaled, at least to some, the ultimate collapse of the vaunted Soviet Empire. Volumes have been written and debated on this topic and what the CIA did and did not predict. I was a part of it, and it was fun.

I was in my third year as an ICBM analyst and looking for a change when a big break came. I applied for and was selected to be the junior intelligence adviser to Ambassador Paul Nitze at the new disarmament negotiations being launched in Geneva, Switzerland. And thus began the best job of my life and to this day the high point of my professional career. The intermediate-range nuclear forces (INF) talks reflected the ebb and flow of the Cold War: a massive Soviet missile buildup followed by negotiated disarmament. Against the relentless Soviet deployments of SS-20 intermediate-range ballistic missiles (IRBMs) aimed at Western Europe, President Ronald Reagan announced that the United States would deploy U.S. Pershing IIs and cruise missiles in four European countries as a counterweight and deterrent to the ss-20s. Moscow reacted with predictable animus, threats, and antinuclear propaganda. Reagan offered the famous "zero option"— the United States would forego its future missile deployments if Russia would dismantle all of its existing ss-20s, including those deployed in the Eastern USSR that the Soviets claimed could not reach Western Europe.

While much has been written about the INF talks and the virtues and vices of Paul Nitze as a negotiator, including the Broadway play *A Walk in the Woods*, suffice it to say that I am ever grateful to the CIA for enabling me to work for this great man during this exciting period of history. I was twenty-seven years old and in Geneva debating the range of the ss-20 IRBM and the relative combat radius of the su-24 Fencer and the F-4 Phantom with General Yuri Lebedev, then deputy chief of the Soviet General Staff. For me, it did not get much better than that.

It was at the INF talks where I made my singular contribution to the course of world events. With only the sketchiest of public information and more intuition than intelligence, I figured out, or so I thought, that Soviet president Leonid Brezhnev would declare a moratorium on ss-20 missile deployments against Europe at his speech to the Trade Union Congress in March 1982. Such a moratorium would be one more propaganda ploy designed to derail U.S. deployments while leaving in place the Soviet force of some three hundred ss-20s already deployed. The USSR hoped the Europeans would lose their nerve and cancel the U.S. deployments. Brezhnev's scheduled speech coincided with the final day of our negotiations in that round of the Geneva talks.

Although the senior intelligence adviser in Geneva, who was my boss, did not agree with my analysis on the moratorium, I raised the idea with Paul Nitze and explained why I thought Brezhnev would do this. Nitze agreed that it was a good possibility. Nitze had the U.S. delegation warn Washington through front and back channels that such an announcement might be coming. The Washington Interagency Group worked through the weekend to get coordinated guidance to NATO capitals warning of such an announcement and offering talking points on how to respond. There was a pool on the U.S. delegation, taking bets on whether Brezhnev would announce a moratorium or not. I was sweating bullets, imagining my humiliation if I were wrong.

Brezhnev's speech in Moscow to the Trade Union Congress was to take place almost simultaneously with Nitze's meeting with Yuli Kvitzinskiy, his Soviet counterpart, in our final plenary of the negotiating session in the spring of 1982. When the day came, our delegation in Geneva had the U.S. embassy in Moscow alerted and standing by through an open phone line to give us a read out of Brezhnev's speech. Bingo! Brezhnev announced a moratorium on missile deployments in the Western USSR and called on NATO to halt its planned missile deployments in response. We ran up flights of stairs in the Botanic Building in Geneva to brief Nitze on the key points of Brezhnev's speech just as he was about to meet with Kvitzinskiy.

Paul Nitze, the showman, played it up. He told Kvitzinskiy that he understood that the Soviet president had just delivered a speech. Kvitzinskiy disingenuously professed not to know anything about Brezhnev's speech, which clearly had been intended to take the West by surprise. Instead, Nitze took Kvitzinskiy by surprise. Nitze outlined the key points of Brezhnev's moratorium announcement, which had taken place just minutes earlier, and articulated why the Soviet proposal was unacceptable. Allied capitals also responded immediately, and having been forewarned by Washington, they uniformly dismissed the moratorium for what it was—a propaganda ploy. It was an intelligence coup! We successfully deflected a major Soviet propaganda initiative in the INF game of cat and mouse. We could not have done better had we stolen Brezhnev's speech in advance!

Some say good DI analysis can replace DO secret intelligence. I do not subscribe to that view, but in this case it was analysis, and hefty speculation on my part, that won the day. I was told that at a subsequent meeting of the North Atlantic Council the allies praised Washington for its foresight and warning of the moratorium. Nitze reportedly told the allied representatives that it was largely due to the work of a young woman on the delegation named Anne Campbell. It was insignificant in the grand scheme of things, but an accomplishment I cherish in the knowledge that I affected world events in my own small way. Geneva also was important because it was where I met my future husband, who was then in Geneva as well.

The INF talks broke off when the Soviets walked out of Geneva once the United States deployed its missiles in Europe in the fall of 1983. My tour in Geneva and with the Arms Control Intelligence Staff (ACIS) sadly came to an end. I had been promoted to a ranking of GS-14 and earned "senior analyst" status. Back in the DI's newly established Office of Soviet Analysis, or SOVA, I finally finished my requisite "long-term" research paper—a fifty-page tome that traced the evolution of Soviet views on arms-control verification. The paper was a thoroughly researched and useful exposition for experts but incorrectly predicted that the Soviets would never accept on-site inspection on Soviet territory. In fact, the INF Treaty, finally signed in 1987, heralded a new age of extensive and reciprocal on-site inspections between the United States and the Soviet Union—and now with Russia—that continue to this day.

Becoming restless with the day-to-day analysis of the DI, I was rescued with an unexpected, directed assignment as a branch chief overseeing the production of raw intelligence reports on the Soviet Union in the Operations Directorate's Domestic Collection Division. As a GS-14, a management position as a branch chief in the DI was the coveted next assignment, but the DO management assignment was the next best thing and exposed me to the DO.

My job was to oversee a branch of DO "reports officers." Reports officers had the responsibility to review all the raw reporting sent in by case officers in the field to determine what, if anything, merited being disseminated as an intelligence report. Reports officers also had the thankless task of editing the reports written by the case officers. In order to separate the wheat from the voluminous chaff of field reporting, reports officers had to have substantive expertise and awareness of policymakers' intelligence needs. In this respect, they had some kinship to DI analysts. Reports officers, however, endured a second-class status in the DO relative to the case officers who had the sexier mission of running operations, recruiting spies, and presumably collecting secret intelligence. It was a fun year as I personally met with individuals who had tidbits of intelligence to share with the U.S. government.

While I did not want to be out of sight and out of mind of my home office for too long, I was floored when I was asked to become the chief of the Soviet branch, the same unit where I had served as a summer intern some ten years earlier. This was the division where the hardcore military analysis and bean counting took place, where women feared to tread. I thought briefly that maybe I was being set up to fail. My experience was in strategic forces and arms control. Although I had written my master's thesis on the tactical air balance in Central Europe and had served as an intern in the branch, I did not think the male analysts in the branch would feel I was qualified for the job. I was a woman and younger than most of them.

Looking back on this assignment, however, it seems like a marriage made in heaven and one of my most rewarding career challenges. Sometimes keen military or technical experts have difficulty writing on complex issues in a way that the layman can easily understand. Fortunately, I had been blessed in my career with senior analysts, branch chiefs, and division chiefs who wrote well and who had taught me how to write intelligence analysis. As a branch chief, I began working on my analysts' papers, some of which had been languishing for years. Working together, we cleaned up the papers and got them published. Analysts today probably cannot appreciate the time and effort that went into writing "long-term" research papers in the olden days and to what extent an analyst's career success depended on finally publishing that brilliant, but long, research paper. Those papers were a much-needed investment in intellectual capital.

Having married a DO officer I met in Geneva, my career came

to a bit of a crisis when he received an assignment to Europe as the chief of station (COS), a reward for having suffered as chief of the DO's Latin American Division in the aftermath of the Iran-Contra affair. I could not imagine not working for three years in Europe, but DO policy did not allow COS's wives to work. To make a long story short, I finally was allowed to work in the station on a tandem assignment after persuading no fewer than eight Senior Intelligence Service (SIS) officers, including the directors of the DO and DI, and the associate director of central intelligence, in short, all the senior managers on the DI side and the DO side starting with my office director. Once in Europe, I functioned as an analyst-in-station and part-time DI representative for SOVA travelers to Europe. Thus, while my tour had a rocky start, I used my expertise to assist the station. It was exciting to be in Europe as the Berlin Wall crumbled, Germany reunified, the Soviet Union collapsed, and the United States undertook the first Gulf War.

After three years in Europe, I returned to the Office of Russian and Eurasian Affairs, or OREA, a newly reorganized office that reflected the splintering of the former Soviet Union. I began a succession of moves slogging up the management ladder. First, branch chief, one more time, this time in a political analysis branch, because that was what was available upon my return from Paris. A year later, in a competitive selection process, I became a deputy division chief in the old Strategic Forces Division, now called Security Issues Division, the same division where I had started my career fifteen years earlier. I almost lost the job as soon as I had gotten it due to an office reorganization that combined two divisions, but I got lucky and was allowed to stay.

Since the Soviet empire had collapsed, Russian military analysis had to similarly evolve. We no longer analyzed the effectiveness of Warsaw Pact plans for an offensive in Central Europe or assessed the prospects of a Soviet nuclear strike. Instead, we analyzed the Russian war in Chechnya, Moscow's military meddling in conflicts along its periphery, and the prospects for a coup d'état by Russian military leaders. We monitored the demise of the Russian military forces as tattered soldiers begged for food in Moscow and Russian submarines, aircraft, and missiles fell into disrepair. We worried about "loose nukes," "suitcase nukes," and the accidental launch of Russian nuclear weapons. We monitored the leakage of Russian nuclear materials and missiles to Iran and elsewhere, enduring endless turf fights with other DI counterparts including the newly formed Nonproliferation Center (NPC).

Oddly enough, some interagency battles fiercely continued despite the collapse of Russian military forces. The Office of Naval Intelligence insisted on attacking our analysis of the sinking Russian Navy. Analysts were outraged when the DDI agreed to include the ONI's one-page dissent in our published paper on the demise of the Russian Navy. Analysts "whined" that this was politicization, but in the end, it was the ONI's dissent that looked silly.

This period of middle management was painful as senior CIA managers began to aggressively downsize the former Soviet military analytic effort as part of the post–Cold War "peace dividend." In a shift of analytic resources away from the Russian military problem, divisions and units were merged, accounts eliminated, promotions denied, analysts forced out of the agency or into other, non-Russian analytic areas. I did my best to protect the troops, but it was a stressful time for Russian military analysts. The consequent loss and dispersion of this analytic capability was significant and irretrievable. Russia became an "issue group" and I a deputy issue manager, overseeing the remnant of Russian military analysts, an analytic cadre that during the Cold War had comprised virtually the entire Office of Strategic Research.

Having endured repeated organizational permutations and downsizing, and nasty analytic wars, turf fighting, and interagency squabbles, I was ready for a change. The next one came when I learned of an opening for the deputy director of the Arms Control and Intelligence Staff, the staff on which I had happily served in my early career when I attended the INF talks in Geneva. At this point in my career I had been a branch chief three times, a deputy division chief, division chief, deputy issue-group leader; I had served in the Directorate of Operations, both at headquarters and in a station abroad, worked for the State Department at a U.S. embassy, and served on an arms-control delegation in Geneva. I had been promoted to the SIS Level 2. I asked the ACIS chief if someone was already in line for the job. He said no and to my good fortune selected me from a pool of applicants.

Compared to the DI analytic war zone, the ACIS was a happy and harmonious place, well run and well regarded—at least that was my impression. I discovered that many of the career officers from other agencies who had worked on arms-control issues fifteen years earlier were still covering arms control. I knew them and the arms-control arena well. A large number of Russian military analysts who had left the DI during its downsizing were now in the ACIS directly supporting arms-control policy and what had become a massive regime.

I was happy in the ACIS, having returned to the interagency policy world that I had loved as a junior analyst. This time, however, I represented the entire intelligence community at interagency meetings chaired by the National Security Council staffers, deliberating on arms-control and treaty-compliance issues. I attended a few meetings in the White House Situation Room chaired by NSC advisers Sandy Berger and Condoleezza Rice. The interagency "squabbles" were at a higher and more intense level. The intelligence community was often the skunk at the NSC's picnic, arguing, inter alia, that the North Korean Framework Agreement and Comprehensive Test Ban Treaty could not be adequately monitored or "verified" and giving NSC staffers the bad news that Russia was undertaking various forbidden activities in violation of this or that treaty. One tenacious NSC staffer insisted on rewriting intelligence judgments regarding chemical and biological weapons; she finally stopped when I chastised her for politicizing intelligence.

Among my most memorable experiences in ACIS, and later in the Office of Weapons Intelligence, Nonproliferation, and Arms Control (WINPAC)—the large analytic entity that resulted from a merger of ACIS and the Nonproliferation Center—were my occasional stints. Even more spectacular to me was the unveiling of the post–boost vehicle of the gigantic SS-18 strategic nuclear missile that revealed the ten glistening warheads that could have wreaked devastation across our continent. A subject of considerable analytic debate in the olden days had been how many more warheads the Soviet Union could pack onto that missile.

One of my last assignments in WINPAC was serving as an adviser to then Deputy Secretary of State John Bolton who was negotiating the "Moscow Treaty." This treaty was signed by Presidents Bush and Putin on May 24, 2002, and ratified in the Senate on March 6, 2003. In contrast to its predecessor, the ground breaking START (Strategic Arms Reduction Treaty), which had some three hundred pages with annexes and multiple verification provisions, the Moscow Treaty was three pages long and contained no verification provisions.

Arms control had come full circle, reflecting the changed geostrategic relationship between Moscow and Washington. In the START negotiations, the United States had demanded strict and intrusive verification measures, including actual on-site inspections, to guard against Soviet "noncompliance." Such Soviet noncompliance with the earlier SALT Treaty had been a subject of intense political debate and analytic scrutiny. By 2002, however, Russian strategic forces were no longer rapidly expanding but were disintegrating before our eyes. The U.S. goal was to preserve its future strategic options and our proposal did that. The Russian military hated the treaty so much that DI analysts incorrectly predicted that Putin would refuse to sign it. I advised DCI Tenet that I believed Putin would sign the treaty because Moscow would rather have something than nothing. That prognostication became reality.

I thus bookended my intelligence career in the arms-control arena, spanning twenty-five years as the world evolved from the SALT Treaty to the Moscow Treaty.

At the end of my career, I was deputy chief of WINPAC for Arms Control and Intelligence Community Affairs and an SIS-4. Moving into the new millennium, however, it was clear that arms control with the former Soviet Union was not high on the policy agenda. Just as SOVA/OREA had been a target for post–Cold War downsizing, so had such attention turned to the remnant of the ACIS that had survived the merger to create WINPAC. War with Iraq was coming and it seemed like a good time to leave.

Through an "early out"—I believe the last one prior to the beginning of the Iraq war—I managed to retire "early," under fifty, and ostensibly young enough to begin a second career. In the fall of 2003, I started law school full time at Georgetown University. After graduating from law school in 2006 and passing the bar exam, I served as a law clerk to the Honorable Gaylord Finch in Fairfax County Circuit Court. That was a marvelous experience that ranks up there with negotiating with the Soviets; but that too is another tale.

Today, I am a domestic relations attorney at a small law firm in Vienna, Virginia, where I negotiate property settlement agreements instead of disarmament agreements and where my clients have weapons of personal destruction instead of weapons of mass destruction. In my former career I had a tiny impact on large, world events. Now, as I represent my clients in their divorces, I have a bigger impact on smaller events, but events most important to those I represent. Having watched for nearly two frustrating decades as nuclear and missile technology leaked out of the former Soviet Union despite the efforts of both Democrat and Republican administrations, I now take satisfaction in negotiating a good settlement for my clients, finding the missing marital assets, nailing the dead-beat dads, and winning the argument before the judge.

I loved my CIA career, and would not have traded it for anything. My fellow students at Georgetown Law School knew little about the Cold War or what all the fuss with Russia was about. I hope that the next generation of CIA analysts will be able to look back as I can with the same fondness, gratitude, and satisfaction in having lived in interesting times and made a contribution.

A Wealth of Options

12

Reminiscences of a Checkered Past

NICHOLAS STARR

I grew up in the Washington D C area, majored in geology at the University of Virginia, and graduated in 1953. Then it was straight on to study more geology in graduate school at Yale. After that, I worked a few years for the U.S. Coast and Geodetic Survey, ending up as acting observer in charge at the Cheltenham (Maryland) Geomagnetic Observatory (now located in Fredricksburg, Virginia). Then I moved west, trying my hand at petroleum exploration with the Continental Oil Company.

After about three years in the oil business, I grew tired of the migratory life, came back to Washington, and started hunting for another job—applying to the CIA and everywhere else I could think of. I must admit that I had no particular expectations or goals—I just wanted to put food on my bachelor table. I certainly had no idea then that some forty years later I would be looking back with pride at a career that had been a lot of fun and a perfect fit for my temperament and skills—and, most importantly, a career that helped to lay the foundation for the end of the Cold War by reducing the threat of mutual nuclear annihilation.

With my background in geology and geophysics, the CIA's Office of Scientific Intelligence (OSI) seemed like a good fit, and, in fact, the OSI gave me my first interview with the agency. As it turned out, they didn't hire me, but then along came another interview with a different part of the CIA. A few weeks later, that office sent a job offer, which I accepted by return mail. When a second letter arrived, imagine my dismay at reading the first sentence—it apologized for offering me the wrong grade. BUT, I breathed a big sigh of relief as I read on to learn that they wanted to hire me at the next *higher* grade.

That was 1961. My first assignment was with the Industrial Register in the Directorate of Intelligence (DI). At that time, most of the CIA was housed in a warren of temporary buildings down by the National Mall. The Industrial Register's home was once a skating rink near the Potomac River, where the Kennedy Center stands now. We were responsible for maintaining a vast card file of foreign industrial sites—everything from spaghetti factories to armament plants. I had been on the job for just a few months when my office moved into the brand-new Headquarters Building in Langley, much of which was still under construction when we arrived.

After two to three years as a glorified file clerk in the Industrial Register, I joined the Office of Current Intelligence (OCI). Its analysts were the DI's reporters, using classified sources to write news stories for the agency's various intelligence publications. I was not given the opportunity to pick my substantive duties before I arrived in the OCI, but found myself in the branch that specialized in outer space, missiles, and other strategic weaponry. That was a fortunate assignment that molded my career for the next two decades.

About three years later, I moved out of the DI into the Directorate of Science & Technology (DS&T), running the midnight-to-eight shift of the twenty-four-hour operations center of the Foreign Missile and Space Analysis Center (FMSAC). My principal job was to create a daily publication that reported on missile tests and space launches.

After that, I had a short tour as liaison officer to the Defense Special Missile and Astronautics Center (DEFSMAC) at Fort Meade, then back to Langley in the early 1970s as the FMSAC representative for National Intelligence Estimates and arms control matters. That was when the Cold War was in full bloom, and the Soviet Union was making major strides in strategic weapons of all kinds. So my job was at the focus of senior policymakers' life-or-death decisionmaking. During that time, I spent a couple of tours in

Geneva providing intelligence support to our delegation to the Strategic Arms Limitation Talks (SALT) that led to the first treaty limiting U.S. and Soviet strategic weapons. For the most part, those assignments involved writing intelligence-related plenary statements and ensuring that the intelligence community's collection and analysis capabilities were protected in the delegation's contacts with the Soviets.

Then I ran FMSAC's Current Intelligence Branch for a couple of years. That was another intelligence reporting job, much like my earlier tour in the OCI, but on a far more technical level.

In the mid-1970s, I moved out of the DS&T to become a full-time arms controller in the Arms Control Intelligence Staff (ACIS). That staff may have been in the DI when I first joined it, but before I left it had become attached to the Office of the Director of Central Intelligence (ODCI). The arms control world was truly an interagency effort, working together with—and sometimes at odds with—the State Department, the Arms Control and Disarmament Agency, the Office of the Secretary of Defense, and the Joint Chiefs of Staff. In most cases, the intelligence community holds itself aloof from the political world of national policy, but—because high-confidence monitoring of the other side's compliance is essential for our country's survival—this was one of the very few areas in which we intelligence officers had a mandate to impact U.S. policy directly. As the DCI's representatives, we had four principal responsibilities:

1. Policy formulation: Ensuring that U.S. negotiating positions did not reveal our intelligence capabilities and that agreements could be monitored to detect any cheating by the other side.

2. Negotiation: Providing on-the-spot intelligence support to the U.S. delegation, as described above.

3. Confirmation: Providing a liaison with both of the congressional intelligence committees (House and Senate), and preparing the director's Senate testimony on the intelligence community's confidence in its ability to detect covert noncompliance.

4. Monitoring: Ensuring that the other side remained in compliance via immediate reporting of ambiguous activity, as well as the production of a periodic monitoring report assessing every aspect of pertinent actions by the other side.

All in all, I spent about twelve years in various aspects of the arms control business—the longest of any of my many jobs at the CIA. I became deputy chief of the ACIS in the early 1980s, but by 1984, the constant interagency meetings to attend and brush fires to extinguish burned me out, so I moved to the inspector general's staff (another ODCI function). I was either a team member or team leader in perhaps a dozen inspections that took me to more than fifteen foreign countries and gave me a glimpse into some exceptionally arcane corners of the agency. Some of those inspections focused on CIA activities. Others assessed the organization and management of offices in the agency's various directorates.

Then I moved into the Directorate of Operations (DO) to run one of the branches in the new Counterintelligence Center. My final job with the agency was as deputy division chief in the intelligence community staff—yet another ODCI function—helping to prepare congressional briefing books to justify the budgets of each of the many elements of the intelligence community.

The intelligence community staff had recently moved from F Street in Washington to Langley when I encountered Amal Kasi and his AK-47. That was in January 1993, while I waited in my car at the stoplight to turn into the agency compound. As some may remember, Mr. Kasi killed two CIA officers and injured three others. I was the most severely injured of the survivors. I lost every drop of my blood and was pronounced dead more than once before the heroes at Fairfax Hospital brought me back to life. My souvenirs of that experience are world-class scars, an essentially nonfunctioning left arm, and an abiding hatred of terrorists of all stripes.

Mr. Kasi's attack threw the CIA into a state of shock. But my colleagues rose to the occasion nobly. I received literally hundreds of get-well cards and visits—from friends and strangers in the agency, from other intelligence agencies, congressional staffs, the State Department, and the Pentagon. And Fairfax Hospital was over-run with CIA personnel wanting to give blood. I was near retire-ment then, but all that thirty-something-year-old blood pumped new vigor into my old body.

The CIA came to the rescue as an organization, as well. All of the bills from my three hospital stays were paid by the agency. That must have cost a fortune. And the CIA paid my medical expenses after I left the hospital, including more than a year of physical therapy. Since the identity of my attacker and his motives were a mystery initially, the agency protected my family and me with round-the-clock armed guards during my first three weeks at home. And I received full pay during the year I was recuper-ating at home before retiring. Most comforting for my finances over the long pull, the agency made sure that I would be eligible for Workers' Compensation.

To finish the account of the shooting, Mr. Kasi immediately fled to his native Pakistan, and the United States offered a multimillion-dollar reward for his capture. After about five years of search-ing, my FBI friend, Brad Garrett, caught up with him near the Pakistan-Afghanistan border. He was returned to Fairfax, where I testified at his trial. The jury convicted him and recommended the death penalty. After five more years—during which his court-appointed lawyer filed interminable appeals—he was executed by lethal injection in November 2002.

Incidentally, Kasi's attack at the CIA came about one month *before* the first World Trade Center bombing, so I believe that the five of us were victims of the very first Islamic terrorist attack on U.S. soil—an interesting point, which has been ignored by the press. Also, the press never picked up on Kasi's perplexing trip to Ham-burg shortly before his rampage at the CIA. Most Americans had never heard of Al-Qaeda before the September 11, 2001, attack, and only after that we learned that there was a major Al-Qaeda cell in Hamburg—so it is tempting to wonder if Kasi's reason for flying to Germany was to get his marching orders from bin Laden's people there.

So what lessons can be gleaned from this rambling account of my thirty-two-year career?

The most important thing is that I enjoyed almost every minute of it. It was important work, but the icing on the cake was being associated with my CIA colleagues—with few exceptions, both my coworkers and my bosses were the smartest and most dedicated people I have ever met.

Not one of my agency jobs involved what my university and private industry training had prepared me for. Luckily, I had an inborn skill for the written word, which served me well in the early days. Later, the more responsible jobs built on the previous ones.

And I should note that—to me—one of the most appealing aspects of working for the agency is the fact that it offers so many, and such varied, opportunities. It is difficult to assess a new job before you move into it—particularly in the intelligence business, where security always gets in the way of detailed description. Sometimes the job that was described to you as an applicant does not live up to your expectations when you come on board. But once in the agency, you will be in an ideal position to move into a job that is a better fit. I am living proof that sampling agency jobs is not a sin, and that it is possible to move between directorates without jeopardizing your chances for advancement.

I was able to keep my enthusiasm by moving to different, ever more challenging jobs. Some people delight in being experts in narrow fields, and the CIA needs people like that. But my interests have always been more wide-ranging. Fortunately, I was able to avoid the narrow, and I think that that breadth of experience made me a more useful intelligence officer for the kinds of jobs that attracted me.

Although I found it invigorating to conquer new worlds, I learned that it is important to give one's best to each job and to stay there a few years before moving on. Job-hopping can blight any career.

Now that the USSR is just a memory, today's new intelligence officers can scarcely imagine the satisfaction that we arms controllers felt at being at the center of the nation's efforts to make the world safer by curbing the Russian nuclear arsenal. Now the bear is stirring again, so perhaps one day it will reawaken and give much the same challenges to a new generation. In any case, given the specter of terrorism and the other uncertainties in today's world, there surely will be no shortage of challenges, wherever they may arise.

After writing this chapter, I sent the following letter to then DCIA Leon Panetta:

> 10 September 2009
> Mr. Leon E. Panetta, Director
> Central Intelligence Agency
> Washington DC 20505
>
> Dear Mr. Panetta:
>
> As an Agency retiree, I received by e-mail today your Statement to Employees on the cowardly attacks of September 11, 2001.
>
> Like all right-thinking Americans, I agree wholeheartedly with everything you said in that brief communication. But I am dismayed that you made no mention of the fact that CIA was the target of the very first Islamic terrorist attack on U.S. soil.
>
> To remind you: The Agency was attacked in 1993, a month *before* the first World Trade Center bombing. Mir Amal Kasi, a Pakistani religious zealot, killed two of our employees and injured three others with his AK-47 on January 23rd. As the most severely injured of the survivors, I owe my life to the professional response of many people that day, not the least of whom were Agency SPOs [security protective officers] at the front gate and Office of Medical Services personnel who rushed to the scene.
>
> An interesting point, which has been almost completely ignored by the press, was our assassin's perplexing trip to

Hamburg shortly before his rampage at CIA. We know now that there was a major al-Qa'ida cell in Hamburg, so it is logical to suppose that his reason for flying to Germany was to get marching orders from Bin Laden's people there. If that was the case, it is an important footnote to the history of terrorism in the United States.

There is no question that the bloody scourge of Islamic extremists' attacks on America began at the Agency's doorstep. That fact should not be forgotten by our country, and especially should not be forgotten by CIA personnel and by its Director.

Very truly yours,
Nicholas Starr

13

Reflections on an Eclectic CIA Career

ALAN MORE

D ecember 10, 1972. It is an unusually cold, gray day in Washington for the prewinter period, perhaps reflective of the mood in town. The U.S. military is trying to extricate itself from the morass in Vietnam, but American soldiers are still dying daily. Richard Nixon has just been reelected for his second term. But the town is in a frenzy over the Watergate break-in and subsequent denials of involvement by the president and his lackeys. On top of this, one of the culprits is a former CIA employee!

This is my first day as a CIA officer—actually a career trainee (CT)—and I want to make sure it is flawless. I have left my apartment in Maryland early for the trip around the dreaded Capital Beltway to CIA Headquarters, maneuvering through traffic with my prized day-glow orange Volkswagen Beetle bought the previous year at the factory in Germany. The trainee program assistant has told me to just drive through the gate off of the George Washington Parkway, so I do! But before I know it, the security folks are all around me and I am out of my car. Once I explain my status as a new employee, they holster their weapons and tell me I need to have a CIA badge to enter the compound. I am eventually directed to general parking and the badge office. Although I'm sure other new employees have pulled this stunt, it is not the best start to a CIA career!

I am finally launching a potentially rewarding career working in the premier intelligence organization in Washington. All my years growing up in Asia and Africa, learning esoteric languages from the locals, and pursuing academic programs focused on geography, economics, and the international arena have gotten me to this point. But questions I have pondered before race through my mind: Is this the right place to start? Can I use my education and experience? What is the job like? Will I find a niche? What are the people like? Can I "cut the mustard" in the highly competitive career system, and on and on? My goal since returning to the United States has been to get back overseas, hopefully working in rural development in the developing world. I long have had visions of working in remote African villages helping subsistence farmers learn to grow better crops and market their surplus in the urban areas. So, where will I find my place now? Intelligence is not rural development by any stretch of the imagination.

On top of this, I am now under cover, something I am a bit uncomfortable with but accept as part of this unusual job. I am headed for uncertain—but exciting—territory: either life overseas in a clandestine role collecting human intelligence or one more in Washington putting the bits and pieces together for the policymaking community "downtown." Time will tell! Little do I know that nearly a third of a century later I will finally throw in the towel and retire, feeling satisfied that I have earned my pay but, more importantly, have contributed something to the CIA's mission and the country.

In the following vignettes I hope to provide the reader with a sense of the range of opportunities that CIA officers are given to use their training, skills, and experiences to do something meaningful, something that will make a difference. Although all federal employees can contribute to the country's well-being, those at the CIA have a unique opportunity to help senior policymakers make prudent decisions about often critically important issues—and to go where others will not go and accomplish things others cannot do. I believe the agency's recruiting slogan, "A mission like no other," sums this up well and reflects the philosophy all employees have about the organization.

Early October 1973

Despite the CIA's and most of Washington's assessment that Egyptian military maneuvers along the Suez Canal are only a training exercise, the Egyptian army launches an offensive across the canal to reclaim part of the Israeli-occupied Sinai Peninsula. Eventually the Egyptians are beaten back, and Washington steps in to resolve the issue of Sinai ownership. Bill Colby is director of central intelligence (DCI) and Nixon is still in the White House—but barely. One bright spot is his national security director, Henry Kissinger, who is running a commendable show at the National Security Council (NSC), particularly in his efforts to get us out of Vietnam, once and for all.

I am fresh out of my career training and assigned to the Middle East-Africa branch of the geographic component of the Directorate of Intelligence (DI)—the Office of Basic and Geographic Intelligence. I have made the difficult decision not to pursue the clandestine operations opportunity, despite my strong desire to work overseas. But I am working with a bunch of really sharp geographers—my core academic specialty—focused on my regional areas of interest.

A ceasefire is brokered in the Arab-Israeli War, and my new branch sees an opportunity to provide analytical support. Kissinger's NSC wants to pursue a staged Israeli withdrawal from the Sinai. We have a good handle on the economic, demographic, and infrastructural situations in the peninsula and start putting together some background reports. The NSC adviser for the Middle East, Harold Saunders, somehow discovers our team, and we become a key part of his effort to negotiate the terms of the withdrawal with the Israelis.

Our small group of geographers works around the clock to give Saunders the ammunition to counter the expected Israeli intransigence at the table, suggesting possible withdrawal points based on the terrain, transport routes, and other factors. The first stage is readily agreed on, but the second stage becomes an issue. The

Israelis want complete control of the strategic Mitla and Giddi Passes in the middle of the Sinai; Kissinger and the Egyptians demur. With our chief, George Russell, a cigar-chomping former military geographer, we take our maps over to the NSC and sit down with Saunders to explain our rationale. After numerous back-and-forths, Saunders feels he has a good grasp of the situation based on our "expert geographic science" and departs for the region. The Israelis finally compromise and the withdrawal takes place.

In appreciation for our work, Kissinger writes personal commendations for each of us, and DCI Colby hosts us at a thank-you lunch in his private dining room. As we leave Colby's suite, we hear that Richard Nixon has resigned. A cheer goes up from the group.

November 1976

A big surprise for many of us—Jimmy Carter is elected president. Here is a peanut farmer, who has never spent any time in Washington, coming to town to run the country. This is in the wake of the Pike and Church Committee hearings that have investigated the agency for supposedly exceeding its authority in the clandestine world, including assassination plots, covert action against democratic regimes, and spying on Vietnam War protestors. Church has even waved a CIA-made poison dart gun at the Senate hearing to make his point about the abuses. Congress eventually establishes the Senate and House intelligence committees to more closely monitor intelligence activities.

George H. W. Bush, DCI for less than a year, is quickly replaced by former navy officer Admiral Stansfield Turner, who brings in a plethora of "blue suits" from his many navy incarnations. He favors technical intelligence—signals and imagery—over human intelligence, so hundreds of clandestine service officers get pink slips. After decimating the Operations Directorate, the rest of us are not sure what is in store as we watch Turner's henchmen running around headquarters sticking their noses in everything.

A pleasant surprise for us in the geographic profession is the new administration's interest in long-term environmental and resource issues, something geographers focused on long before they were popular. The office quickly sets up a new unit, the Environment and Resource Analysis Center (ERAC), bringing together a multidisciplinary team of demographers, climatologists, agronomists, foresters, economists, and geographers. The ERAC's unique ability to bring together expertise and quickly provide answers to policymakers' questions gets the attention of the Council on Environmental Quality (CEQ). The CEQ and the State Department have just been commissioned by the president to oversee a comprehensive U.S. government inquiry into the implications of global population, resources, and environment on future security. The report, *The Global 2000 Report to the President: Entering the Twenty-first Century*, will become a bellwether for many other efforts to assess the long-term global environmental and resource outlook.

I am tapped because of my background in physical geography and quantitative modeling to coauthor the water section with hydrologists from the U.S. Geological Survey. Other ERAC analysts write sections on population, forestry, agriculture, and climate. The study provides a bleak outlook if something is not done by countries and international organizations: population growth must be reined in, alternative energies developed, water carefully used, crops efficiently grown, and forests harvested on a sustainable basis.

It is now late 1980, and the Carter White House sits on the draft study because it is so negative. The campaign season is beginning and the White House is skittish about such a doomsday study coming out as it gears up for its reelection bid. Finally, the administration agrees to release the report, realizing that further delays will hurt it because so many people are already aware of the findings. Although the study is published with little promotion by the White House, it gains widespread attention amongst academics, and international development and environmental bodies. Interestingly, a few years later when I am sitting in a classroom on an academic sojourn, I have my own material presented to me as evidence of the implications of water scarcity for instability and conflict!

ALAN MORE

January 1981

I am bouncing around in a U.S. embassy Jeep in a high-altitude region where opium production is rampant. Many in Washington think a lot of this drug, in the form of heroin, will find its way to Europe and ultimately the United States; there is even talk of a heroin epidemic in the West if something is not done. The State Department, desperate to get a handle on how much is grown and exported, has funded a multidisciplinary effort within the ERAC to develop methodologies for estimating production and flows. So here I am, getting a close look at the crop early in its growth cycle in a remote area where there are few amenities. Come spring, these hills will be covered in beautiful opium flowers and the farmers will be out harvesting the deadly crop.

The ERAC front office has pulled a bunch of us off other duties to form a new branch focused solely on developing a systematic approach to figuring out how much is being grown in several opium-growing areas of the world and how it is being moved. The U.S. embassy agricultural and narcotics officers have been providing estimates for a number of years, but these largely have been based on bits and pieces of information that have been gleaned from their field observations and casual "sources." Our initial model is simple: all we have to do is figure out how much land is cultivated with opium poppies—*Papaver somniferum*—and what the average yield per unit of land is. Then multiply the two and you have a production figure. Easy, right? NOT!

Getting these numbers is where our multidisciplinary team of geographers, meteorologists, agronomists, imagery analysts, and statisticians spends the next few years. The research and analysis involves intensive use of classified and unclassified imagery, weather data, and agronomic modeling, as well as multiple trips to the production areas. I fall back on my rural development and high-altitude experiences—including many years as a mountain climber—to lead the effort.

Our methodology is successful, and we provide Washington policymakers with the most accurate estimate to date. On my last trip into the area, I pick up a severe intestinal bug. The rudimentary hotel we are staying in has run out of toilet paper, so I spend the night running between the toilet and the shower. I later find out that the problem was from an embassy dinner, not the local fare! Before the trip ends, our Jeep is shot at by a bunch of irate farmers who probably have figured out that we are not there to help them!

January 1985

I am working at my desk at headquarters in the Office of Global Issues (OGI), the new incarnation of the office I started in back in the early 1970s. I have recently returned from a year of sponsored—read agency-paid—full-time academic training and am trying to find an appropriate landing place for my next adventure. A call comes from the OGI front office, requesting my immediate presence. OGI director Jim Lynch sits me down and explains how unfortunate it is that the office has never had anyone work on the President's Daily Briefing (PDB) staff. And he wants me to be the first one! He directs me to chat with PDB chief Chuck Peters, a feared senior officer with a reputation for trampling all over analysts when they venture upstairs with their draft articles in hand.

As I walk up the stairs, my mind flashes back to all the wrangling that went on whenever I wrote a PDB article, including my most recent one on South African drought problems. Do I want to be one of those pain-in-the-*@# PDB editors who decimates analysts' fine prose, keeps them at work until the wee hours of the morning, and calls them in on weekends? Do I really want to get up at oh-dark-hundred so I can brief one of the PDB principals at 6:00 a.m.? And what about all my newfound knowledge from my recent academic sojourn—when I can I put that to use?

My chat with PDB chief Chuck is energizing, and despite his reputation, he is a very kind-hearted and affable guy. I end up spending an incredibly rewarding year filling the varying roles of PDB briefer, editor, and senior intelligence officer (SIO)—the night-duty role. My principal briefee is the chairman of the Joint Chiefs of Staff, General John Vessey, a sharp, savvy guy who tells it like it is and is a joy to brief. And I get to ride to the Pentagon in a chauffeured agency car with a secure mobile phone—remember this is well before cell phones! My fellow briefers cover Vice President George H. W. Bush, National Security Adviser John Poindexter, Secretary of Defense Casper Weinberger, and Secretary of State George Shultz

The ritual after all of us briefers return from downtown is a debriefing with DCI Bill Casey, a grizzled veteran of the Office of Strategic Services, the CIA's World War II predecessor. He is wired in with the folks downtown and always interested in their reactions to articles in the PDB. I find out quickly that we need to have a senior officer accompany us because Casey is a notorious mumbler and often misunderstood. In my first debrief, Casey asks me a question after I have given an overview of my meeting with General Vessey. I have no idea what he has said, but fortunately our senior officer jumps in and says, "The director would like to know what General Vessey's comments on the . . . article were." My more experienced colleagues are much better at interpreting Casey's questions, and so I become after several months.

Deputy Director for Intelligence Bob Gates, sensitive to the Reagan White House's staunch anticommunist stance, is very careful about what goes into the PDB and how it is nuanced. We are constantly changing articles because of his view of what should go downtown. Gates has a photographic memory of events, often challenging analysts. In one case where a very senior analyst argues against changes, Gates cites some arcane intelligence reporting from a year ago. The analyst is astounded that Gates remembers this and, after some discussion, agrees to a slight rewording of his article. I am also amazed, but eventually learn how smart Gates is and how to work with him when I have to call him late at night to coordinate changes to the PDB.

The SIO duty is so much fun, I start taking other staffers' nights when I am not scheduled to brief downtown. Nights are far more exciting because the world we are monitoring is awake and up to all kinds of things, including coups, invasions, hijackings, shoot-downs, and other activities of interest to the national security establishment. Moreover, I am in charge and get to make lots of decisions on what to write for the morning briefers, which senior people to alert (including Gates), whom to bring in to craft an additional PDB article, and so on. And I get to work with a lot of dedicated, highly motivated young watch officers, who are on top of their regional areas of responsibility.

On one particular day near the end of my tour, when we have a couple of key countries threatening to duke it out over some border issues, I am a bit frazzled because of the constantly changing situation—and the storyline we need to deliver to the president in the morning. PDB chief Chuck tells me at the end of the long week that I will have great support from a Watch Team I have yet to work with. The senior duty officer for the team is Diane Ching, a long-standing team lead. Sure enough, we have the situation in hand and the PDB set without any issues. I am so glad to end my week of nights on a high note and a well-done PDB article—and I end up marrying Diane a few years later!

April 1994

Rwandan president Juvénal Habyarimana dies in a plane crash and the long-running enmity between the dominant tribal groups, the Tutsis and Hutus, erupts once again in widespread killing. Few policymakers in Washington have any idea of what this is about or even where Rwanda is—some think it is an Indian Ocean island. I am tentatively slated to go to the region because of my language ability and knowledge of eastern Africa from many years of residency and academic training. The genocide is mind-boggling, but the Clinton administration, reeling from the shock of Somalia and the Blackhawk-down incident, pulls back from any direct intervention. My trip is cancelled. Eventually, a quarter of the Rwandan population is killed and many of the others are uprooted and flee to Tanzania, Uganda, and Zaire (now the Congo).

The office, now incarnated as the Office of Resources, Trade, and Technology, assembles a group of us geographers to support the agency's newly formed Rwanda Task Force. Nobody has been following Rwanda closely, but the task force has a lot of long-time Africanists, and we get rapidly up to speed. Our geographic group crafts background studies that support policymakers in town and the peacekeepers in Rwanda. Our work is crucial for determining the resource situation, food aid needs, and where the displaced farmers have settled. Other U.S. government agencies use our material for planning humanitarian relief.

One day, months into the crisis, Vice President Gore's office sends us an unusual request: they want an assessment of the forest reserve in Virunga National Park, which harbors the last of the famed mountain gorillas. Hordes of refugees have settled on the edge of the park and are cutting the forests for firewood. A debate rages within the task force and at senior agency levels over whether this is a legitimate national security issue that should be addressed using valuable intelligence resources. It is finally decided that if the vice president wants it, we should do it. So we put together an assessment for Gore. The vice president's office is happy. And I now know what goes into gorilla habitat management!

Spring 1998

I am sitting in Deputy Treasury Secretary Larry Summers's office waiting to deliver his daily intelligence briefing—which he does not always receive well. And wait I do, since Summers has a habit of wandering around the building after he drives in, chatting with all kinds of folks and disrupting his schedule early in the day. Then he finally strolls into his office, usually an hour or more after he is due to see people. His assistants are in a constant frazzle over his lack of punctuality. It is something I learn to get used to.

I have been seconded to Treasury's Office of Intelligence Support (OIS) as the senior national intelligence officer and am now "officially" a Treasury body. The Asian financial crisis is beginning to roll through the rest of the world, so most of our reporting is focused on the atmospherics in vulnerable countries. Waiting with me is his CIA PDB briefer, David Missert, who will provide a CIA-only briefing. As a Treasury "official," I cannot sit in on the PDB even though I am still a CIA careerist and a former PDB'er! I thank current DCI George Tenet for this absurd situation. Summers, never a fan of the intelligence community, loves to challenge a lot of the reporting and often berates David and me. At least he has not thrown his Diet Coke at us like he did with some of his staffers!

Although this could be wasted time in Summers's reception area, I take advantage of sitting next to people "in the know" to find out what the inside scoop is on Treasury's Third Floor, where the key decisionmakers reside. Summers's two executive assistants are wonderfully talkative and often provide tidbits that are helpful for planning our intelligence support—whom he is meeting with, where is he is planning to go, key speeches he is giving, and other helpful information. I take this back to my Treasury office, so the Watch Team can monitor the incoming intelligence for relevant reports. I am just using the elicitation skills developed in my clandestine training!

While waiting, I meet a fascinating cast of visitors also waiting for Summers to arrive, including Federal Reserve chairman Alan Greenspan, NSC director Sandy Berger, and countless foreign officials. One foreign visitor who cools his heels with us is the head of a major Asian industrial conglomerate. Treasury has just installed new computers that just happen to be manufactured by his entity. The executive assistants are having difficulty getting the computers to work, so the conglomerate chief jumps up and helps them fix the problem. That's customer service for you!

Although my tour is supposed to last a year, I end up staying for three. It is a fascinating but exhausting tour with a dizzying array of issues, continual action on a variety of fronts, and long hours. My greatest satisfaction comes from supporting the boyish-looking undersecretary for international affairs, Tim Geithner. I even get to brief him at his modest home in Chevy Chase and play with his children. Geithner is a straight shooter, and near the end of his tenure he tells me that three-fourths of the "raw" intelligence we provide is already known by the Third Floor from their daily conversations with foreign counterparts. But the rest is very helpful for rounding out their knowledge base and giving them unique insights. I take this back to the clandestine folks at CIA headquarters but am ignored. They think Geithner does not know what he is talking about, so they continue collecting marginal intelligence. What a disappointment, I think, particularly because these valuable human-intelligence resources could be used against more helpful targets!

In my final few months I get to see firsthand the presidential transition to the new Bush administration. The turnover is far more dramatic than what I have experienced in the mostly non-political CIA. The Bush folks rapidly clean house, diving deeply into the deputy assistant secretary ranks, where a large part of the institutional knowledge resides. Alcoa Aluminum president Paul O'Neill is appointed Treasury secretary and seems confused most of the time. His new deputy secretary, Ken Dam, wants us intelligence folks to get O'Neill up to speed on some key issues, but O'Neill seems to be out of touch with the international arena. In a press interview in Europe, he voices uncertainty about the previous administration's strong dollar policy, and the dollar tanks in foreign exchange markets. Perhaps he will learn how powerful his views are in moving foreign markets.

Summer 2001

I am some thirty feet up in the trees at the CIA's remote training facility in Virginia—a far cry from the Third Floor of Treasury decisionmakers. I am using my climbing experience to show a dozen young employees how to get their team safely through the trees and then across a ravine and a river. It is stinking hot and the deer ticks are out in profusion. Everybody is sweating and wondering why they are here in these rural woods. Some ask, Did I sign up for this? They have three hours to accomplish the task. Their rewards will be bragging rights at the bar in the Student Recreation Building that night if they beat the other teams.

This is CIA 201, a four-week course designed to thoroughly steep employees in all the intelligence disciplines—operations, analysis, support, and science and technology. We are giving them some experience on the Special Operations side of intelligence in this first week. It is a chance to understand what a select group of CIA employees does every day, but more importantly, to bond with their team members—an important aspect of CIA life. It is also an opportunity to teach them about the value of leadership, communication, and collaboration when solving problems, which we hope they take back to the workplace.

After the week in the woods, the students return to CIA University's facility in northern Virginia, where we inundate them with briefings from a variety of agency components and put them through another series of realistic exercises so they can get a taste of work in other parts of the agency. Although many employees start the course reluctantly, most finish energized and with a newfound sense of what the agency is all about. They now see how they fit into the overall mission.

My tour at CIA University is tremendously rewarding. I am working with a great team of instructors and helping dozens of new officers see the benefits of an agency career. Particularly rewarding for me are the students I "save"—those one step away from resigning because they see no future for themselves in the agency. Because their perspective has now changed—many now understand their value in the overall mission—they come to me for advice on what to do, how to move on, and how to find their niche. Some of them transition to more rewarding positions elsewhere in the agency, some return to their offices with a new career plan, and some revise their own priorities. And as I will find out much later, some eventually rise to senior positions with wide-ranging authority. As I walk out to the parking lot one evening, I think of how uplifting the teaching experience has been and how it has recharged my batteries.

The morning of September 11, 2001, is bright and clear. Our instructor team has just concluded a very successful course and is meeting to plan the next running. The hijacked planes hit the World Trade Center and the Pentagon, and our world changes. We run several shortened versions of CIA 201, but the course is largely killed off a year later when the post-9/11 management decides new employees cannot afford to spend time away from more productive endeavors. Now everything is focused on counterterrorism and getting more people hired. CIA University management decides the course will be revamped into an online course. I wonder how they will learn teamwork and bond with others in the organization in a virtual environment.

So I decide to move on to another challenge, helping run a recruiting effort to bring loads of new officers on board. The agency lost nearly a quarter of its people during the Clinton era, and our ability to collect, process, and analyze intelligence now is spotty at best—as we shall hear a lot about over the next few years as committees with twenty-twenty hindsight dissect the data. I hearken back to the remark DCI George Tenet made to one of our CIA 201 classes about the dismal state of the agency's resources because of budget reductions: "We're like a patient on life support being wheeled on a gurney to the operating room. It's questionable whether we can survive as a global intelligence organization."

A Career Like No Other

Going back to the concerns I had the first day on the job: was I venturing into what I had hoped for—a rewarding career that tapped my background and experience, challenging me to use all my resources to solve problems, and providing opportunities to explore new territory? The answer is yes! I look fondly back on thirty-two years in which I took on many tasks and assignments I never dreamed I would have been given a chance to tackle—or even liked. At every step, I was asked to tap deeply into my mental and physical resources. And I, like most officers, was given a lot of responsibility early in my career, either to succeed or fail, to excel or stumble, or to learn from my experiences and move on.

Was it all so great? Was I always pleased with everything that went on? The answer to both questions is no. Management was dismal at times. I saw too many officers, who were fairly selected in the competitive process but unable to manage their people and programs. Often these officers were good at substance but had no experience in the vagaries of personnel management. Unnecessary bureaucracy too often wasted time and resources, detracting from the mission and stifling innovation. As a young analyst, I constantly asked questions about why we did things a certain way, often getting the response, Because we have always done it this way! I sometimes wondered how we got anything done. I concede, though, that these issues are endemic to most large organizations, and certainly those in the federal sector. I see this almost every day in my post-CIA career in a university, which makes the CIA look like the most responsive and nimble organization ever!

As I look back, I remember how I was welcomed into the CIA "family." I was joining a special group of officers who were always willing to help—and they always could be relied on. The people I worked with were incredibly talented, dedicated, and smart. My wish from the beginning was that I could contribute something to the agency mission and U.S. national security. I hope I did, but my former colleagues will have to decide on that. The burdens of working in any organization—whether public, private, or academic—are often moderated by how you perceive the value of the contribution you've made to whatever is important—the quarterly sales report, the return to investors, or the bottom-line profit. For CIA officers, it is always doing something that will make a difference for the country.

14

A Geographer Looks Back at Fifty Years with the CIA

WILL ROGERS

In undergraduate school I majored in Political Geography at Clark University in Worcester, Massachusetts. At that time, Clark was known, among other things, as the only place Sigmund Freud ever gave a speech in the United States and for Robert Goddard, the father of rocketry for the United States. However, it also had one of the best geography departments in the country. One of my noted professors, Samuel Van Valkenburg, although born in Java and then still a Dutch citizen, had been called down to Washington to work for the Office of Strategic Services (OSS) during World War II. I think he was probably mapping or writing about Europe. (Later on, we'll see how I met up with him again at George Washington University and how proud he was that one of his students was working for the CIA, the successor agency to his OSS.)

Most people's take on geography is that it involves either making maps or memorizing all the capital cities of the U.S. states. However, political geography encompasses many things, including why countries go to war, or at least have conflicts, because of such factors as boundary problems, ethnic and religious problems, and resource problems, such as rights to water, oil, and minerals. I know most people never use what they study in college, but I hope to show that, in my case, I really did use my studies at Clark in my chosen profession and later added to it at George Washington University, where the agency sponsored me in obtaining my master's degree, also in political geography.

However, the road to working at the CIA had some rocky bumps. After I graduated from Clark, I took a job as a geographer at the

Census Bureau in Washington (really Suitland, Maryland) for the 1960 decennial census. I had taken the Federal Service Entrance Exam and had been offered a couple of jobs before that one, but I wanted to work in the field of geography.

While at the Census Bureau, I met a fellow geographer who had just interviewed for a job with the Central Intelligence Agency and had been offered a position ranking of GS-7. We were only GS-5's at Census. I had never heard of the CIA at that time—remember, it was only thirteen years old then. What little he could tell me about the job, which he did get, interested me almost as much as the prospect of getting a high-level GS-7! I decided to try to get an interview with the agency although I didn't know how. Bill Lewis, the guy that got the job at CIA, had left by the time I had made up my mind to apply.

Luckily, I met a young lady at a Georgetown party who worked for something called the Junior Officer Training Program (JOTP) at the mysterious CIA. I asked her to make a few phone calls for me and to get back to me. Sure enough, she called me with the name of a recruiter for the agency who would speak to me (she, however, wanted nothing more to do with me!). I went to the interview at 2400 E Street N.W. in Washington DC, which was then the headquarters component, or the recruiting component, or the JOTP component, or whatever, as no one informed me who or what I was interviewing for. (As a side note, in 1984–87, I served as the DI's representative to the Career Training (CT) program— the successor to the JOT Program—in the Office of Personnel's Recruitment Division, and we certainly advised the candidates with whom they were interviewing and for what jobs they might be qualified.)

I thought the interview was going well until the recruiter asked me if I had as yet been called into the service. I replied in the negative. He then asked me if I could be considered as draft bait, and that time I had to answer in the affirmative. I thought my chances were ended for an agency career. But there were mysterious things afoot. The interviewer advised me that I could put in an application for employment, the long Personnel History Form, and that they could start on my clearances and other things if I agreed to enter a new army reserve program, under which I would serve six months of active duty and then complete a six-year reserve commitment. I said, I'd apply for the agency and then look into joining a reserve unit.

So after figuring that the best way to get employment with the agency (and my GS-7) would be to go the six months' active duty and five-and-one-half years' active reserve route, I went to an army recruiter in DC. It wasn't that I wanted to shirk my military duty, it was that I wanted the agency job more. The recruiter advised me about a transportation unit that was taking in new people and set me up with an interview with a General Qualls, who in civilian life was a hearing examiner with the Interstate Commerce Commission. I went to his office, obtained all the information, and told him I'd get back to him. That night my mother called from Massachusetts advising me that I had received my draft notice. I called the good general the next day and he agreed to predate my time of joining the reserve. Whew!

I went off to Fort Knox in March 1960. The next month, the Russians shot down Francis Gary Powers. I had told all my army buddies that I was applying to work for the CIA. When the papers reported that Powers had worked for the CIA, I told my friends that I'd probably be taking Powers's place, kidding of course. While still in basic training I received a letter from the agency that I was accepted for employment pending passing the medical and security checks.

I got out of the army in September, went home to Massachusetts, and told all my college buddies and neighbors where I was going to be working. On October 3, 1960, I reported to the personnel building on 16th Street N.W. in Washington—directly across from the Russian embassy. While sitting in the first session, I was called out of the room with the only other two guys (there were about twenty women there) and we were informed that we were to be put undercover. The man asked us if we had told anyone that we were going to be working for the CIA. Being honest, I told him that I had told my army company at Fort Knox and everyone in my home town—but it was a small town! He said, "That's all right, but don't tell anyone else."

As I was now employed in the Directorate of Plans (DP), predecessor of the Directorate of Operations (DO; now the National Clandestine Service, NCS), I had been hired as a GS-5! This with a degree from a pretty good college, ten months at the Census Bureau, and six months in the army. Later on, when I was recruiting for the agency and a potential employee was complaining about the low grade he or she was being offered, they received no sympathy from me.

I was assigned to the 201 Section of the Records Integration Division (RI), which maintained files on suspicious characters throughout the world. Apparently, the records in the Clandestine Service were in serious need of some eager young employees getting them straightened out. Therefore, new employees in the DP had to spend two years in RI before they were eligible for the Junior Officer Training Program. Misery loves company, and even though we were assigned low-level jobs, all the young men and women in RI established a camaraderie that in most cases lasted throughout our agency careers.

After the two years were up and I was accepted into the JOT program to become a case officer, something happened that changed my life forever, and I believe for the better. The Office of Medical Services was under the gun for allowing someone who had a serious medical problem to go overseas and who had succumbed on the trip. Smarting under the criticism, they pounced on my medical records to ensure that I could go anywhere, at any time, in order to qualify for the Clandestine Service. The OMS found some obscure readings in my tests that they said precluded me from serving overseas. However, I have since been to a total of eighty-two different countries with little or no problems. But that was then. Knowing that my career didn't look very bright on that side of the house, I managed to get an interview with the DDI's

Office of Research and Reports (ORR). They accepted me and placed me in the geography division of the office. It came with the stipulation that I would obtain my master's degree in geography in the coming years, which I did. Flunking the medical was most likely the best thing that could have happened to me as I got into a workplace where I felt I could really contribute. Not that I don't hold those who work "on the other side" in deepest regard for the brave and very important service they provide to protect our national security.

I was assigned to the Near East–Africa branch of the ORR at headquarters. My first assignment there was a very interesting one, in which I wrote escape-and-evasion studies on those countries to the south of the Soviet Union. These studies were to be used by pilots still flying the U-2 and other surveillance planes monitoring the USSR. So even though I never took Powers's place, I still was somewhat tangentially involved. I wonder if anyone still uses my report on Afghanistan today.

A year or so later on I transferred to the Soviet branch, still in the geography division. I mostly worked on the "Stans," those countries in the arid southern regions of the USSR. Later on I helped form a group working on analyzing Soviet grain production after the Great Soviet Grain Robbery in the early 1970s. Our Project Upstreet was the first major use of satellite photography for nonmilitary or strategic topics. Officers from the Office of Global Issues (OGI), National Photographic Interpretation Center (NPIC), the Office of Imagery Analysis (OIA), the Office of Economic Research (OER), the Directorate of Science and Technology's Office of Research and Development, as well as a civilian contracting firm, were all members of this group.

Years later, I used my education as a political geographer when I became the agency's principal intelligence officer assigned to work on boundary studies. This may have been my most interesting assignment, and I even got to present an unclassified paper at the Association of American Geographers annual meeting on this topic.

Other assignments included a rotational assignment to the Office of Training to initiate the first analytical training program for new analysts, under the direction of John Chomeau from the Office of Strategic Research. Much of the curriculum is what we use today in teaching foreign liaison analysts.

I returned to the geography division between rotational assignments. In the mid-1980s, I took another rotational assignment as the DI's representative to the Office of Personnel's Career Training Recruitment Division. Traveling around the country we were to select the, yes I'll say it, best and the brightest of the applicants for employment with the agency. That could be either as a direct hire or to go into the Career Training Program. It should be noted that, back then, one never accepted rotational assignments with the thought that they would help your career development. They should only be taken if you found the job interesting and personally rewarding.

After working on insurgencies back in the DI (my office had been renamed and reformed as the Office of Global Issues), I took my last rotational assignment with the Office of Training and Education. They had added the education component after the time of my first rotation. There I ran the Career Training Development Course for the career trainees. That was a most rewarding two years; I still see many of my trainees when I visit stations abroad.

I retired as a staff employee on October 2, 1992, culminating thirty-two years with the agency. Three days later I was on an airplane heading overseas to teach an analytical training course to members of a foreign intelligence service. I have been doing this for the past seventeen years, first in the Special Activities Division, which recently was transferred to the Human Resources Staff.

By October 2010, I will have had fifty years of service with the Central Intelligence Agency. It has been a career—or rather a life—that I would not trade for anything else. Little did I know as an undergraduate student that someday perhaps some very important policymakers would be reading and hopefully making better decisions for U.S. security based somewhat on information I provided. I wouldn't have wanted to have done anything else with my life. In addition to the very interesting work assignments, I might add that the people I encountered in the agency were some of the most intelligent, dedicated, and enjoyable people I could ever have come across in this world. What a rewarding lifetime spent in the CIA!

15

An "Out-of-Body Experience"

Seeing the DI with New Eyes

JON NOWICK

My most memorable, stimulating, and challenging assignment in the Directorate of Intelligence (DI) wasn't in the DI. It wasn't even in the CIA. Yet it shed bold light on the DI's strengths, as well as how the DI benefits from its outreach to others. I'll back up and explain.

Many Careers in One Career

I first joined the CIA—reluctantly—in 1974 as a summer intern at the Foreign Broadcast Information Service (FBIS), now the Open Source Center of the director of national intelligence (DNI). I say reluctantly because, as I was an international relations graduate student in that era, intelligence was a mystery to me and many of my peers, the CIA's reputation was at a low, and I was hoping for a job at the State or Defense Departments.

I soon realized I had stumbled into the right choice. The work was fascinating and fun. My coworkers were bright, dedicated, and welcoming. It was a treat getting paid to do the writing that I had been paying to do as a grad student. When the FBIS asked me to come back the next year full time as an analyst, I jumped at the chance.

I expected to spend a long and probably satisfying career moving slowly up the ranks in one place, the FBIS. I didn't realize how much a person with a gram of spunk could move around within the CIA, take on new responsibilities, work at interesting overseas locations, and keep learning and growing. By the time I retired in 2006, I had enjoyed many different and rewarding careers, all while staying with "Mother Agency." I'll describe some of the highlights in this chapter.

Yugoslavia's Breakup

I started out at the FBIS in 1975 as a Balkan analyst learning to decipher what was going on behind the scenes in communist states by what their controlled media said—and didn't say. Imagine trying to divine a jigsaw puzzle picture when the other side gives you only a few parts. I rejoiced on the many occasions that I found something revealing and of help to policymakers. I also grabbed a chance for a two-year assignment at an FBIS European bureau monitoring media reports from this region.

After returning to Washington DC in 1984, my life shifted into higher gear. A job opened in the DI for a senior Yugoslavia analyst. What had been a sleepy backwater "account" picked up as Yugoslavia began unraveling after Tito's death. My new job allowed me to see more information and travel extensively through the country. With Serbo-Croatian language skills I had learned at the agency, I witnessed firsthand ethnic strains and wrote reports warning about their implications for stability.

I was promoted to my first branch chief job in 1987 and led a talented team of DI Balkan hands. As the violence grew, my teammates spent many evenings working late trying to explain to policymakers what was happening, why, and what the administration might expect next. Members of this team have since gone on to their own successful careers. Two keen young analysts I brought into the DI, supervised, and helped mentor each later directed analytic training for all new DI analysts—in effect helping bring up a whole new generation. The wheel turns. Another star analyst who helped coach me when I entered the DI later wrote key assessments about Yugoslavia's breakup and went on to work on other priority issues.

Central Europe Upheavals

In 1989 I moved on to lead two more teams of analysts scrambling to stay ahead of other fast-breaking events—German unification and the revolutions in Central Europe. My team anticipated growing troubles in East Germany, but I recall standing with my jaw open watching on television as Germans danced on the Berlin Wall. One of these branches included an economic analyst, Jim Lewek, whose geniality helped keep us on an even keel during those turbulent times.

A Hilltop View

When a post-Cold War "peace dividend" in the 1990s resulted in painful cutbacks to the DI size and mission, I served as executive assistant to a remarkable director of intelligence, John Gannon. Gannon worked tirelessly to reassure, restructure, and reenergize an anxious directorate at one of its most difficult moments. His good cheer, sense of purpose, ability to connect with anybody, and speaking and writing skills were a model to me and many others in the DI.

One sad occasion was traveling with Gannon to Dover Air Force Base as the coffin of Jim Lewek was brought back to the United States. Lewek was killed in a freak plane crash in Croatia carrying then Secretary of Commerce Ron Brown—a reminder that even DI analysts can be exposed to danger on occasion. A star for Lewek was chiseled into the Memorial Wall at the CIA Headquarters lobby next to those of other fallen agency officers.

An Early Version of Social Software

I moved on to become communications director to Gannon in 1996, where I was charged with overseeing a controversial precursor to the widely accepted social software of today, a "DI discussion database." This database allowed DI employees to post comments, concerns, and questions anonymously onto a secure site for everyone in the DI to see. Posters would then receive responses from Gannon or whoever else cared to share their views.

Some midlevel managers resisted this database, and I often found myself defending it as a management communications tool. But Gannon embraced it and used it to full advantage, as did his successor, John McLaughlin, who later went on to be acting director of central intelligence. Like Gannon, McLaughlin was and is a master communicator as well as a man of integrity, vision, and courage. His magic tricks and ability to deliver a perfectly executed speech without notes left me spellbound.

Opening up the DI

In that same job, I helped Gannon and then McLaughlin nudge the once-secretive directorate into more openness to the outside world. My outreach coordinator, a bright Middle East analyst just back from a rotation to the State Department, created the first DI site on the agency's Internet website. We also set up and ran a speakers' bureau, bringing DI analysts before hundreds of fellow citizens. I think the website and this personal contact did much to improve public understanding of intelligence, something I lacked as a student, and it also gave our recruitment a boost.

Strength through Diversity

During much of this time I was also working part time to make the CIA a more diverse, representative, and effective organization by leading the agency's largest, most active recruiting team to a historically black university. Some of this school's graduates went on to become overseas station chiefs, senior analysts, human resource directors, and—in one twist—a manager of the overseas FBIS bureau where I had once worked. Had I been there again, I would have reported to her.

My office director at the time it was started, the late George Kolt, was an avid proponent of bringing in this talent, as were two of his successors, John Gannon and Bob Blackwell. They accompanied my team on trips to the school. We enjoyed busy days with students and pleasant evenings with faculty dining on fine down-home Southern cuisine.

Post-9/11 Brave New World

All of these experiences helped shape me, but they didn't fully prepare me for what lay ahead. A jolt came in 2002 when I returned from a second overseas assignment to the post-9/11 tumult, criticisms of the intelligence community, and determination by the community to thwart future attacks. The White House was asking agencies around Washington DC to provide senior hands to plan a whole new enterprise—a department devoted to the security of our homeland. The DI selected me and another colleague.

In September 2002, before Congress even passed the bill standing up the Department of Homeland Security (DHS), a half-dozen other intelligence officers and I found ourselves in an office building several blocks from the White House trying to apply our experiences to this new thing called homeland security. This was what some analysts in the DI jokingly refer to as an "out-of-body experience." This is their characteristically tongue-in-cheek way of suggesting that work outside the DI could be sufficiently different and surreal as to qualify as a near-paranormal phenomenon.

In a sense, they were right. My team, led by my former boss, John Gannon, was charged with planning a joint intelligence and infrastructure protection directorate that would meld the capabilities of both those functions. Working to plan other parts of the department were National Laboratory scientists, computer security wizards, Secret Service agents, Coast Guard officers, and other men and women from many other professions with whom I had previously had little contact. With little precedent to work from, it was an exciting if not always easy sail.

In the end, my team came up with a plan and readied it for the incoming DHS leadership. A high point came in early 2003 when we briefed the new DHS secretary Tom Ridge. Not only did Secretary Ridge approve our overall concept, but he nodded vigorously when I briefed him on a function Gannon charged me to create—an analytic "red cell" designed to think like the adversary and to test and challenge the conclusions of the larger group of mainline analysts.

We would in effect provide DHS leadership and consumers with an independent second opinion on threats, vulnerabilities, and countermeasures. I also put forward plans, later funded by Congress, for an "operational red team" to physically test security in cooperation with infrastructure owners, as well as an evaluation staff to provide the new directorate leadership with candid assessments of the directorate's progress.

In planning the analytic red cell, I interviewed dozens of intelligence officers, diplomats, academics, industry consultants, and foreign government officials in search of best practices. My home agency, the CIA, for instance, had created and used such a unit to good effect shortly after 9/11. At that time, DCI George Tenet stood up a "DCI Red Cell" to look independently at terrorist threats. The CIA also fostered other organizations—a Global Futures Partnership and a strategic analytic group within its Office of Transnational Issues—that were pioneering in reaching out to experts around the world and in using rigorous, creative methodologies to explore outlying possibilities. Our unit would draw from these and other organizations, and they gave us invaluable help and encouragement.

A Difficult Birth at DHS

When our planning staff ended its work and DHS stood up in spring 2003, I had a choice of returning to the CIA or extending my rotational assignment to build and lead what I had planned. The DHS needed help, and I had a thirst for a challenge.

I got the challenge. It was invigorating to start up my own group in the largest new federal department created since the Defense Department. But it came with frustrations that sometimes made me long for the DI. My team and others lacked the workspaces and computers we needed. Many personnel had to work off-site in contractor facilities. The World War II–era naval base and former girls' school near American University that served as DHS Headquarters was poorly refurbished. The heat in our top-floor office soared into the eighties on Washington summer days. A sandwich shop was our cafeteria. Things taken for granted in other intelligence agencies—for example, writing and analytic standards, review and dissemination processes—were nonexistent or just developing.

Another factor new to me was the military culture that influenced the intelligence and infrastructure protection part of the department at its start. This reflected the leadership of a new undersecretary, a retired three-star marine general, as well as the background of many intelligence officers working there. This culture brought with it a knack for quickly developing concepts of operations for new missions, an empowerment of line-level managers, and a sense of camaraderie among the staff with military backgrounds. It also was more hierarchical and formal than the DI. I eventually began to adapt, including calling senior leaders "sir," an almost unheard of term in the DI.

My team and I had several early achievements. We helped prepare the DHS for real contingencies when the leadership asked us to organize the department to take part in two major homeland security exercises—Top Officials (TOPOFF) 2 and a cybersecurity exercise called Livewire. We also issued several analytic red-cell reports. At the same time, we were making less progress than I would have liked. We had challenges getting approval to start red-cell projects, we were not given permission to undertake operational red teaming, and we found little enthusiasm for our proposals to conduct in-house evaluations.

These physical and bureaucratic hurdles reflected in part growing pains faced by other new organizations. Some fifty years earlier, for instance, soon after the CIA's inception, CIA employees worked in Quonset huts on the National Mall. When I recently returned to DHS Headquarters nearly seven years after its start, it was refreshing to see signs of growth and change.

"Employing Imagination" to Protect the Homeland

The fortunes of our analytic red-cell program turned up in early 2004, after a former head of the Defense Intelligence Agency, Lt. Gen. Patrick Hughes (USA-Ret.), came on board as assistant secretary for intelligence. General Hughes called me in to ask me to move the analytic red cell along with me into his part of the directorate. I had to leave behind overseeing the stalled operational red team and evaluation programs but calculated it was worth it if our red cell could gain traction.

Working under General Hughes allowed our work to take wings. For his sometimes bluff exterior, he was and is a warm person with a sense of humor and solid appreciation of the importance of rigorous, creative, independent intelligence analysis. He supported our projects, wrote positive comments on many of our reports, and encouraged us to be proactive in performing our mission. While his eventual successor, veteran CIA hand Charlie Allen, gets much deserved credit for building the DHS's intelligence analysis house, General Hughes before him placed it onto a firm foundation.

My team also was blessed with greater resources. Along with my deputy, Steve Chase, came a CIA officer and a team of contractors under the capable leadership of Kimberly Klein Lynch. We also tapped several facilitators and methodologies from a firm led by a former senior DI manager.

While we made up a lot as we went along, we applied three principles that I had learned in the DI. The first was to employ rigorous, creative, analytic "tradecraft." We regularly used "structured analytic techniques," at the time usually called "alternative analysis," to challenge prevailing assumptions and explore the range of possibilities. The 9/11 Commission encouraged these techniques after identifying a "failure of imagination" as the greatest failure in anticipating that attack. Techniques we used included structured brainstorming, scenario-building, high-impact/low-probability analysis, and most often analytic red teaming (adversary simulation). Our group often simulated terrorist plotters (in conference rooms only!) seeking to harm the homeland. We then identified steps to thwart these plans that our readers could weigh implementing.

Another important principle was to encourage collaboration with a diverse range of specialists and creative people. For our small staff to run exercises, we developed a pool of more than four hundred people around the United States and the world—almost all volunteers—on whom we could call ad hoc. Participants included experts from across DHS and DI analysts, National Security Agency cyber specialists, academic terrorism specialists, industrial security officers, military special operations personnel, law enforcement officers, allied government partners, grad students, and people from many walks of life who think creatively. In a typical exercise, ex-Navy SEALs brushed sleeves with retired Foreign Service officers, trucking industry executives, hard-bitten street cops, psychologists, and thriller writers like novelist Brad Meltzer. They all brought something unique to the table. I'm still impressed by their patriotism and readiness to serve.

A third DI practice that we applied was a crisp writing style intended to get our points across for busy readers. My experience writing and editing hundreds of DI reports for the president and senior policymakers was a help. I shared with my staff pointers I had learned and even wrote a short guide. I later heard that the DHS had adopted many of these practices when it developed its own style guide.

In all, we produced some forty reports in the nearly three years of my tour. Most were distributed not only throughout the intelligence community and federal government—the usual DI "customers"—but also to industry representatives and to state and local law enforcement and homeland security officials. These recipients are where the rubber meets the road when it comes to securing critical infrastructure and protecting the American people. The fact that we kept most of our reports unclassified (but official use only) was essential to this information sharing.

We explored potential threats to special events, such as a national political convention, a G-8 summit in the state of Georgia, and a major sports event. We looked at the security of critical infrastructure sectors, and we considered how terrorists might exploit emerging technologies and weapons systems. Some of our contributions include the following.

Securing Our Infrastructure

We brought together experts who identified a potential vulnerability in a key American cargo shipping sector. Within weeks after we issued a report flagging it to the DHS leadership, DHS closed the vulnerability. We also explored potential vulnerabilities in ferry boat systems. A ferry operator later told us he relied on our findings to protect his thousands of passengers. In another case, we completed a joint study on how terrorists might try to degrade a sector on which Americans and other people depend for their livelihood. Some lower-level officials had assured the senior partner with whom we worked that they could handle various contingencies. After our joint analytic red teaming exposed a potentially dangerous weakness, he looked up with his face whitened and said, "We're screwed" (but using an earthier word). The realization prompted steps to protect this sector.

Identifying measures to reduce risks to cargo shipping and transportation were among the ways the analytic red cell contributed to homeland security.

Reaching Out to Our Youth

In another instance, a prominent youth leadership forum brought twenty high school students from around the country to visit government institutions in Washington DC, including the DHS and our red cell. With their consent, we engaged them in a brainstorming exercise to explore how terrorists might recruit and manipulate American teenagers to perform terrorist acts. The teenagers jumped into the exercise with enthusiasm and highlighted key ways their peers might be seduced or coerced into terrorism. The report we produced, whose conclusions were buttressed by academic research, was distributed to law enforcement nationwide.

Cautioning Against Overreaction

During a heightened terrorist threat advisory in the 2004 presidential campaign, my unit took a contrarian, "devil's advocate" approach to the prevailing view that the nation may be under imminent threat. We marshaled countervailing evidence to produce a study saying why the homeland might be more secure than the government thought it was.

Feedback is something intelligence analysts crave. We were delighted to get periodic comments from around the country showing that our work was read and valued. Some DHS officials told me that our independent assessments might be misunderstood by readers outside the DHS or the administration. But the most appreciative comments often came from state and local police, industry, and military commands. This underscored to me the value of supporting and trusting the judgment of a wider set of "consumers" than the Washington insiders. Even four years after I left the DHS, I learned that state and local officials occasionally ask about our red cell products.

Feedback also came from unexpected corners. At a time when the media had few kind words to spare for the DHS and the U.S. intelligence community, the *Washington Post* in June 2004 ran a story about our red cell, crediting it with "employing imagination"—a reference to the 9/11 Commission's criticism of the government's failure of imagination. It cited the unusually wide range of participants we were tapping. It quoted one of them as saying that "homeland security is on to a good thing" and is "getting at some creative ideas." The article gave me and my team a morale boost.

Summing Up: Relevance for the DI

I left the DHS when my rotation ended in fall 2005, returned to the CIA, retired from the U.S. government, and have since been supporting the government as a contractor. I was honored when both John Gannon and General Hughes attended a CIA retirement award ceremony held for me.

Just before retiring, I wrote an article for a scholarly agency publication, *Studies in Intelligence*, drawing on my DHS experience to point up the value of applying structured analytic techniques against intelligence issues. I don't know if it helped nudge the ball a few more inches down the field, but these techniques have since become a standard part of analytic training and a regular practice in the CIA and other parts of the intelligence community.

Looking back on the DHS experience, it drove home to me how the DI is a crown jewel in the U.S. government for its analytic standards and techniques, ability to draw in-house on an unparalleled and diverse collection of experts, and its presentational style—accompanied by a culture of collegiality, readiness to try new ideas, and sense of mission. Wherever DI analysts go, they bring with them these virtues.

On the flip side, the DI benefits from its exposure to other organizations, cultures, and missions. Sending its analysts on rotational assignments to other agencies, a longstanding DI practice, helps those agencies and the DI. DI pride becomes leavened with humility when its analysts are exposed to the talents of fellow government experts, the military, industry, academia, law enforcement, the National Labs, and the creative arts.

While counterintelligence concerns need to be managed, a robust program of outreach to these people will keep the DI strong and our country and world more secure. So, too, will gaining new employees from the widest range of professions, cultural and ethnic backgrounds, walks of life, and ways of thinking.

16

Peasant at the Creation

The Agency's First Terrorism Analyst and Beyond

EDWARD MICKOLUS

A nd that's what I did for my summer vacation." My colleague in the PhD program of Yale's Department of Political Science finished off a rollicking good yarn about his summer graduate fellowship with the Directorate of Intelligence (DI) with those words back in September 1974, during our department's first brown bag seminar of the semester. Most of us in graduate school were eyeing the consequences of becoming professors soon, preparing for a life of facing down callow eighteen-year-olds every September. But my friend had tried something else—applying his skills in what was a nontraditional field for PhDs: government service. And for the CIA, no less! Most of us knew virtually nothing about the agency beyond the exaggerations of spy-fi movies (did he really work with real-life James Bonds?), wild charges by congressional investigators, and ill-founded "common knowledge" of what the agency "really" does. His description of working on game theory, political-military simulations, and statistical modeling just didn't square with the misconceptions most of us had of spooks parachuting behind enemy lines with a dagger in their teeth, overthrowing governments, breaking into hostile embassies, battling various other no-goodniks, and charming themselves out of tight spots with a smirk and a well-aimed quip.

So armed with my newly minted master's degree and on the way to my MPhil (a degree unique to Yale, which apparently is embarrassed to charge so much for tuition that they keep giving you senior degrees until you ultimately sneak off with a doctorate), I applied for the DI's Graduate Fellow program. Unlike most intern programs in government, CIA Grad Fellows are treated as colleagues, with the same level of clearances (top secret) and the same amount of responsibility as anyone else in the agency. While you're probably not going to brief the president as a Grad Fellow, you nonetheless are likely to contribute to papers he and various other senior policymakers will read. Getting to these heady levels, however, isn't easy. After filling out what seemed like unending amounts of paperwork (which I eventually learned was not as burdensome as in most bureaucracies), several interviews by individuals with whom I would be working, a background investigation during which seemingly everyone I'd ever met was asked about my lifestyle (back then, we didn't know we had "lifestyles," so I was on pretty good ground), a physical exam, a psychological exam, I underwent a polygraph. Many incorrectly refer to this as a "lie detector test." It doesn't actually detect lying, but is still a terrific tool when in the hands of a skilled polygrapher. Many of us also find it a wonderful weight-loss program!

After months of wondering whether I would be back to serving as a lightly paid subject in experiments by Yale's Psychology Department for the coming summer of 1975, I got my welcome letter. I would be assigned to the Office of Political Research as an analytic methodologist.

Armed with the five boxes of computer punch cards that constituted my nascent doctoral dissertation, a slide rule (look them up on Wikipedia's history pages!), a key to a Rosslyn apartment I'd be sharing with my Georgetown undergrad buddies, what I could recall of Bayesian statistics from my econometrics courses, and my two neckties, I walked into the imposing lobby of the Original Headquarters Building. A few steps inside the door, I was confronted by the marble seal of the agency, an eagle on a shield with a compass rose, signifying that the agency stands vigilant watch all over the world. To the left, a statue of General William Donovan, who headed our World War II predecessor, the Office of Strategic Service, guards a Book of Honor of those OSS officers who died for their country. The facing wall features a similar Memorial Wall and Book of Honor dedicated to agency employees martyred in the cause of freedom. As of this writing, there are more than one hundred stars in the constellation, which includes several heroes I had the privilege of working with during my career. The agency is a comparatively small place, and virtually everyone that you meet knows at least one star on the wall.

My initial forays into the world of analysis included developing quantitative methodologies on the United Nations (I simply adapted my MPhil thesis) and international terrorism. One of my doctoral advisors, Bruce Russett, had offhandedly observed that in choosing a dissertation topic, we could write yet another dry-as-dust study of how the Potato Famine affected some godforsaken minor county in Ireland, or we could try something new and look at international terrorism. I took him up on it, and found that the agency was similarly interested in starting to look at the phenomenon. I was delighted to find that precisely what I had studied in graduate school—both substantively, in terms of terrorism, African politics, political psychology, and the like, and skills regarding quantitative methodologies—could be put to use immediately on the job in the DI. Maybe there was a future other than eighteen-year-old faces.

What sealed the deal for me was interacting with dedicated, clever, worldly individuals who were a lot smarter than I was and were enormously patient with my boyish overenthusiasm over everything I saw. Adding to the attraction of the DI was the possibility of knowing virtually everything there was to know—or at least having access to it—on virtually any topic. Imagine being able to call upon the intellectual firepower of the whole of scholarship in an area (which the DI frequently did), put upon it a superstructure of categorization such as Confidential, Secret, Top Secret, and Codeword reporting, and then make sense of it for policymakers who would read your analysis the next day. For someone steeped in research and policy relevance, it didn't get any better than that. So I re-upped for a second Grad Fellowship.

· · ·

By the summer of 1976, there was no turning back and I was hooked on a career as an analyst. Wanting to make this a permanent relationship, I applied to the agency's Career Training (CT) Program, which at the time brought in rookies from all of the directorates—intelligence, operations, science and technology, and administration—to give them a flavor of what the entire agency was about, not just the stovepipe to which we would be assigned. The CT Program also gave its graduates a readymade network across the building that lasted decades. My November 1976 CT class included officers who eventually became the director for operations, director of the Counterterrorist Center, several Directorate of Operations area divisions, an ambassador, senior analysts, you name it. Having friends like these let you get things done quickly by picking up the phone and calling a colleague, rather than having to wait for memos to work their way through several levels of moat monsters.

The CT Program gave us interim assignments in areas in which we would probably not be working initially. I was lucky to serve in the Directorate of Administration's Office of Data Processing (the term sounds quaint today) reviewing software for major collection platforms, in the Office of Training, and back in the Office of Political Research, putting out the agency's first unclassified studies of international and transnational terrorism.

Upon graduating from the CT Program, I returned to the Office of Political Research, this time as the sole analyst on terrorism. For the next few years, I created terrorism databases and founded serial publications that are still in use. Although I was only in my twenties, I represented DI interests in numerous interagency coordinating committees. I was impressed with this aspect of the DI—no matter how junior in age you were, if you were the expert on a topic, you were expected to handle whatever requests came to the agency, from whatever source. This included briefing senior policymakers and members of Congress, giving presentations at scholarly conventions, writing papers (and sometimes books) for academic journals, and flying overseas to meet with representatives of foreign intelligence services and other governmental institutions.

One particularly intimidating trip for a twenty-eight-year-old included a four-day week at Ditchley House, a baronial mansion just outside Oxford University and Blenheim Palace, where members of the British cabinet and other luminaries (the head of British Airways, the head of the BBC, the dean of Oxford, the leader of the UK High Court, assorted captains of industry and ambassadors, even the Spanish interior minister), brought senior visitors from the United States to discuss burning issues of the day. I was part of the American delegation that included the head of the State Department's Legal Bureau, an Ohio Northern University law professor, and Ambassador to the Court of St. James Kingman Brewster. I was easily the youngest by three decades, but there simply wasn't anyone else writing on terrorism back in those days, so off I went. I was particularly excited to meet an individual identified on the guest list as Mr. McNee. I was thinking it was Patrick McNee, hero of the original television series *The Avengers*. Turned out to be Sir David McNee, head of Scotland Yard, but as luck would have it, we got along famously. The Brits did have their chance to tweak the young American, however, giving me a butler named George Washington! The trip later took me through Germany, Switzerland, France, Belgium, and the Netherlands, heady stuff for a kid whose foreign travel had consisted of going over the bridge from Detroit to Windsor on occasion.

During one summer, I filled in as the junior night-shift analyst in the CIA Operations Center, monitoring worldwide developments and updating the President's Daily Brief and the *National Intelligence Daily* as appropriate. The senior analyst and I each night skimmed through three feet of documents (no hyperbole here—we didn't have computers back then, and had to physically dig through that much material), looking for some nugget of reporting that could alter our analysis from earlier that day, or warn of a coup or a war, or update ongoing negotiations on missiles or for the release of hostages.

Looking to expand my experiences as an analyst while drawing upon skills I'd developed at Yale's Psychology and Politics Program,

I spent a year in the Office of Global Issues, writing psychiatric profiles of world leaders, including government officials, leaders of the opposition, or insurgent/terrorist figures.

This analytical wanderlust continued, particularly after my management indicated that the way to get ahead as an analyst was to work for at least some of one's career as a regional analyst, rather than an expert on only one transnational issue, where one had breadth, but not much depth. So off I went to apply my African studies experience from Yale in the Office of African and Latin American Analysis. I worked on political, military, economic, social, and leadership issues in West, Central, and Southern African and Indian Ocean nations. During my early tenure there, the national intelligence officer for Africa (the agency's senior expert on a region) decided to travel through Africa to discuss the policies of newly inaugurated President Ronald Reagan with African leaders. He picked me as his notetaker, so off we went for thirty days to fourteen countries (don't try this yourself—I saw a lot of airports and hotels, but little else), including the United Kingdom, Italy, France, the Vatican, Greece, the Sudan, Kenya, Zambia, Zimbabwe, South Africa, Botswana, the Seychelles, Mauritius, and Reunion. For a visit to one country, I had proudly purchased two suits to wear for our meetings with the president and members of his cabinet. Upon arrival, the chief of station (COS) told me in no uncertain terms that I'd be impossibly overdressed and would embarrass the Hawaiian shirt-wearing head of state. So it was off to the local bazaars to "get local" in the words of my COS (overseas, the COS is God—with apologies to Eric Clapton fans who may be reading this).

One of the most appealing aspects of working for the agency is the opportunity to try something new at virtually the drop of a hat. After I'd been an analyst for a decade, I'd been wondering what it was like on the Directorate of Operations (DO) side of the house. While I'd been happy enough to work in the DI, I also noticed that my outgoing nature was not typical of the more bookish introverts that then populated much of the DI. So while still covering a particularly entertaining coup in West Africa, I got a toehold in the DO by taking a rotational assignment in the Political and Psychological Staff (which later became the Special Activities Staff). When I joined the agency, I'd never imagined that I'd be involved in the world of operations, which was portrayed by Hollywood and in novels as the ambit of smooth-talking, charming cowboys. But I discovered that the DO welcomes analysts for their ability to assess situations and write cogently. I ran several programs and ultimately moved up to branch chief, my first managerial job, and eventually was named Manager of the Year in the DO. While with the covert action folks, I designed worldwide propaganda and political influence, human source intelligence collection and counterintelligence operations on international terrorism, narcotics trafficking organizations, proliferation of weapons of mass destruction, foreign intelligence organizations, rogue nations, and communist insurgencies. Basically, if you were America's enemy, I got to tangle with you. Thanks to the work of some very dedicated officers who worked with, for, and in spite of me, we saved several thousand American lives in our operations—a great feeling! I went on to manage dozens of officers in several components, including the cross-directorate Gulf War Task Force. As many of us were "surged" to the war zones and our headquarters personnel complement was depleted, I often found myself running two, and sometimes three, branches at once. I also chaired promotion and assignment panels, and mentored, coached, and counseled officers as Personnel Evaluation and Management (PEMS) chief for the office.

Specialization in covert action, however, wasn't viewed by promotion panels as sufficiently mainstream for the DO, whose bread and butter is operational collection of human source intelligence, so at the suggestion of my DO career counselor, after a wonderful eight years with covert action, I moved to the Counterterrorist Center, where as a branch chief I conducted numerous collection efforts against high-profile terrorist targets; led, mentored, and directed several officers and wrote their performance appraisals;

and headed liaison with several agencies in the intelligence community. Operations looked at penetrating governments that were supporting terrorists, understanding a Sudan-based multimillionaire who might be supporting terrorists and who was named Osama bin Laden, and tracking terrorist use of high-quality counterfeit U.S. currency.

After nearly two decades of work in the agency as an analyst and operative, the bureaucratic wanderlust struck again. I'd always wondered what the denizens of the seventh floor (the rarified atmosphere of the leadership of the agency) were like, and whether I could contribute. I was fortunate enough to be chosen as the editor of the internal newsletter, *What's News at CIA*, housed in the Agency Information Staff (AIS) and later the Office of Public Affairs (OPA). During the next decade, I interviewed thousands of officers and drafted thousands of articles, broadening the scope of the OPA's coverage and becoming the federal government's most senior editor. The AIS was a very small staff, so during vacation periods of our leadership, I often found myself the next-senior individual, tasked with attending the director's morning meetings. I got to watch the director, the directorate chiefs, and other seniors each day, and was impressed with how one's perspective, no matter how one got to the position, changes when faced with agency-wide issues.

The *What's News* job also allowed me to keep up my public speaking skills. I briefed one hundred groups per year as the seventh floor's senior briefer for visitors to the agency. This could be a captain of industry, a Hollywood star, or the sixth grade from PS 123 in Dubuque. The job included addressing several courses, including CIA 101 (the first class that rookies take upon entry on duty), and Washington Orientation.

What's News also gave me the opportunity to meet celebrities, sports stars, and public figures I never would have met had I stayed in my small hometown in Michigan. I tried to get interviews with everyone of interest who stopped by to meet with the director, or who was visiting for other reasons, be it to give a speech on diversity or charity, or studying to portray one of us in the movies. Among the folks I met:

POLITICIANS: Presidents George W. Bush, George H. W. Bush, Bill Clinton, and George Washington (okay, the latter is a reenactor at Mount Vernon, but still . . .); Barbara Bush, Vice President Al Gore, three secretaries of state (Henry Kissinger, Colin Powell, and Madeleine Albright), three secretaries of defense (Harold Brown, Robert Gates, and William Perry), two secretaries of transportation (Rodney Slater and Ray LaHood), Secretary of Health and Human Services Donna Shalala, ten directors of central intelligence plus Special Services Unit director General William Quinn, FBI director Louis Freeh, Julian Bond (his grandfather was named James Bond!), three Speakers of the House of Representatives (Newt Gingrich, Dennis Hastert, and Nancy Pelosi), Lieutenant Governor John Hager of Virginia, and Representatives Sonny Bono, Heather Wilson, Porter Goss, Alcee Hastings, Larry Combest, Collin Peterson, Jane Harman, Silvestre Reyes, Tim Roemer, Sanford Bishop, John Murtha, Jerry Lewis, David Obey, Norman Dicks, and Norman Sisisky

CELEBRITIES: Will Smith, Patrick Stewart (*Star Trek*'s Captain Picard), Will Patton, Gil Bellows, Edward James Olmos, Barbara Feldon (the original Agent 99 from the TV show *Get Smart*; we held the shoe phone, which she'd never touched during the show), Lou Ferrigno (the Incredible Hulk), John Paul DeJoria (CEO, Paul Mitchell), Miss America Heather Whitestone, Tim Matheson, Tom Berenger, Ron Silver, Dean Cain (Superman), Ben Affleck, Alice Krige (*Star Trek*'s Borg Queen), Dan Aykroyd, Lorenzo Lamas, Rita Moreno, and Paige Turco (*The Agency*)

SPORTS STARS: Cal Ripken (he signed my Lou Gehrig baseball card), the Redskins' Boss Hogette Mikey Torbert—a member of the Football Hall of Fame—Redskins Hog Rick "Doc" Walker, Charley Taylor, Darrell Green, Mark Moseley, and Art Monk, Dallas Cowboy Roger Staubach, Washington Capitals owner Ted Leonsis, Tennessee basketball coach Pat Summitt, and WNBA basketball star Chamique Holdsclaw

I also photographed Sean Connery, Vice President Dick Cheney, Senate Majority Leader Trent Lott, Senator John Warner, and other luminaries during a Scottish National Day at the Capitol Building, before going in to interview Representative Leonard Boswell.

It's quite a list, and I'm sure I've forgotten people whom I didn't photograph at the time of their visits.

The joy of *What's News* wasn't in meeting such worthies—although it certainly had a coolness factor!—but in chronicling day-to-day the accomplishments of America's silent heroes. Every day, I got to meet individuals who had stopped terrorists, derailed drug shipments, captured spies, prevented hostile nations from getting nuclear, biological, and chemical weapons, battled communist insurgents, and ultimately won the Cold War. I met tech geniuses who launched spy satellites, or created bugging devices that looked like insects, or achieved other tech breakthroughs (including Wally Szuminski, whose memoir of incredible courage appears elsewhere in this series). Every day, I got to showcase their triumphs to their colleagues. And because of the extensive network one necessarily builds in such a job, I was able to introduce to each other people from far-flung sections of the agency who might never have met. I thus facilitated numerous interdirectorate working groups on such agency-wide issues as compensation reform, events planning, emergency response, and internal communication.

About midway through my *What's News* tenure, 9/11 occurred. My branch had a unique role in the agency—keeping the lines of substantive communication going, whether it was for thousands or for a handful on a skeleton crew. The thousands were a daily occurrence (and I was always under pressure to get it right every day, because everyone saw my errors in our pages); the skeleton crew I'd experienced earlier when I was one of the few remaining during a short furlough of the agency during a congressional impasse over the federal budget. When the second plane hit, we knew that it was up to us to get the word out to everyone that

America was under attack. Luckily, we had installed an instant messaging system that could get information to the workforce within seconds. It performed flawlessly during that crisis, when the executive director called us to tell the workforce to empty the headquarters compound because two planes were unaccounted for and possibly were heading our way. Once we had sent the messages, however, it was our duty to stay on, ensuring that those few who had to stay—principally the seventh floor and the Counterterrorist Center—were up to date. With emergency shutdowns of several systems, I often was called upon to perform "sneakernet" duties. I will always remember the quiet heroism of those who stayed on, knowing that the Pentagon and World Trade Center were on fire and we could join them at any second.

After more than a decade, 10,000 articles, and 1,200 editions of *What's News*, it was time to pursue what had become a hobby— helping to recruit the next generation of America's heroes to the agency. Perhaps thrice annually, I'd served on recruitment teams because I had a broad overview of the agency and could easily answer cross-directorate questions for applicants. I wanted to try recruiting full time, so I joined the Recruitment and Retention Center's Clandestine Service Hiring Division as a program manager. During my three years there, I recruited and interviewed hundreds of candidates, initiated and coordinated nationwide outreach to universities and professional societies, and addressed thousands of applicants at scores of universities across the United States. During my last year there, I took thirty temporary duty assignments. While the work was fun, travel can be exhausting, and there's only so many hours one can spend stuck at O'Hare during interminable delays before it's time to admit that it's time for something else.

As luck would have it, I was directly assigned back to the Counterterrorist Center (CTC), where I was one of—and later the head of—a small team that orchestrated the CTC's response to congressional and Department of Justice investigations of detainee interrogation procedures. The investigations continue as of this writing.

On October 3, 2008, some 1,539 neckties later, I retired. On

January 23, 2009, I received the Career Intelligence Medal, the Clandestine Service Medallion, and the Gold Retirement Medal. Honorees are traditionally asked to say a few words. Here's some of what I shared with my friends and family:

In thirty-three years, you attend a lot of these ceremonies, and believe me, there's a lot less pressure on your side of the lectern! You wonder if you'll be able to summon up the eloquence and passion that you've seen in your predecessors' valedictories. While I doubt I can do that, I can match them in enthusiasm and heartfelt thanks.

I'd first like to thank my wife of a quarter century, Susan, who has retired the trophy for longsuffering. Let me strongly counsel all you guys out there—the best thing I ever did was to marry up! I've never understood why Susan's had such patience with me, but I'm honored that she has.

It's a great view from here. This is the first time that I've been able to see the highlights of my career, all together for the first, and probably last, time. For while we come for a variety of reasons, usually patriotic, revolving about the mission, we stay for the people we meet. Some of you I've known even before we joined the CIA together, some I've known only for the small time it took to chat with you at a career fair booth, or in the intimacy of the interview room.

Alas, some invitees couldn't make it. The most typical excuse was from COS's, one of whom is twelve time zones away, who couldn't get away from the press of our noble mission. I've always been impressed by how what's exotic anywhere else is commonplace here, where a typical elevator conversation is conducted in Uzbek or Tagalog, and people think nothing at all of saying, "Yeah, I just got back from Ickystan. How 'bout you?"

But still others could not attend because they're now stars on the Wall. Pretty much everyone of my generation knew at least one person who is now in that constellation of heroes. Let us never forget those who made the ultimate sacrifice to our country and our agency.

One of my high school friends once emailed me "Are you a patriot?" It's not something we articulate all that often in our hallways—we don't wave flags at each other—but I think we all know in our heart of hearts what the answer is. You all could have made bigger bucks by joining the private sector, but instead you chose duty and honor. I'm even richer for having worked with you.

My buddy Bob Wallace told me that you're expected to share the wisdom you've accumulated at this ceremony. Over the years, I've learned so much from all of you. A few of these items permit simple listing. Happily for you, the AV system in here balked at my 108 PowerPoint slides. In no particular order, here are the top ten things I've learned working for the agency.

10. Never miss a chance to make a friend. Strangers are simply friends you haven't met yet.

9. Never miss a chance to hear someone's story. There are thousands of inspirational tales hiding in people whom you'll meet in the halls. They'll be happier for having had a chance to impart their wisdom, and you'll be richer for having received it.

8. Never miss a chance to try something new. This place, more than any other, is a wealth of new challenges. I've done things I never thought I'd do when I came into the agency. I thought I'd be a terrorism analyst from Day One to Day 12,308. Instead, I got to work on African political, economics, leadership, and military issues; write psychiatric profiles of world leaders; run covert action programs against terrorists, drug traffickers, proliferation networks, rogue regimes, hostile intelligence services, and anything else that threatened our way of life; meet with thousands of agency employees on countless fascinating programs; rub shoulders with the occasional celebrity, from Agent 99 to Jean-Luc Picard to one of the Men in Black; meet three presidents; and work for ten directors. The United States is often called the Land of Opportunity; the CIA surely deserves that description.

7. When the bureaucracy, or a coordination hassle, or a multitude of temporary reverses might get you down, remember that we serve the most noble mission of any organization on earth.

6. And if that doesn't work, don't forget to laugh and make others laugh.

5. Working well with others is key. There's no James Bond who rushes in to save the world. We're all a team that routinely does so. You get more done at other people's desks than trying to do it all yourself.

4. No matter how the political winds blow and how dire circumstances seem in the world for the United States, or amongst the commentariat and the Hill regarding the agency's future, there will always be a need for our product. In this period of historic transition, it's important to remember that policymakers, no matter what their initial views of us, all eventually come to appreciate how we contribute to them making wiser decisions.

3. We've gone far from the WWII-era definition of a collaborator—someone who consorted with the enemy—although some still view it that way today with the pressure of the Office of the Director of National Intelligence to integrate the intelligence community. Although we believe that our agency, our directorate, our component, and often our branch, defines the word *elite*, there are others, with different perspectives, different sources, different missions, who can contribute to our own. Seek them out. That said, we're still the best by a mile.

2. Take care of your people, whether or not you're a manager. My first management job came with the instructions: "Take care of everything. Don't screw this up." While we're still tying ourselves in knots with various performance measures, it's going to be hard to top those simple instructions. Know how to recognize talent, aim it in the right direction, and then get out of its way.

1. Never forget that what's important in our lives are our families and our friendships.

Some have asked what I'll be doing in life after the CIA. Over the years, I've often wondered that. With the agency as such a clear first choice in my life, what is second choice? As you know, the Horizons course, a wonderful gift from the agency to its employees, gives you a period for self-reflection, to find out what really matters in your life, and to pursue those options. While I have a list of hobbies a mile long, and will pursue some of them, I'd still like the centerpiece of my life to be what motivated me to join the agency in the first place. Happily, green-badgedness lets one keep serving one's country, stay in touch with one's colleagues, and make a contribution to our fellow Americans' safety and national security. I'll be an instructor in briefing, creativity, and collaboration.

God bless you, the agency, and America. I know I've been blessed by being able to call you friends.

Dealing with the Rest of the World

17

Satellite Imagery and the Afghan Task Force

TOM SHERIDAN

I t has been a great honor and privilege to have an almost thirty-year career at the CIA (which I will sometimes refer to as "the agency"). I hope you have been impressed by what you have been learning about the CIA from the many authors of this book. If you are considering a career with the CIA, I hope that you will have the patience for the clearance process and will be hired to work at the agency. You definitely will NOT regret the decision.

Compared to the many occupations we Americans engage in, you may find my career to have been rather unique. But in the CIA it was, and is, far from unique. This type of "uniqueness" is not uncommon in what we do at the CIA. There is the mundane, to be sure, as there is anywhere, but what I have to relate was special.

I start my memoir with a question. What did I—a CIA imagery analyst—have in common with the intelligence chief of a major Middle Eastern country, the chief and senior officers of a major South Asian intelligence service, the ambassador to the United States of a major Middle Eastern country, the CIA chief of station in a major South Asian country, and numerous outstanding CIA operations officers, support officers, and other analysts like me? My memoir will answer that question.

After graduating from Providence College with a bachelor's degree in international relations, I served as a navy officer, including an intelligence assignment in the Mekong Delta in 1969. After I left the navy in 1970, I got a job at the CIA in 1972, thanks in part, I think, to my Vietnam assignment and my navy security clearances, and to an adviser back at Providence who suggested the agency.

I soon moved into the CIA's Office of Imagery Analysis in the Directorate of Intelligence (DI) and in 1983 began my most interesting, challenging, and rewarding agency assignment—using satellite imagery as a member of the CIA's Operations Directorate Afghan Task Force. My work on the task force lasted five years or so. At first the task force work was just part of my duties. Much of my work was the traditional all-source analysis with special emphasis on the study of satellite imagery.

At the time I worked there, the Office of Imagery Analysis was the office that supported the Afghan Task Force and other operational projects, and conducted imagery analysis within the Directorate of Intelligence. Since the 1980s, the Office of Imagery Analysis has been transferred to what is now the NGA (the National Geospatial-Intelligence Agency within the Defense Department) and what used to be NPIC—the National Photographic Interpretation Center. Imagery work for CIA projects continues today and is performed by remote-sensing specialists and by NGA imagery analysts assigned to assist on CIA projects.

In the 1980s we were using only secret U.S. government satellites. Since that period, imagery work has continued and blossomed with the use of commercial satellite imagery and geographic information systems (GIS) technology. Another change is the use of digital imagery. In the 1980s, while the imagery itself was digital, the images were not yet in common use on a computer in a digital format, as they are now. During the period of the task force work we did all our imagery work with hardcopy images studied on light tables. Digital images displayed on a monitor did not come along until the 1990s.

At the heart of the Afghan Task Force was a team at CIA Headquarters in Langley, Virginia. Task force members came from all corners of the agency—all-source analysts, an imagery analyst (me), operations officers to handle agents, logistics officers to handle supply of equipment to the field, and many more. Most of us were in one large room at headquarters, much like the main room of a newspaper. This setup made for an excellent atmosphere where there was a rapid, free flow of ideas and information at the grass-roots level. Problems and opportunities were quickly spotted and dealt with. Synergy was a key to the effort.

We were in effect managers to coordinate agency support to the Pakistanis and to the Afghan Mujahedeen (or the "Muje," as we affectionately referred to the Afghan resistance fighters). We were assisting them in their struggle against the Soviet occupiers of Afghanistan. Originally only I was doing the imagery work, but later my office assigned other imagery analysts to work with me.

At that time the Afghan Task Force was unique in the agency. It served as a model for future efforts. Now within the agency such service—where you work alongside people from other offices, or from other intelligence community agencies—is common. Service on the task force, I think, also showed the utility of having people from one directorate serve in another directorate. Such assignments provide a broadening experience for the career development of the individual.

Up to this point the use of satellite imagery within the agency to support operations, as opposed to strictly analytical work, had been limited. On the task force we would expand greatly the role of satellite images for operational tasks.

On the task force my role—and that of the team back at our imagery office—consisted of using satellite imagery for the following tasks:

- Studying locations the Muje wanted to attack
- Recommending places to attack
- Preparing line drawings of sites to attack
- Evaluating the success of these attacks
- Preparing and delivering satellite imagery-based presentations (we call them briefings) in the DC area and overseas

A critical part of my job was tasking for satellite coverage. There was great competition for coverage, there were sometimes issues of cloud cover in target areas, and there were often questions about the exact locations for targeting the satellites. These considerations often played havoc with obtaining good timely imagery coverage.

Another key aspect of my job was preparing target packages, or having them prepared, and delivering them to the field. The target packages were unclassified, annotated line drawings from satellite imagery of sites to attack. The Muje were insatiable in their desire for these target packages.

For example, we might prepare line drawing studies of ten targets, have them printed on large format paper—say, thirty-six by forty-eight inches—and have fifty copies printed of each target. The Muje would use these line drawings for reconnaissance, for setting up long-distance rocket attacks, and for sabotage operations.

Another part of my job was to carry these target packages to Pakistan for presentation to a team of support for the Afghan Mujahedeen led by Pakistani Brigadier Mohammed Yousaf. During these trips I would brief the targets to the Pakistanis and discuss future targeting. This would form the tasking for further target packages—or line drawings—and the process would begin again. On page 196 of Brigadier Yousaf's book *The Bear Trap* is an example of one of our target line drawings (of Sher Khan). I often dealt with the brigadier on my visits to Pakistan. He recognized my contribution in the inscription to his book. He laughed when he had left a blank after inscribing it "To . . ." (I wrote Tom in there.) He said he thought the name I used when dealing with him was not my real name. He was right.

Once we started to accumulate satellite imagery coverage of the many targets the Muje were interested in and were attacking—garrisons, airfields, buildings, dams, road choke points, tunnels, and so on, I would put together satellite imagery briefings. A picture tells a thousand words. One image in particular was noteworthy—a September 1986 image showing three burned Soviet helicopter fuselages at the western end of Jalalabad airfield. This image showed the successful first use of Stinger missiles by the Muje. (For a description of the role played by satellite imagery in the resistance effort, see pages 93–94 from Brigadier Yousaf's *The Bear Trap*.)

We had been assisting the Muje in preparing this first Stinger attack. We knew where the Muje were setting up, we knew the time frame of the attack and had been imaging the area for a week or more. But nothing happened. We were about to turn off the coverage when the successful attack took place and we got an image of the results right after the fact. Milt Bearden—the chief of station in Pakistan at the time—in his novel *The Black Tulip*, based on the Afghan conflict, refers to this imagery on page 138. Sections of chapters 18 and 19 in Milt's book draw heavily from my work and that of our other CIA imagery analysts. (References in *The Black Tulip* and elsewhere—notably the book *Charlie Wilson's War*—to NPIC imagery analysts, or analysts from other agencies, as doing this work are incorrect. The work was done by CIA imagery analysts.)

These satellite imagery briefings became very popular and very effective. At the task force and at the various CIA offices that were involved in the effort we would pore over the satellite images as evidence that the program was working. We would also present many satellite imagery briefings to Congress and elsewhere in the DC area to show the program was working and to obtain more support.

We briefed foreign officials as well. On a couple of occasions I had the privilege of briefing the Saudi ambassador here in the DC area, Prince Bandar. These briefings were also very effective overseas with senior officers in the intelligence and military offices of our foreign partners. I would travel to various Middle Eastern countries, as well as to Asia, to present these briefings. Those were special occasions. I also briefed Pakistani president Muhammad Zia-ul-Haq and the Army General Staff.

In these short pages it has been difficult to encompass my five great years on the task force, but I hope I have conveyed to you something of the team I was a part of—senior officers in the intelligence community and in foreign governments and many outstanding CIA officers at lower levels who contributed to the success of the Afghan Task Force.

There were at the time, and are now, many analysts, operations officers, logistics officers, and others in the CIA engaged in equally great assignments. For those who decide to join the agency and open themselves to such assignments and experiences, the rewards are many.

18

Slideshow

JERI DiGIULIO

In 1973 Anna Wills, a cartographer in the Directorate of Intelligence, went on a five-week tour of five countries of the Himalayas—Pakistan, Afghanistan, India, Nepal, and Sikkim. She gave such a glowing report of her tour that I thought I might go on the same tour the next year. The decision was made even easier when I read an article about James Michener: when asked where he would like to live for the rest of his life, from among all the geographic books he had written, he is said to have replied without hesitating: Afghanistan. That clinched it. I called a travel agency and made my reservation.

It was a cinch to prepare for the trip. Anna advised me on wardrobe and the CIA Library provided two shelves of books for background. I read *Annapurna* by Maurice Herzog and *Tiger for Breakfast* by a Russian who had fled czarist Russia and wound up in Kathmandu, Nepal, where he opened a restaurant called the Yak and Yeti. I read *Mustang* by a French student, Michel Peissel, who had sought refuge from the rain in a bookstore on Paris's Left Bank. To conceal his real mission, he asked the clerk for a Tibetan dictionary; he bought the book and fell in love with the Himalayas. *Mustang* is the account of his travels through Buddhist monasteries in unmapped regions of Nepal and southern Tibet. I also read the 1963 account of Barry Bishop's ascent of Mount Everest. Besides the thrill of reading about the first American conquest of the highest peak in the world, I found an excellent description of how to winterize a camera for photography at Himalayan altitudes.

My next stop was at the National Photographic Interpretation

Center (NPIC), which was then in need of ground photography of the five southern Asian countries I would be visiting. I was given the use of a Nikon camera, three lenses, and forty rolls of 35mm film. All I had to do was give NPIC the film to process, make notes of where each picture was taken, and allow NPIC to make copies for their files. The original slides were returned to me and several of the most artistic ones were printed for me to frame for use in decorating my office.

The pictures were framed and hung in office after office as my assignments changed. Then in December1979, the Soviets invaded Afghanistan. I immediately remembered my slides in their boxes. I had used all forty rolls of film plus three more that I bought along the way.

I called Winston Wiley, the chief of the Afghan Task Force. I told him about the slides of Afghanistan and offered to bring them in for him or someone from his task force to view, in case they were interested. Winston was busy but said if I could find a conference room to view the slides he would send someone to take a look. After a round of phone calls to find a conference room—no easy feat those days—I called him and we arranged a viewing at 10:00 a.m. on a Friday.

Friday came and I set up my slide projector and screen. A few people came in and sat down to watch the forty or so slides I had selected from the hundreds I had taken. There were pictures of the Khyber Pass and the Bamiyan Valley with its tall Buddha statues, the roads in eastern Afghanistan through the mountains of the Hindu Kush, the unpaved roads nearer to Kabul, and the countryside with its mud fortresses.

The room was dim, so I couldn't see anyone yawning. When the lights went back on, one of the task force members came up to thank me and say that he had no idea of how imposing the mountains were.

An hour later I heard from Winston who asked if I could show the slides again. I said sure, though not knowing if I could get a conference room on such short notice. Fortunately the same room was available at 2:00 p.m. When the time came, I went into the conference room. Every chair was filled and it was standing room only. I didn't have time to count heads. We went through the slides for the second time that day. This time many people came up to thank me and ask questions. What time of year were the pictures taken? October. Did I know the altitudes of the mountains? More than ten thousand feet. Had I seen any airfields outside Kabul? No. Any other transportation system? That one I could answer because I had read Paul Theroux's book *The Great Railway Bazaar*, which pointed out that one could travel across Afghanistan only by bus or taxi. Theroux chose to fly from Iran to Pakistan.

As the Soviet invasion of Afghanistan went on, it became clear how important the country's terrain was. Invasion itself was difficult because of the miserable roads that became mud slicks in winter. And Moscow had chosen to begin its invasion in December. The Afghans used their time-tested defense tactics of hiding in caves and making surprise attacks on the invaders going through mountain passes. Even the Soviet use of helicopter gunships was thwarted because they were not designed to operate at such altitudes. Later the Afghans were equipped with shoulder-mounted Stinger missiles.

The rest is history well known to us all.

19

Meanwhile, in Asia . . .

MERRILY BAIRD

Although born in Honolulu toward the end of World War II, I was raised in the boroughs and suburbs of New York and, like many of my compatriots there, grew up knowing little of the United States west of the Hudson River or south of New Jersey. At the same time, the Holocaust's legacy drove our family to be preoccupied with modern European history, while my father's business as an importer and exporter of chemicals made far more exotic locales familiar household words as well. Throughout my childhood, an interest in Japan was particularly strong, for my parents had been exposed to that culture while living in Hawaii, and Japanese businessmen periodically came to dinner. Later, once my father built an explosives factory in West Africa and became a prominent collector of African art, that continent became a more dominant interest and members of the Liberian cabinet grew to be intimate friends.

In 1962 I went off to college expecting to become a public school teacher, a common goal of young women of that era. Still, I sensed that this would not satisfy me and decided to feast first on a more unusual diet of courses. Four years later any thoughts of teaching in public school had been lost in the mists of time, and I graduated with a degree in anthropology and minors in Japanese studies, African studies, and geography. In a similar vein, I began graduate school intending to earn a doctorate in anthropology, but in this instance I was seduced by both the allure of studying ancient Japan and a desire to help shape the modern world. The result was that I left graduate school with a master's degree in Japanese studies plus a year's experience as a teaching fellow and signed on with the agency's Career Training Program in 1970.

Building an Analyst's Career

Agency hiring practices are always a work in progress, and in those days you were hired by the Career Training Program without reference to a future assignment. Only in the course of the basic six-month training, which focused heavily on operational matters, were we sorted into groups destined either for the Clandestine Service or the Directorate of Intelligence. There was no question that I, as the only female hired for the Career Training Program that year and something of a hothouse flower, would become an analyst. I was offered two positions in the Office of Central Reference, and I chose to be the biographic analyst for Japan.

I realize now that the gods of good fortune smiled on me at that juncture. After all, by third or fourth grade I was a devoted reader of the *New York Times* obituary section, which traced the arc of fascinating lives, and by junior high was addicted to creating files on five-by-eight cards. As the sole Japan analyst in the Office of Central Reference, I was mistress of an astonishingly large array of files, including those prepared by the U.S. military authorities who occupied Japan after the end of World War II. Far more important, the assignment offered me the opportunity to become acquainted, albeit at a distance, with hundreds of prominent Japanese and all of that country's key institutions.

Around 1972 I relocated to the Office of Current Intelligence, which covered the globe from a broader political perspective, and I remained in this office and its successors through the mid-1980s. The assignment to the Japan politics desk involved everything new analysts learn about identifying key developments and writing articles worthy of publication in the *National Intelligence Daily* and President's Daily Brief. It did not, however, demand that I penetrate a veil of secrecy to acquire information or that I work an intellectual acrostic complicated by partial and misleading clues. As one of the world's most open societies, Japan, I concluded after three years, offered little ground for forging methodological breakthroughs or taking on seemingly impossible tasks.

On the other hand, North Korea, a country not then covered by my office, did seem to offer challenge aplenty, and I asked to be switched to that account within the same branch. Everyone, especially the analyst covering South Korean politics, warned me that to work on the secretive North would be to commit career suicide. Little did my colleagues understand that such dire warnings would only harden my determination, and in January 1975 I began to reinvent myself as an analyst of what the intelligence community calls a hard target.

By imitating the analytical approaches of my office's talented sinologists, I prospered and in late 1975 visited selected Asian capitals to brief local officials regarding political developments in P'yongyang. Although it will seem laughable now, the simple fact that I had identified and ranked the members of the North Korean Politburo was viewed as something of a minor miracle, and the U.S. ambassador in Seoul responded by asking that I immediately be assigned to his embassy. This did not work out, but other opportunities quickly came my way. So quickly, in fact, that in January 1976 I packed my pens for a one-year rotation to the State Department's Bureau of Intelligence and Research. Hired by the bureau as the senior analyst for Japanese politics, I also picked up the North Korea account there, served as the Japan-Korea branch chief, and mentored the three seasoned Foreign Service officers who ran the bureau's Northeast Asia Division without prior intelligence experience.

Midcareer

As almost always occurs with rotational assignments, especially those to another directorate or agency, the time spent at State brought considerable personal growth. Among other things, operating away from home strengthened my sense of being a CIA asset, and I would never again think of myself as a narrow specialist. Virtually all agency managers have made this mental leap, and they view such a transition on the part of junior officers as a marker of future success.

In the decade that passed after I returned to the Directorate of Intelligence from the State Department, my assignments rarely lasted more than a year or two. Serendipitously I began to specialize in a priority area—nuclear proliferation—and in the production of an intelligence format—the lengthy, interagency National Intelligence Estimate—with which not all political analysts were comfortable. As a result, I now handled special projects, usually on commission from senior agency officials who worked outside my own office's chain of command, and I now more often than not addressed issues unrelated to Asia. I can assure you that such a "have gun will travel" lifestyle is not the best way to ascend the bureaucratic ladder rapidly, but it satisfied my preference for varied challenges and my newly discovered love for managing complex projects. It also reinforced my belief that the agency, while being a highly disciplined organization, is remarkably flexible in supporting officers determined to blaze unusual career paths.

The years between 1977 and 1987 involved considerable training. Among the highlights of this training were a week spent at the Oak Ridge nuclear facility, five weeks flying about the country with other analysts to study weapons manufacture, and a week spent at Harvard's John F. Kennedy School studying the often fractious intersection of intelligence and policymaking. Travel to Asia was also frequent, so that by retirement I had spent nearly three years abroad and had worked extensively with the Clandestine Service. Last but certainly not least, this period provided my first opportunity to manage an analytical branch within the Directorate of Intelligence. This was the unit of the Office of East Asian Analysis that covered the two Koreas from a political, economic, and military perspective.

During my second year as chief of the Korea Branch, I was invited to serve a one-year rotation with the Product Evaluation Staff within the Directorate of Intelligence. This staff assessed the quality of each analytical office's longer publications and kept book on how well the offices met their research plan commitments. While Robert Gates was the deputy director of intelligence, the tracking tasks were fascinating, for he used the force of his personality and intellect to upgrade the quality of work in general and the direction of analysis on the Soviet Union in particular.

Just as interesting was our staff's more substantive research, especially when I was tasked to judge the success of a regional office in handling a high-profile issue. Director of Central Intelligence William Casey requested this review because a senior cabinet member had complained repeatedly that pessimistic agency analyses compromised the ability of the White House to achieve policy breakthroughs. My study indicated that the regional office had been prescient and on the mark in its analyses, but the findings also helped illustrate how often intelligence community findings clashed with the more values-driven policy imperatives of our nation's top decisionmakers.

Toward the end of my year with the Product Evaluation Staff, I returned from a single day of leave to discover that the staff chief had unilaterally mapped out my future. To improve the quality of the directorate's longer papers, she told me, the deputy director of intelligence had accepted her proposal that I should personally tutor every directorate branch chief on how to review and edit longer papers. Her optimistic calculations indicated that, by working with one branch chief daily, I could complete the task in eighteen months. Lady luck, I am happy to report, intervened before this doomed-to-fail plan could be implemented: the staff chief was tapped to head the directorate's newly created Office of Leadership Analysis and I became that office's chief of the Africa branch.

Golden Years in Analysis

In the Office of East Asian Analysis, I had headed one of the directorate's most senior branches, as measured by grade, age, and experience in the relevant intelligence field. Now, in the Office of Leadership Analysis, only a few analysts and intelligence assistants were older than twenty-five, a mere two had been to Africa, and not a soul, other than me, had any academic background related to the continent. This posed special challenges, and I still smile as I remember how I sent all the analysts downtown to dine at an all-too-authentic Ethiopian restaurant, invited special guests to visit the branch each week, and arranged a robust schedule of overseas travel. The exposure to outside speakers and travel transformed even the most junior of our branch members, and I departed the branch a year later having accomplished what I regard as the ultimate goal of a manager, that is to say, making one's subordinates so competent and self-assured that you are quite dispensable.

Getting to know the African continent anew had been a great deal of fun and quite a challenge given the fact that we covered better than fifty countries, but the most valuable aspect of this assignment was separating two jobs that had been meshed in the Office of East Asian Analysis, namely those of senior analyst and branch chief. This separation of functions is critical and became even more pronounced when the Office of Leadership Analysis asked me to manage officers who specialized in the behavioral analysis of foreign leaders and had clinical and even medical experience that I lacked.

This was a major learning experience, and all that I absorbed from the remarkable officers in that branch was put to good use when I decided later to return to analysis. The Office of Leadership Analysis gave me a great deal of freedom regarding my use of time and choice of research topics as a senior analyst, and during my last year there I even spent a portion of each week on loan to the agency's Office of the Executive Director.

On the substantive front, I pursued two paths: describing the decisionmaking culture and institutions of North Korea and promoting on an office-wide basis the application of leadership analysis to strategic weapons issues. These years were, bar none, the most productive I had in the agency, and, although I no longer had subordinates to supervise, I was able to create a dynamic cluster of analysts who worked with me to break the code of North Korean leadership and prepare for the not-too-distant death of the aged leader Kim Il-song. I also worked tirelessly to assure that other offices were vested in my success, and, in the case of a study of North Korea's trading entities, I convinced colleagues at the National Security Agency to reassign analysts to assist me for several months. The resulting research report included a guide to specific trading entities and is the analytical project of which I am most proud. Within two days of its issuance, requests from the Commerce and Treasury Departments forced a second printing of the report as well as the creation of a CD version that could be sent to every Customs Service office and port of entry. It was this type of collaboration combined with my work on strategic programs that led to my being awarded the intelligence community's National Medal of Achievement in 1994.

A Challenge Unlike Any Other

In late 1993 I traveled to New York City to attend a fundraising dinner that honored a favorite cousin. The very city was a tonic, and my cousin's diverse range of friends impressed me. By this time I was moving into the final chapter of my career, and I returned to work inspired to finish that career by doing something radically different.

If you are ranked as a GS-15, as I was at that juncture, and have had broad agency experience, a logical place to conclude a career is in the Office of Inspector General. Initially I visited the Inspections Staff. This group, drawn from all directorates, assesses the functioning of agency offices and recommends constructive change. Openings were not available, but I was advised to consider the Investigations Staff, which handles criminal matters, instances of failed management, and grievance cases. At the time, no analysts worked there but a chat with two investigators convinced me that the focus of the work and intensity of the operating style would suit me perfectly. When a vacancy occurred a few weeks later, I made my very last change of assignment.

The Investigations Staff hired me as a grievance officer, and I actually put in one eight-hour day as such before being reassigned to an investigation of administrative failure that would keep investigators as well as the inspector general himself engaged full time for better than eight months. This was the inquiry into how the agency, over a decade, had failed to uncover the spying of Aldrich Ames on behalf of the Soviet Union. Given my background, I was assigned to study the details of Ames's career and to supervise a specialist from another office who assessed Ames from a psychiatric point of view. I also helped edit the massive Ames report, and thereafter I did a lot of editing and even rewriting of reports for other investigators. During my last two years in the office, as special assistant to the inspector general I enjoyed varied investigative and administrative assignments, many of which allowed me to forge win-win solutions for pending managerial disputes. Family issues forced me to take an early retirement in late 1997 and to relocate outside the Washington DC area. Otherwise, I expect, I might still be juggling an ever-fascinating mix of challenges in the Office of Inspector General.

An Analyst's Career in Perspective

Twelve years after the departing the agency, I can look back on my career and consider it in the context of a full life. This has been a gratifying journey of recollection, for I realize what dividends accrued from the work habits passed on by my businessman father and appreciate how the passions and interests of my childhood and youth were fulfilled at Langley. Not every working relationship I had in my twenty-seven years at the agency was ideal or necessarily sustainable, but I judge my career overall to be one of remarkable blessings and know that the independence I so treasured and won in great measure was envied by even the most senior of my peers.

Every day I quite consciously use lessons learned at the agency to enrich and guide current activities. In my postretirement years these have included, most significantly, researching and writing on subjects long familiar. To date I have published a book on Japanese art (titled *Symbols of Japan: Thematic Motifs in Art and Design*) that was, in truth, the product of a cultural anthropologist's encounter with the symbolic roots of both Japanese and Chinese art. I have in addition contributed a chapter on North Korean strategic thinking to a book issued by the Air War College. I ruthlessly edit my own writing, reminding myself of the guidelines I shared with my analysts, and apply in public speaking contexts lessons learned from having given hundreds upon hundreds of official briefings. I can remember almost verbatim many gems of advice shared by supervisors and colleagues at the agency, and to those wise friends whose counsel continues to benefit me I dedicate this brief memoir.

TWO

Heroes Behind the Heroes

CIA Support Officers

A Quick Look at Oversight

20

On Planet Congress

MARTIN PETERSEN

Testifying before Congress is one of those things that goes with the job. It is almost always painful. It takes an enormous amount of preparation. The agency and agency officers take it very seriously. They prepare. They write statements. They revise them. They fact-check them twice. Internal "murder boards" are run for important testimony—question-and-answer sessions where other officers play the part of Congress and grill the person who will be testifying. In short, many hours of careful preparation are spent to present testimony that is accurate, responsive, and nonpartisan.

We are testifying to an audience—how to be fair?—of strong personalities. There are many strong personalities in Washington, but there is no greater egotistical, self-centered population than Congress. It is dominated by people with a very well-developed sense of entitlement and convinced of their superior intelligence and skills—which they demonstrate at hearings by stumbling through questions prepared by their staff. Congress is a body of 535 independent actors unified by one common value: what is in it for them and how they can gain a political advantage from the activity at hand.

It is a different culture, to be sure. The person testifying is frequently more prop than actor. Congressmen often talk to one another—which is to say, score points off one another—by means of the questions they ask. The testifier is the wall the shot ricochets off of before it strikes "the honorable gentleman from wherever" between the eyes. What most want is to make a speech—especially if there is a camera running—and then have the testifier express agreement, if not awe.

All of which leads to some incredibly convoluted questions. A colleague and I were testifying on the Chinese economy when we got one of these rambling expositions from a gentleman with a bee in his bonnet. It had been a very long hearing. We had been at the table for hours without a break while members and staff wandered in and out. To make matters worse, it was an open hearing, which guaranteed an audience of Asian intelligence services, mainstream media, political junkies of all stripes, and a liberal assortment of one-issue true believers—all pretty much looking for tomorrow's headline or gotcha moment and it was all red meat to any congressional representative looking for some ink.

In this case, the good congressman was recognized by the chair and got his turn on stage. He began a series of rambling questions all couched in "his impressions" about things Chinese and ending with the same question: "Would you agree?" Most were easily dealt with, and then he launched this one, which reads better in print because you cannot see the pauses or the hand gestures:

"One other general impression I have had is that the Chinese have perhaps had a long history, a long pattern of almost absorbing whoever is trying to govern them. So that it sort of takes on its own momentum, unlike the Soviet Union, which seems to be the opposite."

(I looked at my partner and there was bewilderment—and fear—in his eyes. Where is he going with this and please don't say that my partner will answer this question?)

"It never seems to be able to overcome its own political leadership to do what it otherwise might have the capability of doing."

(At this point, I lost the thread. I had no idea what the first pronoun referred back to—the Soviet Union? China?—or what the second half of the sentence was all about.)

"Maybe that is instructive, in terms of what is going on. I don't know whether this is accurate information or not, but I have even heard that when the Chinese nationalized some basic industries back in the early 1950s or late 1940s, that they even issued bonds on the acquisition or the takeover of those enterprises, often retained some of the management of those enterprises to run them, and have honored the repayment of that indebtedness."

(Okay, we seem to be edging back into China industrial policy, although I had no clue how any of this related in his mind to the statement about "absorbing.")

"Is that accurate?"

I gave a five-word answer that my colleague at the table still refers to as one of the single best answers he ever heard at a hearing: "Some of that is accurate."

The congressman got what he wanted, apparently, because without missing a beat he launched into his next series of questions, which were more focused.

A colleague and senior military officer friend of mine once suggested only half-kiddingly that the best strategy when testifying on the Hill is to "go dumb early." It isn't an effort to withhold information; it was an efficiency, he explained. It got the conversation down to a level they were used to. Mark Twain would have endorsed the approach. (Mark Twain once said, "Suppose you were an idiot, and suppose you were a member of Congress. But I repeat myself.")

In Support, You Never Know Where You Might End Up—and What You Might Learn along the Way

DAN KING

These personal reminiscences are written to illustrate just a few of the experiences one might have as a support officer for the CIA and a few of the "lessons learned" along the way. In many ways it is a personal journey back over a career, but it may also convince you that the Directorate of Support is the place for you. Times change, requirements change, organizational structures change, but the essential elements of support haven't changed since the Roman legions. I served as a support officer for the agency from 1964 to 1994.

The lessons learned may seem obvious, but as my father the lawyer always said about contracts, "reading the fine print is an education, not reading it is called experience." The same goes for support lessons learned.

Recruitment

The card on the university bulletin board said, "Are you bored? Do you want adventure and a new and exciting career? Call this number." At the time I was finishing graduate school in engineering at Lehigh University and was burned out from two years of eighteen-hour days studying and working part time. I needed a change. I called the number in Philadelphia and the gentleman who answered wouldn't tell me who he worked for or what was involved, but said to come down for an interview.

On the appointed day I went for the interview to a nondescript office in downtown Philadelphia. There was no sign on the door. I knocked, heard a buzzer, a click, and I just stood there not knowing what to do. Finally a secretary opened the door, explained to me how to get "buzzed in," and then let me in. The office was full of safes, all kinds of phones and machines, and posters of exotic locations and attractive women—I was hooked before the recruiter ever said a word.

A Matter of Faith

The recruiter, G. G. Zitrides, explained that he had just the program for bored engineers—a Junior Officer Training Program (later called the Career Trainee Program) for future CIA officers. This program had only recently been opened to officers who would serve in a support role. Support, he explained, included engineering, personnel, security, training, logistics, communications, finance, and medical services. I would have a chance to use my engineering, live abroad, and move into a management role if I was successful. I would undergo a year of training before being placed in a permanent position. But first, had I been in the service? No, I had not been in the service. Well, unless I had a military background he really wasn't interested but, if I was willing, he had a solution for that as well.

All I had to do was go to the nearest recruitment office of any of the services, sign up for officer candidate school, go wherever they sent me, and in one year I would receive orders reassigning me to Washington DC for training. Of course, if I didn't make it through officer candidate school, I would never hear from him again. Having a father who was an attorney, I naturally asked if I could get all of this in writing. No, he said, it was a matter of faith. You had to trust that the agency could and would do what was promised. Trusting, I signed up with the air force and served as a combat defense and base police officer in Cheyenne, Wyoming. Sure enough, one year later, like magic, orders arrived assigning me to U.S. Air Force Headquarters in Washington DC. The squadron commander commented to me at the time that he had never seen a set of similar orders. Within the agency, it is an article of faith that promises are to be kept.

A Willingness to Serve

For the next year I underwent the usual organizational and operational training both in the Washington area and at "the farm," an agency training facility located outside the Washington area. However, for the first time a course was included on support services, primarily for those who would be serving as support officers in agency stations or field offices located abroad. A long-time support officer, I believe his name was Tom Kelly, taught the course and had a bit of wisdom that I still recall. He said that to be a good support officer, you had to have a willingness to serve. By that he meant that if you wanted to be the center of attention or had an enormous ego that needed to be stroked, then support wasn't the area for you. On the other hand, if you took pleasure in the success of an operation and enjoyed working as a member of a team while serving others, then you had found a home. Serving others, he explained, is not the same as being subservient. Making your voice heard on critical issues, bringing your expertise to a problem, and giving honest opinions at all times are demanded but all successful support officers still have a willingness to serve others. (My wife believes that there are as many big egos in support as anywhere else, but what does she know.)

A Chinese Prison

When I finished training, it was decided that it would be wasteful not to use my engineering education, so my first job was to design a copy of a Chinese prison. At the time, there was considerable concern about "brainwashing" of persons who had been taken prisoner (including both agents and officers), so it was thought that our officers should be exposed to what they might experience. The prison was constructed at the farm and later turned into a museum. I recall the challenge of researching the subject, talking to people who had experienced imprisonment, and doing the actual architecture and engineering design. Other support officers were involved in everything from recruiting Chinese-speaking guards to raising cockroaches to put in the cells. The experience was to be as realistic as possible. Within the agency, you never know what you will be working on next.

People Are Still People

Another project I remember well during this period was a temporary duty assignment to the Middle East to construct a facility on a particular border monitoring missile launches from a test site. What I remember most is not the engineering that was involved (although it was very challenging) but rather the people I met along the way. I lived at the construction site with several hundred workers, a German contractor, and a Greek foreman. It was a time to learn that most of the world doesn't think the same way we do about things and that you need to listen and see the world through their eyes if you are to understand them. While doing that you have to always remember who you are, what you believe in, and whom you work for.

While building this facility, I remember an invitation I received from one of our workers to visit his home. It was a small village that could be entered only by walking along a mountain path for several kilometers. His home was a single room with a dirt floor and only rugs on the floor. It was snowing outside and his poor wife and children had to wait outside, barefooted, while I visited (as was the custom). He had nothing, but he managed to provide tea and a little food and I remember his kindness to this day. Kindness is universal to the human condition (as, I'm afraid, are a few less desirable traits).

A Few Good Mentors Are Hard to Find

Returning to the States, I was visited by Glenn Brewer, who was then a senior support officer (engineer) working for the Directorate of Science and Technology. He said he had heard that I did good work and that he had a project on which he needed help, but he couldn't tell me what it was, where it was, how long I would be gone, or what I would be doing. However, the job was mine if I wanted it. As I've said before, you have to have faith, so I took it. It turned out to be the construction of a major overseas facility involving a very large and complex technical collection facility and hundreds of houses for workers. More important than the work I did there was that Glenn Brewer then became a mentor who was able to provide guidance and support for the remainder of my career. On this same project I also worked for Jim McDonald, later director of logistics, Harry Fitzwater, later deputy director for administration, and John McMahon, later deputy director of the agency, and I consider them all mentors who supported my career at one time or another. Those relationships that you establish early in your career may last a lifetime. Do good work for your superiors, make some sacrifices for them, learn from them, and the good ones will take care of you as well. Finding good mentors involves a little luck and a lot of hard work.

One experience that I recall from this period following the initial overseas facility construction was John McMahon telling me that he wanted to initiate another major construction effort but not to say anything about it to anyone. I was worried that I would need additional engineering support so I went to the then director of logistics, asked that he not say anything, and told him that McMahon would be initiating a new construction program and I thought I might need additional help. He immediately grabbed the phone, called McMahon, and read him the riot act for not telling him first that he had this in mind. As I left his office, the director's secretary gave me a note that McMahon wanted to see me immediately. I went to McMahon's office; he let me stand there for several minutes and finally said, "You are number one on my s#&t list. I told you not to say anything." I said, "John, you're right and it will never happen again (and I meant it)." He said, "I know it won't. By the way, I'm going overseas tomorrow, if you'd like to join me." Now John knew how to mix the "carrot" and the "stick." The message is, as a support officer you will often have a "home" office and you will often work for "others." Don't violate the trust of either.

Lifelong Friends and Missing Relatives

Once the overseas facility had been built, John McMahon asked me if I would like to serve abroad in a generalist support position. This would be a major departure from engineering because I would also be responsible for supply, procurement, transportation, housing, and other generalist functions. The director of logistics at the time did not support the assignment because I had no experience in those areas. But McMahon insisted that I get the job and I got it—that is what mentors are for.

While on that assignment, I made a number of foreign friends and even discovered some "long lost" relatives of my wife. We are all still friends to this day. As a support officer, try to go abroad, make friends, and you may be lucky enough to have them for life.

The Special Assistant and the Boss's Secretary

Returning to the States, I worked as a special assistant to the director of logistics. His secretary and I were constantly arguing about my memos—she kept changing them, even the substance. The boss heard us arguing one day and I had had enough. I asked to see him and explained the problem. He said, "A secretary (today he or she would be called an executive assistant) like Polly is hard to find. She knows how I like to work, she anticipates my needs, she protects my flanks, keeps my calendar, and she has my ear. She can't be replaced. Young men like you who want to get ahead are a dime a dozen. Now, what do you want?" Wisely I said, "Nothing." It never pays to get in a contest with the boss's secretary—you will lose.

A Good War Always Helps Promotions and Provides Challenges

One day the director of logistics called me into the office and asked if I'd like to get my GS-15 ranking. (Always worry when they start with the carrot rather than the challenge of the job. Get challenging jobs and the promotions will take care of themselves.) He said that they were having trouble filling the chief of logistics job in

Vietnam and that if I would take it, the GS-15 (a promotion) would
follow. He also said that if I didn't want the job, nothing would
ever be said (don't believe that). So, you guessed it, I took the job.

In Vietnam we had a large number of Americans and Vietnamese providing logistics support to agency operations in country. The
ambassador was saying that "peace was at hand" and that families could return from offshore safe havens (mine was one of the
few families arriving directly from the States). I always remember that on our first day in country, I met socially an Agency for
International Development (USAID) officer who spoke Vietnamese and who had lived in the country ten years. I told him of the
ambassador's view that there would be peace and the USAID officer replied that his view was that within six months we would all
be out of there. He was right. Try to learn the language and listen
to those who best know the country and its people.

Within months the country was falling apart, the evacuation
of Americans was being planned, and our ambassador was assur-
ing me and other managers that all of our Vietnamese employees
would be evacuated with us. I met with them, and about 150 of
my Vietnamese employees wanted to evacuate, which I promised.
They sold their homes and had our assurances of evacuation in
return for their loyalty and commitment to us until the end. They
did help and support us until the end, but we left them behind. I
did what I could to get them out but events (bombardment, riots,
etc.) on that last day made it almost impossible to do so, and I will
always feel that I didn't do enough, that I failed them. There may
come times in your career when there will be moral dilemmas
that you may never resolve. Just do your best.

Over the next several years some of these same employees
managed to reach Thailand and wanted the agency to confirm
that they had worked for the U.S. government (and hence get
priority entrance into the States). The agency refused to do so
and my boss told me not to interfere. For probably the only time
in my career, I disobeyed orders and went to friends in the State
Department who took my personal assurance that these were

former agency employees, which got them out of Thailand. It pays to network.

Telling You What You Want to Hear

After a period of getting my head together and decompressing after Vietnam, I was asked to serve as director of logistics.

At its core, logistics is providing a needed service or materiel at the right place and at the right time, worldwide. Services include things like transportation, procurement, supply, and facilities. Materiel includes all of the things needed for the success of agency operations (from pencils and paper to boats, trains, and planes). Of course, we could all go to the "yellow pages" for such things, but what makes it more complicated and exciting for agency support personnel is that most of the time you do not want the agency's hand to be visible and some of the time you even want your work to be attributable to others. There is no lack of opportunity for creativity.

I recall that shortly after taking the job, I happened to meet Harry Fitzwater (one of my mentors) on the steps to the Headquarters Building. He asked how I was doing and I said that I was having trouble getting people to do what I wanted them to do. His response, "After all these years, you are finally starting to understand the problem." As a manager, that is what it is all about; having a vision of where you want to go and how you want to get there and then getting other people to make it a success. Obviously, I think a lot of good things happened during the time that I was there (who doesn't think thus?) but we also learn from our failures.

One of my failures during this multiyear assignment was the development of a Logistics Integrated Management System (LIMS). The concept was well ahead of its time, involving the integration of data processing systems supporting all of the separate logistics functions. The project was well funded and had management support but got into an overrun position, and deployment dates continued to slip. I spoke with the people heading the project and they continued to assure me that all was well.

About this same time, I was asked to head up the Office of Communications upon the promotion of the then head of that office. As soon as I had done so, my replacement in logistics cancelled the LIMS development project (its objective was later met, but in a more limited fashion than I had envisioned). Some months later I happened to run into several of the people who had headed the LIMS effort and asked them how their assurances to me of continued success could be reconciled with the failure of the project. Their answer was "that I had wanted the project to succeed so badly that they didn't have the heart to tell me that it was not succeeding." On any major project, never again did I depend on what I was told without verification. Surround yourself with people who are willing to tell you the truth (*the emperor has no clothes!*) and set up systems to verify the facts. Management 101, but it is easy to be misled.

First In, Last Out

Communications was a new and exciting world for me. If logistics is about "things," then communications is all about "technology and dedication to the mission."

It was about technology because communications officers were always at the forefront of the newest technology (satellite and computer) well before that technology was generally available. It was about dedication to the mission because agency communications officers were always the first people in and the last people out on any major operation. Communications officers probably have won more medals than any other group of support officers. They have also had to show more discretion and vigilance since they are exposed to more secrets than anyone else in an overseas station other than the chief of station (head of an overseas office). Because of this access to station communications, communications officers are a natural target for recruitment by foreign intelligence services.

I recall at one point the chief of the Soviet Bloc division telling me that there was a traitor in communications leaking secrets to the Soviets. I just didn't believe it. It turned out that Aldrich Ames, one of the Clandestine Service's "own," was working for the Soviets and the Soviets had spread disinformation regarding a communications officer working for them to deflect attention from Ames. The fact of the matter is that there have been far more operations officers who have "forgotten what they stand for and whom they work for" than support officers. This is understandable because it is the clandestine services officer who has the greatest exposure to foreign intelligence services. There are times when it isn't clear who is recruiting whom.

The point is that communications is critical to the success of all agency operations. Intelligence that can't reach the policymakers is worthless. And without worldwide, secure, uninterrupted communications, command and control is equally impossible.

Eventually the time came to move on and in the tradition of former heads of communications, I assigned myself to run the European area office for communications for three years. Living, dining, and traveling all over Europe for three years was a tough job but someone had to do it.

If the Tab Is Big Enough, Everyone Will Let You Sign

After returning from Europe, I was told that it was time to get back to work (Europe was work!) and was asked to head up the Office of Finance. I was now a "bean counter." Actually, bean counting can be a lot of fun for a couple of reasons. First, virtually nothing can be done without money and as a finance officer you get to be included in everything. Second, where else can you legally learn how to "launder money and manipulate funds," worldwide? Now that doesn't sound like your normal CPA activity, does it?

But if logistics is about "things," and communications is about "technology and dedication," then finance is really about "integrity." Finance officers have a responsibility to ensure that every penny is expended for the purposes authorized and they take that role very, very seriously. To that end, certain finance officers are designated as "certifying officers" to review and approve the expenditures of others. As a prerequisite, they have to have attained a certain level of experience and training. I may have been the head of the office, but the standing joke was that I didn't have the experience or training to certify anyone's accountings (which was true). However, I always noticed that at year end, when the agency had to "certify" in writing to the Office of Management and Budget and to Congress that the total funds made available to the agency had been legally expended and accounted for (both the dollars and penalties for failure to do so were very large), everyone was more than happy for me to sign that letter.

When it comes to the handling of money, agency officers are expected to practice the highest standards of integrity and it is the responsibility of agency finance officers to ensure that they do so.

How Far Do You Have to Go to Be Happy?

After a year or so in finance, I was asked if I would like to serve as the associate deputy director for administration, which was the second most senior support position in the agency at that time. My ego wouldn't let me say no, but the truth was that I wasn't truly happy serving at that level. One of my own corollaries of the Peter Principle (which states that in a hierarchy every employee tends to rise to the level of his or her incompetence) is that within the agency, if you love your work and do a good job, eventually you will be promoted to a level which has nothing to do with the reasons for which you came to the agency in the first place. Certainly senior management positions afford the opportunity to impact general policy directions and to lead, but for my part at least, I wanted to be closer to the action and as the head of a functional office one could still do that. At a more senior policy level, while there are greater opportunities to lead, one still spends much of the time attending meetings, haggling over resources, and keeping the politicians on Capitol Hill happy. So, unless that turns you on, stay at the office level.

I asked myself if there was anything in the agency that I still wanted to do before I retired—and there was one thing. I wanted a tour in a particular European country. Why there, you might ask? Well, the short answer is that my wife is from that country, we speak the language, and I wanted to experience the reality of that country's independence. One thing about the agency, once you are in the door you can go virtually anywhere. So . . . .

The Clandestine Service—Another Culture, Another Language, Another Set of Values

I approached the then deputy director of the Clandestine Service and asked if an assignment to Eastern Europe as chief of station (COS) might be possible. It was a considerable step backward in rank but something I truly wanted to do. He reluctantly agreed, as it was shortly after independence, there was a dearth of that local language's speakers, and he anticipated that the role of the COS would be primarily a liaison, not an operational role. I wasn't totally ignorant of the requirements of the job, having taken some introductory courses on operational training over the years, but I certainly wasn't an experienced operations officer either. So, it was agreed that I would take three months of additional operational training and move into the job. However, between the time that I went into training and the completion of the course, there was a new head of the Soviet Bloc division within the Clandestine Service and the new head was very reluctant to support the assignment. He clearly wanted his own person in the job, but it was too late and he did not have a language-qualified candidate to fill the job. Hence, I was off to the assignment, but with no real enthusiasm or support from the home office (always a mistake).

I remember well my reception by the local service. In order to monitor and control our activities my family was placed in housing in a former compound. The housing itself was fine (it had previously been used to familiarize Soviet agents with American life styles—although there was no hot water for the first six months we were there), but it was located on a compound surrounded by barbed wire with guards on the gates and dogs that were released every night at dark. Not exactly the "liaison" environment that I had envisioned.

During the year that I was there I certainly got the station up and operating and there was some intelligence of value (the degree of the local government's control over nuclear weapons located on their soil was the question of the day), but not the kind of continuous stream of reporting that the Clandestine Service would have liked. Also, I didn't really have the support of the division chief since I was not his candidate for the job. As a result, little operational guidance or support was forthcoming from home. In fact, important information on existent assets in country was withheld. Be that as it may, it was certainly the prerogative of the division chief to replace a COS with whom he was dissatisfied, and after one year I was called home based on the argument that someone with more operational experience was required (which was for the most part true as the "liaison" environment had changed to a much more traditional "operational" environment over that period of time). So the tour was less than a total success but if I had failed to go for it, I would never have forgiven myself. For better or worse, the agency had given me the opportunity to do everything that I ever wanted to do. The only message here is that every directorate of the agency has its own distinct culture and set of values and to be successful in that environment, you should be very certain that you understand it and have the support of those you work for—something that I had always done in the past but failed to do in this case.

Family Values

Little mention has been made in this monologue of my family—a wife and four children. We often underestimate the impact that working for the agency has on families, but the high divorce rate should be evidence enough. During my career my wife had to do everything from formal entertaining in Europe to standing in bread lines in Eastern Europe to being shot at by the Viet Cong as she and the children took the last commercial flight out of Saigon. She also had to do most of the raising of our children. If there is one change I would have made in my agency career, it would have been to spend more time with my family and given up a few promotions along the way. Always think about how much you are willing to sacrifice for that career.

Moving on to the Private Sector

A final question that we all face is whether to retire or go for a second career. For my part, I always wondered how well I would do in the commercial sector. Following retirement from the agency I worked for a large information technology firm for another nine years before truly retiring, and I learned a few lessons there as well. Maybe I should have known them already but here are a few:

- The CIA puts more emphasis on career planning and preparation than most commercial firms.
- Contrary to the negative view of government employees held by many, CIA personnel are truly a breed apart. They are just as aggressive and intelligent as any I met in the private sector and are far more dedicated.
- In private industry (at least where I worked), you lived and died by "the numbers," that is, profit targets. The day after winning a major contract for the company, the vice president treated me to lunch and said, "Thanks for the win but that was yesterday. What have you done today?" And he meant every word of it.
- The private industry work was just a job, but the CIA was a career.

Giving Back in Retirement

If you made it through this paper, then there is still time to contemplate one more issue—what will you do when you really retire? If you had a great career, then you have an obligation to give something back. Volunteer at your local thrift shop or food kitchen, teach children to read, help your church or synagogue or mosque; do something positive to give back.

22

What Is a Promise Worth?

DAN KING

During my thirty-year career with the CIA, the Vietnam evacuation troubled me more than any other single event. I like to think of myself as person who tries to do the right thing—a person who keeps his promises. But sometimes we have to see ourselves as we really are.

At the time of the Vietnam evacuation, I was in charge of logistics support for agency operations in Vietnam. Even though the major campaigns of the war were over by the time I arrived there in 1974, we still had a significant presence supporting both agency and Vietnamese paramilitary and covert activities. Numerous Americans and Vietnamese supported logistics activities throughout the country, from the Delta in the south to Da Nang in the north.

Our main logistics compound, near Tan Son Nhut Air Base, was our primary transportation hub. Logistics encompassed everything, from the supply of weapons and munitions to housing and transportation. As chief of logistics, I reported to the chief of support, whose responsibilities also included such other functions as communications, security, personnel, and finance. He in turn reported to the chief of station.

In the months before the evacuation, there was little indication of what was to come. As late as February, the logistics branch's major problems were finding accommodations for families that were planning to return (many had been moved to "safe havens" in other countries) and resuming cargo shipments to the coastal cities of Da Nang and Nha Trang.

Then things started to fall apart. In mid-March, President

Nguyen Van Thieu made the decision to abandon the Central Highlands. Vietnamese troops started streaming south, along with thousands of refugees who feared a communist bloodbath. Enemy pressure forced the agency's officers in Hue and Quang Ngai to evacuate to Da Nang.

On March 28, Da Nang itself was evacuated under the worst possible circumstances. Rioting and looting were widespread. In many cases, agency officers had to literally fight their way out. Our logistics officer there managed to escape by motor boat to one of the barges sitting offshore; our ordnance officer was rescued by helicopter from the Da Nang airport, which had been closed by mobs on the field. Others came south on a coastal freighter and had to barricade themselves in the wheelhouse to save their own lives—while deserting South Vietnamese troops robbed and raped women and children in full view.

Things were not going well in Saigon, either. To add to the confusion, as thousands of refugees arrived, a renegade South Vietnamese pilot bombed the palace in early April. We sent the remaining American dependents home, including my wife and our three small children. They had come to Vietnam because the State Department and the ambassador had assured them that the situation was becoming more stable and that it was safe for American families to return.

On the day after the bombing, I thought about those assurances as my family boarded the last commercial flight out of Vietnam. I watched helplessly as tracers arched up toward their departing aircraft. And I remembered the U.S. Agency for International Development worker I had met on our first day in country, six months earlier. He had lived there for ten years and spoke Vietnamese. He had told me that we would all be gone within six months. He was right.

In this chaos, we received conflicting messages from the higher-ups. The ambassador felt that we could maintain stability only by keeping our Vietnamese employees as calm as possible and at work until the last moment. The Defense Department attaché believed the best course was to save their lives by starting to move them out of country as quickly as possible. The ambassador disagreed, ordering all embassy elements to keep their Vietnamese employees in country until he gave the order. Ignoring the ambassador's command, the Defense attaché began quietly—and successfully—airlifting his employees out of the country.

At the agency, we listened to the ambassador. We paid a heavy price for doing so.

During a meeting with the ambassador, I had the opportunity to express my concern. He assured me that I had his word: all our Vietnamese personnel would be evacuated when the time came, and I should tell them so. Over the next several days, I met with those employees and promised them that we would get them out. Of our large number of employees, about a quarter of them and their families wanted to leave with us. They sold their homes, all their valuables, to get what gold they could for the journey. In return for our promise of safe evacuation, they promised to continue to work for us until the time of departure.

They kept their word. During the last few days of April, conditions continued to deteriorate. So many refugees streamed into Saigon that it was almost impossible to move through the crowded streets. However, our employees stayed with us, continuing to provide us with transportation, housing, and materiel.

Meanwhile, the Defense attaché continued to move out his remaining Vietnamese personnel until all had been evacuated. At that point, a personal friend of mine, a Defense Attaché Office (DAO) air operations officer, called me. Was there anyone I wanted moved? I knew one Vietnamese family well from meeting their daughter in the States and visiting them and their other children while we lived in Saigon. The next morning, I got them to the airport and, with the help of the air operations officer, on a plane out of country.

Other moral dilemmas, dilemmas that trouble me to this day, also began to confront me. Senior station officers insisted that their personal possessions be moved first, before anyone or anything else, even before the possessions of State Department personnel—and even if I had to pay some bribes to make sure it happened. I did so. But weren't we supposed to all be in this together? What were my superiors worried about—our Vietnamese employees or their "things"?

I wanted to start moving out my Vietnamese personnel. But I had been ordered not to do so. Meanwhile, I knew from some of the station's Chinese Nung guards that key Vietnamese agents—and the mistresses of certain senior station and embassy personnel—were being evacuated. Agents, yes; but mistresses instead of loyal, long-term employees who were facing death because they worked for us? Hadn't we all agreed to wait for the evacuation order?

Of course, the answer had a double edge. Was I really any better? When I had a chance to use DAO aircraft to move a few people, what did I do? I moved my Vietnamese friends first, not my Vietnamese employees.

By the early morning hours of April 29, the end was at hand. I was living near Tan Son Nhut Air Base, where the bombardment began. It was targeted on the base itself, and it was plain that the North Vietnamese had just gotten tired of waiting for us to leave. The message was clear—get up and get out.

I sat for a while on my apartment roof, watching the bombardment and not knowing what to do. Some of us got together and made our way to the embassy. At that early hour, we made it in without difficulty. Even then, mobs had started to form, masses of people trying to get in and be evacuated.

At the embassy, I contacted our Vietnamese employees, who had gone to one of our compounds located elsewhere in the city, just as we had planned. Their families and children were with them, and they had access to radios that we stored in the compounds. Of course, they immediately wanted to know when we would send vehicles to pick them up. They assured me that they were still protecting the compounds and waiting for evacuation. I assured them that the ambassador would honor his commitment.

I went to see the chief of station and told him that we needed some of the remaining buses and other vehicles to get our employees to the embassy. He responded curtly; he "just didn't have time to talk about it." I got a similar response from our State colleagues. For the rest of the day, in constant communication with our Vietnamese employees, I listened to their frantic pleas and tears as they waited for us to come get them. They begged for help, the help we had promised.

I was the one who had promised to get them out. Even though the ambassador had made the actual promise, I was the one who had talked to them. I was the one they expected to honor the commitment. But as time went on, it became ever more obvious that I wasn't going to be able to help them. What could I do? I had promised. I had always prided myself on keeping my promises. I thought for a long time. It seemed to me that the right thing to do was to go out and try to get at least a few of our Vietnamese employees into the embassy. The marines would probably let them in if I were with them.

What about my obligation to my American colleagues? I had been ordered not to leave the embassy, where I was collecting and issuing side arms and flak jackets to our officers and helping to destroy classified files that identified our employees and agents. Shouldn't my responsibilities keep me in the embassy? Which obligation was the greater?

But more than anything else, I was afraid. I thought of my wife and kids and, mostly, of myself. I wavered between going after my Vietnamese employees and trying to get us all back into the embassy—and staying in the embassy, where I was also needed. The mobs around the embassy were getting bigger and bigger. If I did go after my employees, I probably wouldn't get back. What would the North Vietnamese do to any agency officer they caught? Was the ambassador's promise worth dying for?

Late that evening, I left by helicopter from the embassy roof with the few remaining station officers. As we flew out to sea, I started to cry quietly. I cried for the Vietnamese I had left behind.

People who, until the very end, had done everything that we had asked of them. People to whom we had promised protection and evacuation but, in the end, had walked away from. I was crying for myself, too. Until the day I die, I will always wonder if I did the right thing. I'm not sure. It still eats at me. I think about it a lot.

23

An Adventure in the Far East

ROBERT A. MORGAN JR.

I t was a typical hot and muggy afternoon in Laos. Overhead, whipped by the wind, the clouds formed majestic intricate patterns as they rushed by. As usual, the locals were busily going about their business. Yes, it was another typical day in Long Cheng. It never ceased to amaze me: "What I was doing in this godforsaken place"?

Long Cheng was one of a typical number of valleys in Laos. However, there was a difference because the valley was 3,500 feet above sea level, and at the western end was a strategically located one-thousand-foot asphalt runway. The valley was also home to General Vang Pao, the leader of the Meo people. His features were those of a typical local: short in stature, brown skinned, with a rounded Asian face. But he was different, possessing the aura of authority of a natural-born leader. From Long Cheng, he controlled the war effort against the communists in Laos, and the valley was the base of his operations.

The Laotian terrain was unique, and our valley was no exception. It was six miles long, and on both sides thousand-foot-tall mountains reached to the sky. At one end a karst—a solid sheet of rock—shot up several hundred feet. Lush green foliage lined the hillsides. Thatched huts pockmarked the hillside.

As a logistics officer, my job was the direct support of the general's sixteen-thousand-man army. I spent twelve hours, seven days a week, between the airstrip and my office supporting the war effort. Logistical support was coordinated from my office, which formed one end of a wooden l-shaped structure that was located at the western end of the valley. The building was built above-ground on a bed of wooden supports. It also had its own special character. The office floor was made of rustic wooden planks, and the roof of tin sheets. Routine office work was conducted under true field conditions. Puffs of dust would filter up through the floor boards covering everything in sight, as vehicles of assorted sizes bounced over a dirt road less than fifty feet from the front door of my office.

Since arriving in Long Cheng, days became fleeting moments. Only fifteen months earlier, in August 1968, I had arrived, two suitcases in hand, by jumping onto the runway from the tailgate of a C-123. As a cargo aircraft, the C-123 was small by today's standards. It had twin engines and a large cargo ramp for on-loading and offloading cargo. Flying in Laos was always something to behold. The plane was usually filled to capacity with fifty-five-gallon drums of hazardous high-octane aviation fuel. Every flight seemed to have a contingent of Asian passengers. Most locals didn't comprehend the dangers of smoking on an aircraft, and they always smoked during the flights. Thermal air currents and rain were also problems, and flying during the rainy season was by the seat of your pants. Blankets of low-hanging storm clouds covered the mountains, obscuring the pilot's view of the ground from the cockpit as he scanned the horizon to gain his bearings. Navigation was by compass, and descending to a landing strip required nerves of steel. The pilot would locate a hole in the cloud cover, start circling, and spin through the hole like he was in a funnel to get his bearing. Once under the cover the plane would follow the valley with less than two hundred feet to spare, from wing tip to tree line. Thus I formed my first impressions of the jungle and mountains, as the plane navigated the valleys when I first landed at Long Cheng.

I arrived at the end of the rainy season. During the day temperatures hovered at ninety, and in the evening would fall to sixty-five degrees. During the dry season communist activities would increase, because the lack of rain made the roads and terrain passable.

Fifteen months later, nothing had changed. Two days ago the U.S. Agency for International Development facility at Sam Tong, twenty miles from Long Cheng, was raided. Not to worry, though, I was told, because "the locals had always contained the bad guys."

Dusk in the mountains was especially enchanting. The sun slowly sinks, and the night becomes alive with jungle sounds, and this evening was no exception. After a hard day's work, I always managed to find my refuge at our bar, which was built over a bear cage at the rear of our barracks. Our living quarters were constructed of stone and wood, and the bear cage had a front and sides of iron bars, and a back section that was attached to a rock formation. Forming the back wall of the cage was a small cave, and some jagged rocks which were home to four black bears.

By now I was on the patio, but not alone. Several officers were also present, and as we talked our conversation drifted toward the day's activities. The officers served as field advisers to the local units and reported on their activities. They were the liaison between the general's forces and the American effort. By 7:00 a.m. they were usually at the airstrip boarding aircraft for their field positions. Field work involved monitoring military actions and supporting the effort by resupplying frontline units with food and ordnance. Resupplying field units was hazardous for both the Americans and the locals. Rice was the main staple of their diet, and delivery was by cargo aircraft. Because of the jungle terrain, there were few if any landing strips for the cargo aircraft, especially for those transporting rice.

Rice was supplied by rigging it for airdrop and repacking it in double-sacked forty-kilo bags. At a predetermined time, the aircraft would circle the drop zone, and free-fall the bags from five hundred to seven hundred feet above the ground. Problems would often occur on the drop zones when the locals would try to catch a free-falling sack of rice. If they misjudged the drop, the impact of being hit by an eighty-pound sack of rice would kill them. What a way to go: "killed by a falling sack of rice."

Another danger was the helicopter landing pads. In mountainous areas the pads were usually hacked out of jungle terrain and were located on the side of a hill, or at the bottom of a depression. Upon landing, the tips of the chopper blades were fairly close to the slopes of the banks, and because aircraft was in such short supply the pilots would leave the engines running and the blades rotating. In the excitement, passengers would sometimes scurry down the banks to board. More than once the chopper blades had a different idea, thus ending the life of an unlucky soul.

Another very important guest was also present: Floyd, the senior member of our bear family. Floyd also sensed the day was long and started rattling his cage. Our bears included Mamma, Baby, Little Baby, and Floyd, all gifts from the general. Black bears can weigh up to 250 pounds, and each has its own personality. Of all the bears Floyd was a true character, because he had a drinking problem. When it was beer time, all five feet of that large black frame would stand up, and with paws gripping the bars, he would rattle this cage. Floyd would consume this daily beer ration of twelve cans, by standing at the front, or by reclining on a rock at the rear of his cage. Drinking time called for a black snout to be poked through the bars. Then, through the bars, we would pour the beer into a large black gaping mouth, and deep from within a loud belch could be heard by all. Like a typical lush, Floyd's eyes would become glazed—appearing as two small red marbles. When he had enough, he would waddle back to the rear of the cage, drape himself over a rock and fall fast asleep.

The night was crystal clear. A pale moon had risen, illuminating the mountains with a soft yellow glow. It was nine in the evening, and after three beers it was sack time. We drifted our separate ways, some back to the bar for a few more drinks, and others to bed. Tonight a light breeze was blowing, an excellent night for sleeping, I thought, as I slid under the covers. Thoughts of my next leave in Bangkok danced through my mind. It had been over two months since my last leave, and working seven days a week, twelve hours a day, it now was time for an R&R to regain my sanity. Noise from the ground floor drifted slowly upward, and I could tell from the heated discussion that drinking was taking its toll. As the sound grew faint, I couldn't care less as I drifted off to sleep.

Call it a quirk of fate, but in the middle of a good dream, somehow, I always manage to wake up, and tonight was no exception. Less than three hours had passed, and now there was a knock on the door. "Everybody up, the bad guys are on Skyline Ridge," the duty officer yelled as he ran through the barracks. At 1:00 a.m., what a way to wake up! This time, they really must mean business. By now I had one leg in my pants and was lacing up my boots. Several thoughts flashed through my mind, all seeming to center on, "Why was I in Long Cheng, and not somewhere else?" They call it prior planning, and I sure was glad I had taken all the necessary precautions. Just two days ago I had prepared for such an emergency. My field pack had been repacked and a new map added to supplement my rations, compass, and first-aid kit. I also had a folding stock carbine, two hundred rounds of ammunition, and two fragmentation grenades.

Flanking our billets, on two sides, were two concrete pill boxes, and halfway up the side of a hill, partially hidden from view, was a small cave. As I reached the cave, I could see illuminating rounds fired by a 105mm howitzer arching high above Skyline Ridge. The mountain ridge was parallel to the valley and less than a couple hundred of miles from North Vietnam. A dull yellow glow lit up the ridge. The bad guys were on the ridge, but how many was not known. We had a field phone in our defensive position, and we totaled five, all armed.

Slowly the minutes ticked by and more illuminating rounds were fired. Several thoughts flashed through my mind, and I felt isolated from the world. We were 130 miles from Udorn, and if necessary could walk out, but it would be risky. Hidden along those jungle trails were the Pathet Lao, and no telling what they would do. By now it was starting to get light, and still no bad guys. It was 6:00 a.m., and the sun was slowly creeping over Skyline Ridge. Apparently the firing of the howitzer had deterred the attack, but our chief wasn't taking any chances. The word was passed over the field phone, "Evacuate Long Cheng." It was now 7:00 a.m.

Evacuating Long Cheng was not going to be a simple process, but only involved the Americans. The Thais and Laos would remain, but no Americans could be on the ground at night for political reasons, because that is when the attacks would occur. Thus I found myself in my office, deciding what paperwork to destroy. Across the street from my office was a 2,500-square-foot stone/wood, communications/office facility. In the center was a courtyard where we had fifty-five-gallon sodium nitrate drums, which we used to burn classified information. Everyone went through safes and file cabinets, emptying contents into the drums. Once loaded, all were ignited. Because we couldn't stay overnight, all aircraft on the runway had to be flown to Udorn or Vientiane. All American personnel were flown to Udorn.

The plan was to fly to Udorn, overnight, and then return the following morning, depending on the condition at the site. We had radio contact with the site and could confirm the previous night's activity. If no activity, we would return by 8:00 a.m. each morning and leave by 5:00 p.m. The flight took eighty minutes, and was by Porter, Helios, C-123K's, H-34, and Huey helicopters. This went on for about a month. Our chief then decided to reoccupy Long Cheng on a continuous basis. This flying was dangerous, and on one occasion I was on a Huey returning to Udorn at 5:00 p.m. It was monsoon season, and after crossing the Mekong River it started to rain in torrents. It became so bad that the pilot couldn't see and we had to open the side doors and lean out and provide directions. Anytime you fly in a hostile area, it completely drains your strength, because of the up-and-down drafts, chance of accidents, and plain pressure. In Udorn we would eat dinner, be in bed by 10:00 p.m., up by 5:00 a.m. and on the runway by 6:00 a.m. After a while this really started to get old. However, all went well and within a month we were back in Long Cheng, and the enemy didn't make another attack. Thus my tour at Long Cheng ended.

24

First Tour Adventures

The Mysterious Case of the Missing Missionary

HUGH S. PETTIS

Fresh out of college and keen for foreign adventure, I was sent off to a really remote outpost. So remote that there was no PX or commissary, and with just one airline flight in per week and a tiny foreign colony of Brits, Americans, fugitive Nazis, and French—mostly of medical persuasion. There was little to do except study the language, swim (in the American pool), and play tennis (on the British and American missionary hospital courts). Nighttimes it was bridge with the French (and to this day I still talk to myself in French when playing bridge, to the complete and useful distraction of others).

Single folk in this foreign colony numbered six bachelors and two young ladies, one a governess for the British consul general's kids, the other a medical technician at the Presbyterian mission hospital—a missionary no less. Competition for attention from the governess was, to put it mildly, fierce. I naturally entered the lists. And utterly failed to score to any degree with this attractive young lady from Seven Oaks, Old Blighty. Hard on the testosterone-laden American ego.

"Aha! I'll date the missionary, make the other insanely jealous, and SCORE with a bank shot off the mission tennis court." Great scheme. (We ops types are always thinking, scheming, or plotting.) And it worked—like gangbusters as we used to say.

The only glitch was that by the time Miss Governess-if-you-please awoke to her competition I had become completely swept off my feet by my American missionary lady friend. When I invited her to play tennis on her tennis court, she demurely agreed, if I would teach her the "fascinating game of chess." One thing led to another, and within two months I'd completely forgotten the British one and fallen in love with the American one (with whom church-going was added to tennis and chess). It wasn't until my missionary and I were picking out our china pattern in the bazaar and ran into the British contingent that the Great Light dawned: the governess had been aced on Life's Tennis Court of Love.

Three months later saw the biggest bash in town—our wedding, to which ALL were invited, prominent locals, dignitaries, a trainload. The Presbyterian Mission was losing one of its own, an unprecedented event in its hundred-year history. A brief honeymoon followed (one afternoon) at the nearby birthplace of a famous local poet, then we settled down into our apartment for our first year of married life—one furnished with a new passport for the bride, and notification duly sent to the Ministry of Foreign Affairs (to wit, I now had a wife with me).

Several months later the Ministry of Justice contacted the mission hospital and the American consulate reporting that this American medical technician had either (1) failed to renew her resident's visa, or (2) had left the country illegally.

"No no," we all said. "She got married."

"We know about her," was the officials' response. "It's the medical technician we're looking for. What's happened to her?"

We never really satisfied the authorities as to the whereabouts of the American medical missionary. Every month or so they'd come around, snooping, and quiz the locals, who would say of course they'd seen her—she married another American. This just did not compute (as we'd say today) and the Ministry of Justice never got it straightened out.

I suspect the name change threw them. They could never equate the Miss of one surname with the Mrs. of another surname.

We rotated out a year later, back to Stateside, leaving a suspicious officialdom still convinced that they'd lost an American medical missionary. Indeed they had. She was now mine—and is still happily so after sixty-three years of being a mysteriously missing missionary.

25

Out of the Barn, Into the Beltway

HAZEL HARRISON

Dwight Eisenhower was president, Elvis Presley's "All Shook Up" was tops on the Hit Parade, and the Randolph-Henry High School class of '57 was on its way to New York City for a weekend senior trip. I was a senior that year, but I could not be part of that trip. We did not have the money for such luxuries. It was also my responsibility to help the family milk the cows twice a day. We lived in one of the most rural areas of Virginia. Besides milking the cows, we pitched hay, gathered eggs, and helped Mom can enough garden vegetables to get us through the winter. Mom and Dad expected each of us to work our share around our home and at the same time get top grades in school. If I received an unsatisfactory grade, I knew Daddy would deal with me as soon as I arrived home. In our home, we had the bare essentials of electricity, but no telephone, no bathroom, and no television. Our family of six lived on less than three thousand dollars per year.

I started thinking about what I would or could do in June when I graduated. In retrospect, I know that God answered that question for me when I arrived at school one cold January day and an announcement was made that any seniors who would like to talk to a government recruiter could meet in study hall at one o'clock. I figured that I had nothing to lose. About thirty-five seniors gathered to hear the recruiter talk. A few of us took the application packets, and on the way home, I decided that this was my chance to leave home with a secure job and future. I decided it was worth the risk to approach my dad for his permission.

The next few days were tense in our house as I filled out this extremely long and complicated application. I needed sixteen references. I didn't even know that many adults who could be a reference for me. I also had to furnish several business people as references. I listed the local country store owner as a reference and later learned via the community grapevine that she was totally befuddled when FBI (she said) agents came in to check me out. This was the biggest event that our little community had ever experienced.

I mailed the application to the Central Intelligence Agency and about three months later, they sent me a request to call them on a certain day to tell them when I could report into their pool of applicants. This was very exciting and scary for me because I had never talked on a telephone. I could not call from school because a long-distance call, in those days, was very expensive, and they would not let me use their phone. I remembered there was a public phone booth in the village about two miles away. So, at the appointed time, I walked the two miles and made the call. When I heard a voice on the phone, every truck in the county decided to pass by, and I could not hear a word being said. After much yelling into the phone and asking the poor fellow to repeat instructions, I knew enough to know the address and day that I should report to the CIA as a potential secretary who would test and train in a pool of applicants. When I left the phone booth, I was so nervous, my legs trembled the two miles back to school and that night, my parents learned that their oldest child would soon leave for an unknown destination, an unknown career, with unknown people, and with an unknown agency. At that time of our lives, we had never heard of the CIA.

My parents were surprised, but proud, that I had snagged a job at $3,400 a year with health benefits. This was almost beyond their comprehension. But I knew there was a huge world out there that I knew nothing about, and I was ready to discover something more than I had ever dreamed. I had never traveled over one hundred miles from home and the only way I could get to Washington DC was via Greyhound bus. Dad made arrangements for me to live with relatives in Alexandria and he signed a two-hundred-dollar loan for me at the local bank in order to have some funds until I would get a paycheck. On the designated day, I got up at two in the morning, milked seventeen cows, and left by five o'clock to catch the bus headed north to the big city.

As I rode north to Alexandria on the Greyhound bus, I thought about my life. My teeth chattered thinking of all the scary things I was about to encounter, but I had goals in mind. I knew I would have to learn a lot of things from friends as time passed. I knew that I would have to succeed because there would be no turning back for Mom and Dad to rescue me. They had enough problems with four children still in school and one more to come. Most of all, I wanted to make Mom and Dad proud of me. Dad had raised me to stick with whatever choices I made in life. He told me that if I could eventually work up to ten thousand dollars per year that I would never have any financial worries. That was the way country folks felt in the mid-1950s.

On June 12, I reported to the old CIA Headquarters off Twenty-Third Street in DC where the Personnel Office was located. After processing me through the system, they informed me that I should report to the training pool on Sixteenth Street. During the next two months, I mastered the IBM Executive typewriters and practiced using a telephone along with other greenhorns. I passed my first shorthand test with flying colors but I really had to work on the details and use of that electric typewriter. To me, it was the ultimate machine loaded with the latest technology! Little did I realize that within five years, I would be using a typewriter that didn't even have a carriage, only a little ball that literally flew back and forth as I typed!

During my time in the pool, I met a very sophisticated, tall, raven-haired girl named Shirley. She was raised in northern Virginia and was beautiful, with gorgeous clothes. I developed a friendship with her that served me well during this very stressful time of my life. I shared my story and it was obvious that I needed her to teach me lots of "girl stuff." We discussed makeup and went shopping for some inexpensive basics which she taught me to use. She took me shopping to a nearby ladies dress shop and helped me purchase my first professional working dress and a pair of high-heeled shoes to match. The whole deal cost less than twenty-five dollars. I couldn't wait to write home and tell Mama.

I successfully completed my stay in the pool and was called into the Personnel Office to be assigned. They told me that I was to report to the Office of Logistics in Quarters Eye on Ohio Drive. I nodded and said, "Okay," but I had no idea what they meant by "Quarters Eye" or "logistics." Those words were absolutely Greek to me but I wasn't about to let them know that. That night I looked up "logistics" in Webster's Dictionary to discover that I would probably be in a supply or procurement group. My pool friends explained that Quarters Eye was the name of a series of buildings on the street next to the Potomac River. Little did I know that I would be working "down on the river" for the next few years.

I was assigned as a temporary secretary to a military officer because his secretary was going on her honeymoon. I trembled when I realized that I had to sit at a desk and act like a secretary. Suddenly, I would be forced to use the telephone frequently for eight hours every day. I might as well have been sitting at the desk in the Oval Office for the way I felt at that moment!

When the permanent girl briefed me about the position, my head swam with new terms, new requirements, and unfamiliar responsibilities. I had never heard of keeping a calendar, noting appointments, and, worse of all, I had to make an original and twelve carbon copies of every memorandum. Any mistake had to be carefully erased, corrected, and unnoticeable on the original. Talk about being nervous! Every time my boss was faced with my naïveté and ignorance, he became exasperated and let out a long string of words that would make a hardcore master sergeant say, "Yes sir!" One of the worst days of my life came when he discovered I did not understand what chronological filing meant. He paused a few moments before he showed his soft side and then, with patience and understanding, he explained everything I needed to know. Eventually, he became like a second father to me as he took the raw material of an inexperienced girl and molded her into a real secretary.

My only secretarial asset was that I could type and take Gregg shorthand like a whiz. From my boss, I learned proper telephone usage and manners, how to operate business machines, record-keeping and filing, letter writing and formatting. He would not tolerate crying, giving up, or feeling sorry for oneself. Soon I could prepare his letters in advance. When he sat down at 8:30 each morning, he had a twenty-four-inch stack of memoranda to sign with every signature page properly tabbed. His desk was newly waxed, a cup of black coffee ready, and two packs of Camel cigarettes were ready to go. I knew that I was becoming so important to him that he would find it difficult to replace me. In my heart that was exactly the position I wanted to hold. I worked nights, weekends, and holidays. I wanted to become indispensable. My plan for survival was working.

As it turned out, the secretary who was on her honeymoon decided not to return to work and my temporary job became a permanent position. The captain sure didn't want to train another greenhorn. One day, the captain suddenly realized that my eighteenth birthday had just passed and he asked, "Did they give you a polygraph?" I had no idea what a polygraph was and when he explained that I had to take a lie detector test because I had several top secret documents in our safe, I panicked. I certainly didn't have anything to hide, but the image of being wired up was a little more than I could fathom. When I checked into the Security Office to take the polygraph test, I was asked for my birth certificate. That was when I knew I was in trouble. My birth certificate was in the family storage box, along with Mama's quilts, on the second floor of my family home back in southern Virginia— and they didn't have a telephone. The security fellows seemed to understand and agreed to move on with the test. But that evening, I wrote a letter to Mama asking her to mail the certificate to me. Forty-eight hours later, it arrived.

When the captain moved on to another job, he gave me some fatherly advice to grow professionally and reach for the stars. He made me believe that I was ready to grow. With him leaving, I wanted to control my next assignment. So I headed for the Personnel Office and asked for an overseas assignment. With a simple verbal request, I was given an assignment in Frankfurt, Germany. My plan to succeed and grow professionally kicked into high gear and the next phase of my education began.

I still had not flown in an airplane and I was really scared of that long transatlantic flight to Germany. Somehow I made it through the NYC Airport and about ten hours later, I landed in Frankfurt. My new boss met me and took me to a small hotel on Reimundstrasse. He had warned me that the community bathroom would be on the main hall. When he dropped me off, it was dark and I didn't know a word of German. The bed was made with fluffy down covers instead of regular American blankets. I didn't know how to use the telephone, and for the entire night, I heard German sirens constantly whining in the street. It was a relief when daybreak came, and I could see that everything was normal on the street.

The next day I was assigned to a one-bedroom apartment, picked up my new red convertible car that had arrivèd intact, and reported to my new office. The next two years literally flew by. As a single girl, I was living an enviable life traveling to as many places in Europe as possible. My office had a package that needed to be delivered to Berlin in November 1963. I volunteered to carry it because I knew that I could fly up on Friday, enjoy the weekend, and return on Monday. When I landed at the Berlin airport, the first thing my contact said was, "The president has been shot." It took a few minutes for me to realize that he was talking about President Kennedy. My trip then took on a somber tone as I witnessed all of Berlin turning out their lights and putting candles in their windows to honor our U.S. president. At the hotel, I ran into several other Americans on temporary duty assignment and we grouped together as meal partners and spent the entire weekend close to the hotel since not much else was open. While there, we did venture out to view Checkpoint Charlie at the Berlin Wall and the Brandenburg Gate. It was an awesome sight for this country girl to experience during this sad period of our nation's history.

In the next eighteen months, I traveled through Austria, Italy, Spain, France, and Holland, and became interested in international affairs. At night, I studied accounting at the European Division of the University of Maryland and took German language classes. I began to realize that working for the government was turning into a lifetime career. When I returned to the United States, I had enough rank for assignment to a "paraprofessional" position at the GS-7 level. Of course, I grabbed the opportunity.

By the early 1970s, the professional women's movement was reaching into all government offices. Like many other professional women, I had experienced subtle discrimination in the office. Every organization was taking a close look at the females who had the potential to move into management. I seemed to be in the right place at the right time and I took full advantage of it by accepting assignments as fast as they came along. I wanted to be a supervisor that was respected and loved and yet could get the job done faster and more efficiently than others. In fact, I wanted to be a role model. I took every management course offered and on my own initiative, completed several self-study courses. I volunteered for committees, developed workshops, wrote articles, and worked on projects. I constantly developed ways to make my superiors aware of my capabilities. I was growing personally and professionally during this time, continuing my educational opportunities, managing my money, and was even able to send financial help home to Mom and my younger siblings. I was enjoying life!

As a GS-9, I was considered "supervisory level" by the logistics people, but because I did not have a college degree, I was not being considered for promotion when the review cycle came around. I began to wonder whether I had a chance to move further up the ladder. By this time, I had gotten married. After the next review cycle, I asked my supervisor to quietly look into why I was not promoted after several years in grade. The word came back that the deputy division chief had said, "She's married and doesn't need a promotion." That statement was clearly discriminatory to me. So with about ten years of service with the agency, I started checking for other available government jobs.

I ran across an ad for a secretarial position in another government agency with a lady who traveled around the country giving training. The job was a logistical position working as her front-person setting up travel arrangements, conference rooms, meals, and general preparations. I was offered the new job on the condition that I could work out the details within a week. When I arrived back at the office, I informed my supervisor that I was seriously considering this offer. She immediately went to the "front office" to see the division chief. I believe the events of that day forced division management to take a closer look at my work performance and they soon realized that I was considering my own solution to the problem of stagnation. I was then transferred to a more responsible position and from that year on to the end of my career, annual performance reviews and promotion cycles came within reasonable time frames.

During each of my assignments, I would attempt to find a project in which I could save the government money or in which the division could be made more efficient in providing logistical support to other parts of the agency. For example, during my stint as the junior supply officer in the McLean Headquarters Building, I discovered a pile of broken typewriter fonts gathering in our stock room. The fonts cost about twenty dollars each and our supply room had to keep various type sizes in stock at all times. I started collecting the broken fonts rather than trashing them. I looked through several catalogs and found a small company in New England who had engineered a system of repairing broken and chipped fonts. I contacted them and worked out the details to send a shipment of a dozen fonts each month for repair. When the first shipment of repaired fonts was put back into our stock, I put a stripe of red fingernail polish on each one. This way, I would be able to determine some level of confidence in the repaired products. After about six months of weekly repair shipments, my division chief realized that I was saving the agency thousands of dollars with this recycling effort. About a year later, I was honored to receive a monetary award in recognition of my efforts on this project.

During these years, I was appointed as a supply officer in different assignments throughout the agency. Most of my postings would be located geographically away from the main logistics office; therefore I could work and make decisions independently. These situations served to increase my confidence and professionalism.

About this time, my husband had reached retirement age and took a medical retirement in his early fifties. I knew that this would be the opportunity for me to accept my second overseas tour in order to retire under the agency system stipulating five years overseas service, twenty-five years of federal service, and no earlier than age fifty. He agreed that this would be a good idea and he would accompany me; however, he definitely wanted to live in an English-speaking country. He was extremely pleased the night I came home from work and asked if he would go with me to the South Pacific.

When we arrived in the South Pacific for a tour, my husband was the first male spouse to accompany a staff member to that area. The next day's event was a welcome party at "The Wives Club" meeting. It was changed to "The Spouses Club" overnight. George attended and enjoyed it immensely. When he left the meeting, he was on a first-name basis with most of the wives. While in the South Pacific, my husband worked for a newspaper company as a salesman. He became a well-known Yank spouse.

Working in the South Pacific, I came to realize that being the only senior female on the staff was a problem. It became apparent that I was not being included in staff meetings. I was not invited to sit with the male staff members at lunch. I was not being briefed or included in any major office situation. Without causing hard feelings or office unrest, I decided to talk out the problem with the security officer with whom I was carpooling. He was very interested in what I was experiencing because this was a new situation for the local staff. As it turned out, I realized that the staff from the commanding officer down did not realize their own discriminatory behavior. They immediately made positive changes when they realized that incoming female staff had to be an integral part of their management team.

After my husband and I returned to the States, I worked another six years in staff positions of the Supply Division. On my fiftieth birthday in 1989, I returned to the Personnel Office to ask for my retirement application. That day was the culmination of thirty-two years working for the Central Intelligence Agency. I was retiring at a senior grade, considered fairly successful in the Office of Logistics, and yet, I had the strong desire to move on to another phase of my life. I entered retirement by enrolling as a full-time student at Longwood University in Farmville, Virginia. I graduated thirty-six months later as the oldest graduate of the class of '93.

I could not have had a more interesting and satisfying career. My prescription for a happy and fulfilled life in most any career is to set goals and readjust them about every five years. Continue your education throughout your life. Don't get derailed. Be the first to volunteer to give of your time. Be the first to come up with new ideas and possible solutions. Look at life with a positive attitude. Be thankful for family that supports you. Be thankful for a good home, good schools, and good transportation and roads. Cultivate close friends that you can rely on. Know that God loves you. Thank Him every day for His blessings. You'll never be lonely. You'll always have something to do. You'll always have friends. Believe that you can do it. As my dad told me, "Stick with it. Don't ever give up."

After I finished my degree at Longwood University, I taught General Equivalency Diploma (GED) Prep for six years, and since then, I've really been retired. I have done a lot of charity work; the biggest project was helping to build an eight-bedroom home for disabled adult men here in Farmville. It is now operating full-time and managed by HopeTree Family Services where I am on the board of trustees. In recent times, I've had to care for my parents and now that Dad is gone, my mother lives with us. I'm enjoying every minute that I get to spend with her.

26

Ed and a Secretary: How I Ended Up at the CIA

MARTIN PETERSEN

I was at a crossroads. I had started my graduate program in Asian Studies with an expectation that I would pursue an academic career. But I got drafted in the middle of it, and after a year in Vietnam, I realized the college environment was not where I wanted to spend my life.

I still had a few months to go to complete my degree when I started to seriously consider my career options. I weighed journalism and took the State Department exam. I knew I wanted to use my Asia expertise and Chinese language, but I had no real idea of where or how.

One evening over a beer, I commiserated with a fellow Vietnam vet named Ralph, who was an air force intelligence officer. It was Ralph who suggested that I talk to "these other guys," as he put it, and he got me a single-page, standard government, résumé-like form and a post office box address. I filled it out and dropped it in the mail.

A few weeks later my phone rang. "Hi. My name is Ed. Are you Martin Petersen?" My quick, but suspicious yes was followed by, "I got your form. I'd like to meet. I'll be in Honolulu next week. If you're interested, meet me at this address at 10:00. Keep it to yourself." Ed spoke in short, staccato sentences and hung up promptly after my weak "okay."

I didn't know what to think. After he hung up, I realized I hadn't asked whether he was calling for the CIA. I didn't know who else it could be. The form Ralph gave me was the only one I had filled out and mailed.

I checked out the address that weekend and it was an old federal building near the Honolulu waterfront. I arrived a half-hour early on Tuesday and quickly discovered that the room number could only be reached by an outside staircase that opened up into a long, narrow hall. The room was at the end of the hall. I took a breath and knocked on the door.

"Come in." Ed was sitting in a bare room at a folding card table. There was a single chair opposite Ed. I sat down and we started to chat, just breaking the ice I thought. I cannot remember what we talked about other than my interest in Asia and military experience. I kept waiting for him to tell me about the agency or job openings or to begin the interview. After about thirty minutes, Ed leaned back and said, "I've heard enough." He reached into his briefcase and dropped the thirty-plus-page application on the table. "Fill it in and mail it, if you are interested"—the undercurrent was more like "if you have the guts"—"and don't call us, we'll call you." I was thinking, "I don't know *how* to call you," when he unscrewed the top of his enormous pen revealing—a small stapler!—and nailed some notes to my form with one quick motion. It wasn't Q, but I was impressed.

I filled out the application and dropped it in the mail. And heard nothing. I graduated that December and returned home to Arizona where I found temporary employment. I had passed the State Department exam and was now waiting for the orals but still looking around.

In late winter I received another cryptic phone call. "Hello, are you Martin Petersen? Do you know who this is?" I said, "I think so." Who else could it be? "We'd like you to come to Washington for some interviews. Can you get here the second week of March? Expect to be here five days."

I quickly agreed but had no idea how I was going to do it. "Strapped" did not even begin to describe my financial situation. My temporary employer fronted the plane ticket, and I bought a truly horrible, light blue suit on the one credit card I had. I arrived in Washington with the credit card for the hotel and twenty dollars in cash to last the week.

This was 1972, and that was stretching it even then, especially since the cab ride from National Airport came to seven bucks. I figured I needed another seven to get back, which left six to eat on for five days. My grad school days and army experience told me it would be a tight fit, but that it could be done.

The motel was within walking distance of the building where I was told to report—a break for my finances. I showed up early, was processed by security, and then escorted to a waiting room where a secretary presided from behind a steel desk.

She looked tough, no-nonsense, simply the hardest, middle-aged, middle-school librarian you have ever seen. She looked up from her desk, took in my electric blue suit over her eyeglasses, and with a voice that must have chilled generations of lesser beings, asked with slow, deliberate precision, "Young man," (I shrank two inches) "precisely how much money do you have in your pocket?"

I told her six dollars and a credit card. With a look that spoke volumes about my ability to make my way in the world, she said slowly and clearly, to compensate for my limited intelligence, "At the end of the day, take this blue ticket and go down to the curb. Get on a blue bus and only on a blue bus. Show the driver the ticket and get off where he tells you." I didn't know what to think other than that I may have failed a means test or something and I was being ushered out before I ever got in.

At the end of the day, I did as I was told. The Bluebird bus wound through wooded areas and very nice neighborhoods to the gates of headquarters and stopped near the front steps. I walked into the great marble lobby for the first time and took in the seal and the atrium. I felt a chill. I showed my ticket to the guard, who directed me through a door just off the lobby.

I still had no idea what was happening when I sat down opposite a young lady, who asked my name, pulled out some paper, punched an adding machine, and then unlocked a drawer full of money. She paid me for my plane ticket, my ground transportation, and a per diem to cover my other expenses.

I was totally shocked. I thought, "This is where I want to be. They are cryptic and secretive—what did you expect?—but they take care of people, even people they haven't decided to hire yet, like me." The gruff old secretary saw to it that something that normally happens at the end of the week happened at the start of the week for me. Undoubtedly, she had done it many times before.

I got through the rest of the week without incident and with one last "don't call us, we'll call you" ringing in my ears, I went home, where I promptly cancelled my plans to go to LA for the State Department oral exams. I knew where I wanted to work, and I was willing to pass on other chances while I anxiously waited for the call. It came a few weeks later, and a month after that I was in Washington beginning thirty-three years with the CIA.

During those wonderful years, I saw the same level of caring many times—however brusque—the same sense of family—however distant the cousin—that I experienced from a secretary whose name I cannot recall. Organizations like to talk about employees as family. At the CIA it is a value that is lived.

Traveling with the President

FRANK RYAN

In the mid-1960s, an associate and I were called upon to provide technical assistance to the U.S. Secret Service (USSS) in support of President Nixon's trip to Bucharest, Romania.

Things were somewhat dicey. No president of the United States had been behind the Iron Curtain since Roosevelt attended the Big Three meeting at Yalta in 1945.

We were part of the "advance team," and after the initial meetings with Romanian Security, the USSS was still not satisfied with the security arrangements for President Nixon's arrival. For instance, Nixon was not allowed to ride into town in the USSS armored car. Instead he was required to use an armored car provided by the Romanians.

The day before the president's arrival, a high-ranking officer from Romanian security entered a conference room to address the concerned officers.

Everyone present was silent in anticipation of his remarks. In short order, he listed the details of all of the security measures that had been taken to protect Nixon during his stay in Bucharest.

In closing he assured the USSS that Nixon was safer in Bucharest than anywhere else in the world.

Finally he said, "You need not worry about the safety of your president in my country. For you see, in Bucharest, even the birds do not fly unless I let them."

Alas, President Nixon's trip to Bucharest was uneventful.

KH601

RICHARD IRWIN

O n December 31, 2004, I officially retired from the Central Intelligence Agency (CIA) after twenty-eight years of service. When I joined the agency, little did I know that this journey would take me to eighty-seven countries around the world; afford me the opportunity to become fluent in Spanish, Italian and French; work under eight directors of central intelligence (DCIS); go to the White House to serve a president; and end at a newly created domestic agency known as the Department of Homeland Security (DHS) as part of the largest U.S. government reorganization in the past fifty years. As a CIA covert operations officer, I had the opportunity to serve at the "right time and the right place" on several historic occasions and was fortunate to have been involved in some of the most successful operations in the annals of the agency. Along the way, I battled communism with the Contras in Central America; witnessed the rise of global terrorism, Al-Qaeda, and the events that led up to 9/11; and laid my life on the line in Afghanistan.

While growing up, I always wanted to be a Pennsylvania state policeman. Although I applied in the fall of 1976, during my junior year at York College of Pennsylvania while studying Police Science, I was not accepted. Initially crushed, I took the advice of one of my college professors and decided to apply to several federal agencies (the CIA, the FBI, and the U.S. Secret Service). My interest in the CIA was further piqued after seeing a recruitment advertisement in the *Philadelphia Inquirer*. I officially applied in August 1976. At the time I was a twenty-one-year-old junior in college with a 3.00 grade point average, whose only job experience was as a construction worker, a security guard, a bouncer, and a bartender. After receiving a letter from the CIA in May 1977 saying that due to my age and lack of experience it would be very difficult for me to join the agency as a full-time staff employee, I was asked if I would be interested in working as a contract security guard in the Washington DC area following my college graduation. When I replied that I was interested and would do just about anything to get my foot in the door with the agency, I was informed that they would begin processing me for the position at GS-5 at $9,303 per year. Although a year had passed since my initial application, when I finally received the phone call directing me to report to CIA Headquarters in Langley, Virginia, in late August 1977, I was twenty-two years old and did not have a clue of what I was getting into. The only thing I knew about the agency was what the recruiter had told me, what I had read in books and newspapers, or heard on television and in the movies. I later found out that, despite receiving over one hundred thousand applications, the CIA had only hired fifty-four people that year (1977) and I was lucky to have been one of them. With the exception of my immediate family and several close friends, no one knew that I had applied and was accepted into the CIA. Thank God, in that I was told from that day forward that I would be undercover and would not be able to reveal my agency affiliation until the day I retired.

I reported to CIA Headquarters in Langley, Virginia, on September 11—a date not only affiliated with a new beginning in my life, but also one that twenty-four years later would forever be immortalized in history with the attacks on the World Trade Center and the Pentagon. Although I was expecting to work at the CIA Headquarters compound, I was surprised when told that I would be working at a covert agency facility in Northern Virginia. During the initial check-in with my security supervisor, I received a uniform, a schedule, and a badge (number KH601, as the chapter title hints), and was told that I would have to work rotating shifts since the facility operated twenty-four hours a day, every day of the year. The facility, I quickly learned, was the U.S. government's premier satellite reconnaissance facility. Much of the work performed at this location was eventually compromised when William Kampiles (who worked as a watch officer at the CIA operations center in Langley from March to November 1977) took a copy of the technical manual for the KH-11 reconnaissance satellite system, after resigning from the CIA, and sold it to Soviet intelligence for three thousand dollars. Kampiles was later caught, tried, convicted of espionage, and sentenced to forty years in prison.

One year to the day after serving as a security guard, I accepted a staff position with the agency as an intelligence assistant in the Directorate of Science and Technology at a GS-7 ranking. My job consisted of retrieving and filing target folders and building target packages for photographic interpreters who spent hours analyzing and interpreting rolls of satellite imagery pertaining to the Soviet Union, the Middle East, and other "hot spots" around the world. Ten months later, I was promoted to a GS-8 and became a research assistant, editing reports, which the photo interpreters produced.

After serving at the aforementioned site, my goal was to become a security officer in the Office of Security within the Directorate of Administration or an operations officer in the Directorate of Operations (DO), now known as the National Clandestine Service.

During the spring of 1980, while playing rugby for a local Northern Virginia rugby team (NOVA), I fractured my right shoulder and had to have extensive surgery to repair it. While recuperating from the surgery, I received a phone call from the Office of Security informing me that I was going to be interviewed as a candidate. The next day, I departed Pennsylvania at 4:30 a.m. and drove to Langley in a 1976 stick-shift Mustang. Fortunately, I was not pulled over by a police officer that morning because if I had been, they would have seen a young man dressed in a three-piece suit with a tightly wrapped bandage around his upper body trying to shift gears by placing his left hand through the steering wheel. As I arrived at Langley for the 9:00 a.m. interview, I realized that I was running late. I parked the car and raced to the interview room only to hear voices from inside the room say, "I guess that we can proceed with the next interview in that it appears that this candidate is not coming." Upon entering the room, the three interviewers, two men and a woman, were aghast to see a sweating young man with a bandage wrapped around his entire upper torso, talking at a hundred miles per hour trying to explain why he was late. For the next twenty minutes, I then proceeded to tell everyone about the injury and the lengths to which I had gone to get to the interview that day. Several months later, after being selected on April 28, 1980, I was told by one of the interviewers that the impression I had made on the panel that day was the reason I had been selected.

My Special Agent class consisted of five men and five women. Following graduation, I packed up my things and drove to Boston, Massachusetts, on June 23, 1980, the field office where I had been assigned. In those days, the Office of Security had field offices in Boston, New York, Washington DC, Miami, Chicago, Los Angeles, and San Francisco. As a special investigator, I was responsible for conducting background investigations on individuals applying to the agency or being considered for access to classified information at the agency.

During the summer of 1983, after serving three years in the Boston Field Office, I was assigned to CD-5, a section of Clearance Division responsible for clearing contractors that have staff-like access within the agency. This meant that a contractor had to undergo the same security processing as that of a CIA staff employee, which included a full background investigation and polygraph. Our jobs consisted of opening new files on contractors being considered for staff-like access and scheduling their polygraph test. The process is known as the "whole person" concept to ensure that the agency is looking at the entire person and not just a portion. When all of the information was received from the various offices and the polygraph completed, we had to decide whether to approve or disapprove the candidate. If no derogatory information was identified in either the background investigation or the polygraph, we would fill out a sheet recommending approval and send it to the chief of CD-5 and his superiors. If all three of them concurred with the recommendation to grant the individual access or clearance, it was then granted. If negative information was found on the candidate, we had to write up a short report.

After a year and a half of serving in CD-5, I received word on February 22, 1985, that I was to be assigned to the Overseas Security Support Branch (OSSB) whose mission was to conduct comprehensive, physical security surveys to identify vulnerabilities at our DO offices and bases. Additionally, OSSB officers were taught to develop and implement a variety of contingency plans. OSSB security surveys included a threat-and-vulnerability assessment, information on the emergency destruction equipment used to destroy classified information, and the security containers used to store classified information. During a survey, photographs were taken of all of this equipment as well as the compound, entrances and exits, and the entire agency office. Before their departure, OSSB officers frequently wrote emergency plans and, in some instances, emergency evacuation plans, while ensuring that these plans were integrated into any existing plans on hand. The second phase of the OSSB survey consisted of conducting residential security surveys for all of the agency personnel to ensure that they had adequate security and appropriate emergency egress.

The first few months of 1985 were spent in training in that our boss wanted to create security generalists who, in addition to conducting surveys, could be called upon for additional support to the DO, such as providing personal protection. In four months, I trained in locks and safes, personal protection, firearms, high-speed defensive driving, clandestine operations familiarization, crisis management, explosive awareness and recognition, post-blast investigation, travel awareness, information security, and fire fighting, to serve as a first responder.

In early February 1986, I was notified by the director of security that the agency was creating a Counterterrorist Center (CTC) and the next day I was asked to report as its first director of security. I recall after leaving his office that this was the first time in my career I had been told that the reason I had been chosen was that I was the best candidate for the job. Since I had traveled to more than fifty countries while with the OSSB, I was confident that the experience I had acquired combating terrorism during these trips would assist me greatly in my new assignment. During my tenure as the first director of security in the CTC, I had the opportunity to set up and administer two covert training sites, several proprietaries, safe houses, and limited access "bigoted programs." (My time in the CTC also provided me with a thorough understanding of using cover, backstopping, alias documents, and accommodation addresses.

In December 1987, I received a cable from the chief of our office in Tegucigalpa, asking me to report to Honduras to help oversee the "phase down" of the supply program of the Nicaraguan Democratic Force (FDN; one of the largest of the various Contra groups). I was sent to Swan Island, the principal storage and supply base supporting the Contras, to ensure the safety and security of the inhabitants on the island. At the time of my arrival, there were 68 Americans assigned to Swan Island, 100 members of the Honduran navy to support Honduran sovereignty, and 180 FDN Contras with full logistic support, communications, and administrative facilities. Because we were concerned about the potential of an attack from the Sandinistas, I prepared emergency evacuation and destruction plans. All Americans were issued a "bug out" kit and we designated an area of the island where personnel would report in case of an emergency. In addition, we made sure that all of our emergency equipment was in good condition and in close proximity. During my time on the island, we began to reduce our files and all nonessential classified materials were destroyed on site or shipped back to our office in Tegucigalpa. Although tensions were running extremely high with respect to moving the lethal and nonlethal material off the island, we moved approximately 340,000 pounds of material by air and another 360,000 pounds by sea during the next few weeks. Following the February 29, 1988, deadline mandated by Congress for the U.S. government to cease supporting the Contras, I remained on the island for two more months as part of a five-man contingent to ensure that our interests were protected on the island while it remained in a "mothball" mode.

I returned to the United States in April 1988 in time for my son Matthew's birth. I soon learned that I was being assigned to Tegucigalpa at the request of the chief of our office. After ten weeks of language training—enough to order a cheeseburger, a beer, and get my face slapped (not necessarily in that order), I arrived in Honduras in August 1988 with my wife, Karen, who had just given up a lucrative career as a conference planner with Electronic Data Systems; our fifteen-month-old daughter Kelly; and our three-month-old son, Matthew. Prior to our departure, Karen had to sell our townhouse, purchase a new house, pack and unpack—all of this while pregnant and working full time while I was on temporary duty assignment in Honduras or in language school. To make matters worse, Karen had never even been outside of the United States except for our honeymoon to Acapulco. Within days after our arrival, both of our children got deathly ill due to contaminated water and were diagnosed with parasites known as giardia and amoebas. Fortunately, with the assistance of Pedialyte (a dehydration fluid), Flagyl (an antibiotic medicine used against bacteria and parasites), and a host of other medications, they eventually got better.

At the time of our arrival, the agency had employees assigned to Honduras. Half were assigned to a compound in the capital while the remaining half were assigned to an operations base in the country on the outskirts of Tegucigalpa, and at a large warehouse north of the city. Some of our officers were also deployed to several forward bases located together with Honduran military units along the border with Nicaragua. As the first agency security officer assigned to Tegucigalpa, most of my time was spent securing our operations base and forward sites. After conducting surveys at each of these locations, I followed up by implementing security measures, evacuation plans, and emergency destruction plans. When constructing new forward sites we had to fence the entire compound, construct living quarters, mess facilities, and latrines, put up lighting, construct guard posts, and ensure that the facility had plenty of emergency power.

I worked with a team of local male and female police officers that monitored leftist groups who were trying to harm the U.S. embassy and American citizens in Honduras. The team included analysts who analyzed the information collected by the police officers. Due to my special relationship with the Honduran bomb squad, I was immediately notified anytime a bomb was discovered or exploded. I was most interested when the U.S. embassy, the American School, one of the U.S. companies, a residence housing Americans, or the Peace Corps (which was bombed on December 19, 1988) was involved. In Honduras in 1989, it was not unusual for two or three bombs to detonate in the capital of Tegucigalpa or the northern cities of La Ceiba and San Pedro Sula in one night. Restaurants, banks, shopping centers, and supermarkets were favorite targets of the Honduran left.

Our residence was located near the Honduran First Battalion and the Honduran police and intelligence services, and my day usually began by visiting these sites before driving to the operations base or the U.S. embassy.

For entertainment, on weekends we would frequently visit several of the small villages surrounding the capital of Tegucigalpa. Once, my wife, the kids, and I rented an entire island off the coast of Honduras named Sandy Key for fifty-two dollars per night and stayed for five days. On Wednesday evenings, we bowled on a U.S. embassy bowling team; on Thursday evenings, we played darts in an embassy dart league; and on weekends, we played golf at the local country club, or basketball and football at the American School. During periods of increased threat, we played golf with our pistols attached to our hips. These activities were eventually curtailed, however, when a walk-in to the U.S. embassy advised that a leftist group was planning to attack the bowling alley and, sure enough, it was determined that he was telling the truth.

In late June 1989, although I was a security officer, I was asked to work with the Honduran government, using mobile search teams (MSTs), to stem the flow of arms entering Honduras; and a training program to look for weapons, ammunition, explosives, and drugs in false compartments. In three years, the Honduran MST program had grown from 48 to 144 members, with some individual teams expanding from 12 to 24 members. In addition, it had expanded from four teams to eight. The Hondurans had thirty-two major arms and narcotics seizures during this period.

During my tenure in Honduras, our medical services officer had assembled an emergency rescue team. At weekly meetings, each one of the all-volunteer team was trained in fundamental first aid and the use of specialized emergency medical gear. As a unit, this six-man team had practiced various rescue techniques, including rappelling from helicopters from as high as three hundred feet and using special rescue gear. The team consisted of a medical officer, our branch chief, two operations officers, a communications officer, and me, as a security officer. In November 1989, this team responded to a Tan-Sahsa Boeing 727–200 that had crashed into a six-thousand-foot mountain known as Cerro de Hule, some five thousand feet from the runway at Toncontin International Airport in Tegucigalpa. Organized to support agency projects, the team was activated during the crash because local emergency resources were completely overwhelmed.

When we arrived at the crash site the scene was chaotic. Ill-equipped, unprepared, and disorganized, local authorities appeared unable to deal with the emergency and could not stop the looting that had begun. Our arrival immediately brought a sense of order and purpose to the scattered rescue efforts. Starting in the aircraft, we systematically searched for survivors. Individual team members climbed into the still-burning wreckage, maneuvered around pieces with razor-sharp metal fragments, and pressed into sections that were precariously perched on the mountainside.

Afterward, we quickly established a security perimeter around the aircraft and searched the remainder of the wreckage-strewn, half-mile crash site. When all possibility of finding other survivors was exhausted, we returned to the fuselage where most of the bodies remained. Throughout the day, we battled the fire and slowly moved forward through the wreckage to remove the bodies before the intense heat destroyed the remains, collecting all personal items that might assist with identification. This crash killed 123 of the 138 passengers on board and half of the eight-member crew, including several USAID (U.S. Agency for International Development) employees from the U.S. embassy. We extricated and identified seventy victims, including a U.S. Marine security guard watch stander from the U.S. embassy in Managua who was aboard the flight. In addition, with some local assistance, we located and retrieved the black box as well as some official documents that were part of a classified pouch.

Looking back on that day, our team was the only organized, purposeful, and properly equipped rescue effort at the crash site that morning. Although we were organized for agency support, we quickly mobilized in a lifesaving effort that was carried out with great courage. In the best tradition of agency employees, we stepped into a disintegrating situation, took charge, and pressed forward at great risk. I believe that our response that day was a model of what the agency is all about—anticipating problems, preparing collectively, and collaborating to achieve a common goal.

In May 1990, President Callejas presented me with the highest Honduran civilian award the country provided. This was a special day for me in that my wife, Karen, and my brother, Jim, attended the ceremony. When I departed Honduras and returned to the United States I had over twenty commendations in my file, including two from the president of Honduras; two from the former chief of staff of the Honduran Armed Forces; two from the former director of the Honduran Intelligence Service; and one from the chief of operations of the Salvadoran Army General Staff. In my last performance evaluation, it was noted that "my talents had been applied to meeting objectives far beyond that expected of a security officer" and that "my performance, although lacking any formalized training as such, was of a very high caliber."

After serving in Honduras for three years, my family and I returned to the United States to reacquaint ourselves with our parents, family, and friends. Although I had notified the Office of Security six months previously that I would be returning to Washington and had filled out a "dream sheet" naming my top three choices for assignment, no one had taken any action. When meeting the new director of security and his deputy, I was shocked to learn that they had not even focused on the fact that I had returned and was ready to begin a new assignment. As I began to protest that it was not fair that I did not have an assignment, they told me, "The new Research and Analysis Division in the Gloucester Building is looking for people. Why don't you go over and see the division chief." Arriving in the Gloucester Building, you cannot imagine the pain I was experiencing to be placed in a sterile vault with no windows after my time in Central America. More depressing was the fact that I soon learned that I would be supervising several analysts that the Office of Security had just hired to form this new division and that my branch was going to focus on Africa and Central and South America.

Unfortunately, the Research and Analysis Division was new, and the Directorate of Operations (DO) did not even know that we existed. Although we all had brand-new computers on our desks, the phones remained silent. Because I had just returned from Central America, had traveled extensively throughout South America and Africa, and was well known in the DO, I took it upon myself to try to convince the DO that this new Research and Analysis Division was a great idea and could be beneficial. To help our cause, with the blessing of a new supervisor we resurrected a program that I had implemented in Honduras referred to as a Personal Protection Survey. This survey looked at the daily patterns and routines of our CIA officers living overseas. The second portion of the survey involved writing and implementing emergency and evacuation plans concentrating on rally points or staging areas, safe havens, emergency communications, and emergency supplies such as food and water. After these plans were written, we made sure that they were integrated into all existing plans. Having successfully implemented this program in Honduras while serving there, I was asked by the support chief in the Latin American Division to conduct similar surveys throughout Central and South America. In addition, after briefing the support chief in the Africa Division, I was asked to take on a temporary duty assignment to a high-threat post in Africa for several weeks in February 1992 to conduct the Personal Protection Survey there.

In late May 1992, one of my former supervisors, who had transferred from the Office of Security to the Directorate of Operations, asked the director of security for me to work on a special program he had been assigned to in the DO's Special Activities Division (SAD) for ninety days. When I left the Gloucester Building, I knew in my heart that not only would I never return, but that it was time to try to transfer from the Office of Security to the DO.

On my first day in SAD with my former supervisor, I learned that for the past several months he had been supervising a sensitive program whose mission was to provide direct support to the UN Special Commission (UNSCOM) implementation and enforcement of UN Security Council Resolution 687, resulting from the cessation of hostilities following the 1990–91 First Gulf War. In August 1991, he had been called to the seventh floor by the deputy director of operations at the time and asked if he would put together a group of agency and U.S. Special Operations Command (USSOCOM) personnel to support UNSCOM. Prior to this time, the State Department had been responsible for coordinating the U.S. involvement in these missions to include target selection, mission planning, and security. The agency was being brought into the equation after an Iraqi defector reported that several of the UN inspection books naming the locations of all of the proposed inspection sites had been left in a hotel room by someone from the UN team during a recent inspection. This was found by the Iraqis—and the inspectors wondered why all of the sites were always empty when they arrived.

Following his appointment, the first thing my former supervisor did was visit USSOCOM and ask for several of their top operators and analysts to support this initiative. He then integrated the personnel with a group of specialized agency officers. Their mission was to gather as much intelligence as possible on the Iraqi WMD (weapons of mass destruction) program so that sites that supported these efforts could be recommended to UNSCOM for inspection. Once the sites were selected, the analysts would make a detailed target study of the site. The operators then devised a training program for the UNSCOM team members, under the direction of the chief inspector, to learn to conduct a thorough, methodical search of a site, building, or room to look for items of intelligence value.

Following my transfer to the DO, in addition to managing the USSOCOM operators, analysts, and the specialized agency officers, I was made a branch chief in a newly formed group within SAD. I was thirty-seven years old and was as happy as I could be now that I was finally out of the Office of Security and embarking on a new career in the DO. Although the two other branch chiefs in this group were in their late fifties, along with the majority of the branch chiefs in SAD, I was accepted into the ranks because of the backing I had from my former supervisor and the chief and deputy chief of SAD. Since my branch was brand-new, we were asked to design training programs to support the Counterterrorist Center and the newly formed Counternarcotics Center (CNC). Relying on my past experience in Central America and the new mission of the USSOCOM operators, analysts, and specialized agency officers, we helped design a program that uses a thorough methodology to search for items of intelligence and law enforcement value. This methodology ensures that discovered items are recorded and logged so that the "chain of evidence" is not broken when dealing with items of law enforcement value that could be used in a court of law and items of intelligence value that could be used to expand the amount of information and knowledge known about the participants. With the success of the course, my branch developed several additional courses and by the time that I departed the group, we had a stable of independent contractor instructors who were providing this training worldwide to the DO. In addition, with the success of this group, my branch was called upon to plan and support several counterterrorism and counternarcotics raids and "takedown" operations. One such operation in South America involved taking down a kingpin narcotics trafficker in 1992, while another one involved a sensitive counterterrorism operation in Central Eurasia.

In August 1993, the deputy chief of SAD was selected to be the next chief in one of our European posts and wanted me to accompany him as one of his branch chiefs. Several days later, when the chief of SAD was selected to head our office in another European post, the deputy chief was trumped and the chief of SAD asked me to accompany him as one of his branch chiefs. Shortly thereafter, in September 1993, I returned to language training in preparation for my PCS (or permanent change of station).

I arrived in my first European post with my family on July 12, 1994, and was asked to set up and manage a new counternarcotics program for a year before taking over the branch chief position in that the country where we were assigned. That country, and one of its neighbors, were increasingly becoming the gateway into Europe for Latin American–based cocaine. As the counternarcotics program manager, I worked closely with the two police services, one civilian and one military, and in close coordination and cooperation with U.S. law enforcement representatives, including the Drug Enforcement Administration and Federal Bureau of Investigation, in the U.S. embassy there. Our goal for establishing this program was to provide the host country with intelligence from the CNC, other headquarters components, Latin America, and European sister offices, as well as technical equipment and training. Shortly after establishing this program, we started providing "lead" information, notably from Latin America, due to the increased amount of cocaine shipped to and through Europe, and convinced the civilian and military police counternarcotics services that it was more important to focus on disrupting entire networks rather than individual traffickers.

During the three years that I was assigned to this European country (1993 to 1997) the country doubled the amount of cocaine, heroin, and hashish seized during the previous year, ranking them at the top in European seizures for three straight years. One of the highlights occurred in 1996 with the seizure of more than one thousand kilograms of cocaine following a one-year investigation by the police. In addition to the cocaine seizure, numerous arrests were made, residences and companies were raided, and several bank accounts were frozen. This was one of the largest and most important operations to dismantle a narcotics trafficking organization in this country's history. While public credit was given to several services, the equipment and training that we provided proved invaluable in carrying out this operation. The HF intercept equipment was crucial in locating and tracking the vessel while cellular telephone intercept systems used to monitor the mobile telephone conversations of the head of the organization eventually led to his capture and arrest. Our assistance clearly enhanced local efforts to combat narcotics trafficking and organized crime during my three-year tour. The lead information, equipment, and training we provided produced solid results and enabled this country subsequently to develop its own capabilities. In February 1996, our office was recognized for outstanding achievement through training and, when I departed in the summer of 1997, the counternarcotics program in this country was responsible for more than 60 percent of the office's intelligence reporting. Lastly, in addition to focusing on counternarcotics during my tenure in this country, we added organized crime to our charter and in addition to targeting Italian organized crime, we targeted Russian organized crime, which was rapidly expanding outside of the borders of Russia.

In the spring of 1997, during a visit to the post where I was assigned, the chief of our European Division asked me if I was interested in being a branch chief in another European post. Before accepting the assignment, I asked if I could do my language study in country instead of returning to the United States for a year with my family and then transferring back to Europe, to which he agreed. Studying abroad in this fashion was not the norm. In August of 1997 I moved my family to my second European post, settled in a beautiful villa outside of the capital, and began my language immersion. Although I was authorized a full year to learn the language, after ten months I tested at a level indicating working proficiency in speaking, reading, and writing and decided to forgo the last two months in order to begin working. The cost of the ten-month program was twenty-five thousand dollars—less than the cost of a full-time language student at our language school in Washington DC. In early July 1998, after completing my language training and testing in Washington, I reported to work ready to assume a branch whose focus was to spot, assess, develop, recruit, and handle targets unilaterally and with liaison. Even though our relationship with our counterparts at this time was tenuous at best, my goal was to outline a plan similar to that which I had developed at my previous post to offer training in an effort to establish close ties with them, which was no small task thanks to Aldrich Ames, the infamous CIA spy.

No sooner had I begun working when we received a cable from our office in London informing us that an Al-Qaeda cell in Ireland had called a telephone number in the country where I was serving. We later learned that the cell was believed to be affiliated with a plot to blow up the U.S. embassy in Tirana, Albania. After I brought this to the attention of the FBI's legal attaché and the head of the civilian police counterterrorism section, the police identified the residence and immediately placed it under surveillance. After receiving authorization, a wiretap was placed on the telephone and shortly thereafter, on October 2, 1998, the police raided the residence and arrested several Yemeni and Egyptian Islamic Jihad members. Indeed, they were part of a plan to blow up the U.S. embassy in Tirana, Albania. Following the raid, all of the local newspapers and television channels reported that the police searched the apartment and found beards, wigs, weapons, gold bullion, contact numbers, and mobile phones, which the police were able to exploit. Within hours of the raid, numerous FBI agents and a U.S. attorney from New York City arrived to assist the police with their investigation.

Looking back on my three-year tour in this European country, I am proud to say that we doubled our repertoire of liaison contacts and used these contacts to open doors to several services not previously met, particularly in the area of law enforcement. These efforts paid huge dividends in that prior to my departure we enjoyed strong relationships with three intelligence services and three law enforcement services targeting counterterrorism, organized crime, and counternarcotics. In addition, while I was stationed there, we increased the intelligence production and quadrupled the number of counterterrorism intelligence disseminations to the point where we ranked third in the DO in 1998 and ranked second in the DO in 1999. More importantly, we increased the number of recruitments. Lastly, I am most proud of the fact that shortly after my arrival in October 1998 we orchestrated the takedown of the aforementioned Yemeni and Egyptian Islamic Jihad members.

As I arrived back in Washington DC during the summer of 2000 after being overseas for the better part of six years, I was shocked to see how morale in the agency had plummeted during the years of the Clinton administration. Not only because of the Aldrich Ames scandal—the experienced counterintelligence officer who turned out to be a Soviet mole, and whose activities resulted in the deaths of ten Soviets working for the agency—but also due to the appointments of two very unpopular directors of central intelligence. I arrived in the Counternarcotics Center in September 2000. Although the director of the CNC promised me a group chief position during an overseas visit earlier in the year, on the day I arrived, he told me that it was his last day and that he was being reassigned as the chief of the Far East Division. When I met with his replacement, I was shocked to hear her say that she did not feel obligated to stand by the commitment made by her predecessor and was appointing her own group chief. I was then offered the deputy group chief position, which I accepted since I did not have a choice.

The group where I was assigned had a huge budget and was divided into three branches consisting of agency officers from all four directorates and one FBI detailee. One of my first assignments after assuming my new position was to travel to Central America in an attempt to convince a country to target a major money-laundering group with ties to one of the largest narcotics trafficking families there. In order to support this initiative and others, I developed a training program for CNC officers who needed to know how to support and conduct counternarcotics and organized-crime operations. In early January 2001, I returned to Central America in an effort to convince another government to resurrect their mobile search team program after receiving information that Colombia's largest guerrilla group (known as the Revolutionary Armed Forces of Colombia, or FARC) was trading cocaine for weapons and explosives, which had been buried along their border during the Sandinista regime.

On August 7, 2001, at 5:00 p.m., a fire erupted in the CIA's Original Headquarters Building when sparks from welders working on the roof went down one of the airshafts, igniting some paper. The following day, I was called to the executive director's office on the seventh floor and was asked to serve as manager of the agency's Emergency Preparedness Program, responsible for developing and implementing contingency plans to ensure continuity of operations and continuity of government. For the next few weeks, I tried to get my hands on every agency emergency plan ever written. What shocked me was the fact that there were volumes of plans but no one had ever taken the time to implement them or, more importantly, test them. I took it upon myself to rewrite several of the plans and design a system to implement and test them. The first step in developing the emergency preparedness plans was ensuring that we had the proper equipment and radios on hand to respond to, mitigate, and recover from a major incident. Unknown to everyone however, the clock was ticking, 9/11 was approaching, and we were running out of time.

During the morning of October 22, 2001, while sitting at my desk, I received a phone call from the chief of a new operational element within the CTC responsible for tracking down Taliban and Al-Qaeda members and transporting them to prison. Upon arriving, I received a quick overview of this new group and, afterward, was told that the agency was looking at sites to hold captured Taliban and Al-Qaeda members. Although the U.S. military base at Guantanamo Bay, Cuba, was being considered, I was told that the agency wanted me to visit an island in the Caribbean and conduct a survey on whether it could be used to house the prisoners since I was only one of a few employees still working for the agency with an intimate knowledge of the island. The following day I departed with a member of this new operational group under the guise of conducting a survey of this Caribbean island to support a counternarcotics initiative using my previous position as the chief of special operations for the CNC as cover. Returning to headquarters several days later I turned in my report, complete with photos, suggesting that if the CTC could convince the host government, both sites could be used to construct secure detention facilities. Weeks later, I learned that the CTC had decided to use Guantanamo Bay, Cuba, to house prisoners under this program instead of the island or the U.S. airbase.

On New Year's Eve, December 31, 2001, at 3:00 p.m., I received a call to report to the executive director's office on the seventh floor. The executive director informed me that he had just left a meeting with the DCI, who was deeply concerned about the safety and security of the CIA officers we had in Afghanistan. George Tenet's comments were along the lines of, "I just lost one officer (a reference to Mike Spann), and I don't want to lose anyone else." Following this exchange, the executive director came straight to the point. "Richard, I want you to go to Afghanistan to provide force protection measures and harden our facilities. I am not looking for a survey but rather someone who can implement security measures in Kabul and several of our forward bases. Based on what I have observed from you over the past few weeks, you are the most qualified officer we have." Although I knew that my wife would kill me for accepting this mission without first checking with her, I responded by saying of course I would go and then thanked the executive director for his confidence in me. The next day, January 1, 2002, I boarded an evening flight from Dulles International Airport to Uzbekistan. Over the next few weeks, with the assistance of ten Afghan nationals we had hired, and several of our officers, we began to harden our facilities, making them more difficult targets. I arrived back in the United States from Afghanistan in early February 2002. In a cable, the chief of our office in Kabul, had written to the Near East Division, stating, "The hotel where our officers are staying is now one of the most secure facilities in Kabul." When asked by Tenet how many agency officers we had in Kabul and how much money I had spent, I told him the number of employees and that we had spent sixty-eight thousand of the hundred thousand dollars, to which Tenet smiled and said, "I would say that was money pretty well spent, don't you agree?"

Tenet went on to say that he had just met Governor Tom Ridge who, following 9/11, had been appointed as the Homeland Security adviser to the president on October 8, 2001, as part of Executive Order 13228, which established the Office of Homeland Security and the Homeland Security Council. During this meeting, Governor Ridge told Tenet that he was looking for some CIA officers to assist him in establishing this new entity and, therefore, wanted to know if Tenet would be interested in detailing several officers from the agency to Homeland Security. Telling Tenet that I would be excited about working for Governor Ridge and supporting such an entity, especially in light of the fact that I was born and raised in Pennsylvania, the next day I traveled to the Eisenhower Executive Office Building on the White House compound to meet with Governor Ridge. Hearing me discuss the reasons why I was there, and after a quick overview of my background to include my recent activities in Afghanistan, Governor Ridge told me that following 9/11 he had been summoned to Washington DC by the president to be the first adviser for homeland security. During this initial meeting, President Bush had told Governor Ridge that on 9/11 he had received conflicting reports of what was happening in New York, Pennsylvania, and Washington DC from forty different federal, state, and local officials. The president went on to say that from that day forward, he was going to look to Governor Ridge to keep him informed as his new assistant to the president for homeland security. Following this story, Governor Ridge looked me directly in the eyes and said, "From this day forward, I am going to look to you, Richard, to keep me informed as my new director of incident management." My mission would be simple. When dealing with major disasters, emergencies, terrorist attacks, terrorist threats, wild-land and urban fires, floods, hazardous material spills, nuclear accidents, aircraft accidents, earthquakes, hurricanes, tornadoes, tropical storms, war-related disasters, public health and medical emergencies, and other occurrences requiring an emergency response, I was to run every threat and incident "to the ground" to see if there was a terrorist nexus, especially during periods of increased threat, and to report my findings back to Governor Ridge.

In addition to coordinating National Special Security Events, I soon discovered that in my new role I would also be involved in continuity of operations and continuity of government. This refers to the efforts within individual executive departments and agencies to ensure that primary mission-essential functions continue to be performed during a wide range of emergencies, including localized acts of nature, accidents, and technological or attack-related emergencies, and secondly, the coordinated effort within the federal government's executive branch to ensure that national essential functions continue to be performed during a catastrophic emergency.

On September 24, 2004, I put my retirement paperwork in at the agency, the same day that Porter Goss was sworn in by President Bush to be the new DCI. As I sat in the auditorium that day with the executive director and heard Porter Goss speak to the packed auditorium, my mind drifted to the first day I arrived to work in the agency and sat in the same auditorium hearing Charlton Heston on a video providing a "welcome aboard" speech. My, times had certainly changed. Jennifer Garner is now the celebrity providing the same speech. My mind also raced to many sad memories that the auditorium evoked, including the ceremonies honoring the former chief of our office in Beirut, William Buckley; Larry who was killed in East Africa; and Mike Spann who was killed in Afghanistan.

On December 31, 2004, I officially retired from the CIA and entered the agency's transition program. During the twenty-eight years that I spent with the CIA, the agency had been very good to me and I had a great career. Thanks to the agency and Uncle Sam, I have stood on the equator in both South America and in Africa; visited the Cape of Good Hope and the Cape of Good Horn; visited Mayan, Aztec, and Inca ruins; and even the Pyramids. Everybody kids me about the fact that my wife and I lived in two European countries for six years during the 1990s, while few remember the fact that we also lived in Honduras for three years while our two children were infants and when Honduras was the second most impoverished country in the Western Hemisphere and Americans were being targeted and killed. Few people also remember that I spent an enormous amount of time in Central and South America during the 1980s.

The only sad memory that I have when reflecting on my agency career, which spanned almost half of the CIA's existence, is that I know almost half of the individuals who died in the line of duty and who are represented by the 101 stars on the CIA's Wall of Honor today.

A Hero's Story

29

Our Man in Havana's Jails

A Temporary Duty Assignment in Hell

WALTER E. SZUMINSKI

The Cuba of the early 1960s was a watershed for Americans and American foreign policy on many levels. The menace of communism, thanks to the overthrow by a small band of rebels of a corrupt dictatorship in a Caribbean island on New Year's Day 1959, suddenly was no longer an ocean away, but was rather a mere ninety miles from the coast of Florida. Rabid anti-Americanism led to a break in diplomatic relations after Fidel Castro demanded that the U.S. embassy be substantially cut back on January 3, 1961. Relations with the nascent Castro government quickly soured, and the rookie Kennedy administration adapted the rollback policy of the predecessor Eisenhower administration, leading to a failed attempt to oust the Castroites with the Bay of Pigs invasion in April 1961. Tensions continued, including quiet, and again failed, efforts to remove Castro himself. These strains culminated in the October 1962 Cuban Missile Crisis, dramatically bringing home to the American in the street the danger that the communist regime could pose to the country's safety.

Since those early years, the Castro government has held on, despite continuous American-led economic sanctions and the fall of Havana's communist patrons in the Soviet Union and Eastern Europe. As we await the eventual fall of the Castro regime and the restoration of democracy to Cuba, Havana has begun a "charm offensive" to ensure that the post-Castro regime has a "soft landing" back into the fold of world nations. As part of the regime's attempt to gussy up in the eyes of world opinion, we've seen some easing of human rights abuses, a rolling back of the more egregious examples of oppression of the Cuban people, and piecemeal introduction of capitalism and concentration on the foreign tourist trade. The Cuba of millennium's end has come to mean many things to many people: a potential boon to the tourist and hotel industry, a possible return "home" to a generation of Cuban Americans who have never set foot on the island, a gold mine for consultants of every stripe seeking to assist the new regime to move in new directions, and even a new market for Major League Baseball. But for others, it may mean a disinclination to remember the lessons of the past at the price of perhaps someday having to repeat those mistakes.

With that in mind, I've decided that it's now safe for me to tell the world about the abuses I saw firsthand as a CIA officer during my 949-day stay in Castro's jails. Many of the people I met have since died. To protect those who are still alive and in danger, I have given aliases.

This chapter is based upon the extensive notes I made upon being released from Castro's prison in the summer of 1963, an earlier article by the late Nathan Nielsen in *Studies in Intelligence* on my experiences, and interviews with the numerous individuals who assisted me during that time. I have also read numerous other Cuban prison memoirs, many written by people I met in the jails, to fact-check these events.

Many of the individuals I shared space with will be surprised to discover the true names and true nature of the work of the three Americans they knew for so many years. While we were able to share so many of our thoughts and feelings with them, we could not share our true identities. Any wavering from our flimsy tourist cover story would have meant our death by firing squad on charges of espionage. Counterrevolutionaries, never mind CIA operatives, were routinely dragged to the wall and shot. To those friends from so many years ago, I send my best wishes and hopes that they aren't offended by those then-necessary lies.

There are several other books written by survivors of Castro's prisons, including by Armando Valladares, Lawrence Lunt, and John Martino. As they have already extensively described the unbelievably bad treatment one experiences in these jails, I won't go over ground they have already plowed. Suffice it to say that, yes, conditions were very, very bad. In Havana, the political prisoners and criminals were all treated the same, Geneva conventions notwithstanding. At the Isle of Pines, the common criminals were allowed freedom of the prison compound, while political prisoners were kept locked in the circulars. I will concentrate my narrative on some of the personalities we met, the ways the human spirit can overcome such adversity, and some of the methods we used to continue to conduct intelligence operations, even from prison.

Setting the Scene

In 1960 Fidel Castro had established his rule over the island of Cuba, and his true communist spots were beginning to show. His 1959 takeover against Batista was undeniably popular, despite his having had only eighty guerrillas under his command two years earlier. Although he began as a Man of the People, he soon turned into an ideologue, as earlier tentative feelers to more middle-of-the-road politicians were brushed aside and the rebels' revolution had nowhere to turn but the Left. An exasperated Washington became more and more concerned about the establishment of a Russian beachhead in Latin America. Communist China, the other bête noire of the West, had also begun to embrace Castro.

With all this swirling around, the ops folks decided that a team was needed to go to Havana to install audio equipment. This looked like a pretty straightforward, low-risk operation. So just like in *Mission: Impossible*, David C., Thornton A., and I were picked to go to Havana for a few days.

I had joined the Central Intelligence Agency in October 1950. My first assignment was as a communicator assigned to East Asia. It was a great assignment and provided the challenge I needed at the time. For the next seven years I spent time in the Middle

East and Central America with only short visits back to the States between two-year assignments and short TDY (temporary duty assignments). It was during my home leave period in the late summer of 1960 when this story begins.

I had been visiting my parents in Dorchester, Massachusetts (a suburb of Boston), for about a week when I received a call from the Washington office to report for a TDY. I left for Washington DC the next morning.

Dave C., to be later known as Daniel, came from Tamaqua, a small coal-mining town in northeastern Pennsylvania. He married a girl from Wisconsin that he met in a military school. He and Wilma lived in Bethesda, Maryland, with their six children.

Dave was the new division chief trying hard to be accepted as one of the audio techs. He came from an engineering group, where he had spent his entire previous career, to an operational group. This was an environment markedly different from the slower-paced, methodical engineering climate of development and engineering. In the operational environment, the tech had to improvise under constantly changing conditions, and go to alternate Plan B even if you didn't have one. Dave, by nature, was the consummate optimist.

Thornton A., later known as Danny and Andy, was born in Baltimore, Maryland. He has one brother, Ronald, an artist in Connecticut. Andy and his Florida-born wife, Gayle, had two sons, and lived in Springfield, Virginia.

Andy was a former marine who had a penchant for volunteering and concentrating on detail to the extreme. He also had an engineering background and volunteered to come on this trip to see firsthand why the equipment was breaking down in the field.

I was born in Boston, Massachusetts, the only child of immigrant Lithuanian parents. At the time of this adventure, I was thirty years old, single, six-foot, blue eyes, and blond. My hobbies included flying, ham radio, and driving my 1955 Ford Thunderbird. By nature, I am easygoing and laid back.

Getting Ready for the Mission

So the word went out to the three of us. I had just completed my second PCS (permanent change of station) assignment (late August 1960) and was enjoying a thirty-day home leave break between assignments. I had been home for about one week. Already the newness was wearing off and I was getting bored and lazy. It was a relief to get a call from Elsie C., the cute secretary in the DC office. She stated that Dave C., the division chief, wanted to talk to me about going on a TDY. She stated that whatever time I spent on this trip would be added to my home leave time when I returned to Boston. I hopped on the Eastern Airlines flight from Boston to Washington. On arrival I called up an old friend who had a spare bed in his apartment, so I headed there instead of staying at a hotel.

The next day, a Thursday in early September 1960, I checked in at the office in the Technical Services Division (TSD) but it was like a tomb. My previous boss had checked out and was getting ready to leave for overseas. Everybody was someplace else.

I wandered around and finally ran into Dave, who didn't know me but, after I said "hi," fielded pretty well. We went into his office and, after the customary greetings, we started talking about various items of interest—my chance for a promotion, future assignments, the latest in eavesdropping equipment, and people in general.

After about an hour, Elsie came in with a priority cable from Havana saying that another country had broken relations with Cuba. It looked like we would have a chance to install some equipment in the facility while its owners still had control. When they moved out and others moved in, they will have been wired for sound.

After no more than a few minutes of discussion, Dave decided to go to Havana for the TDY, which was then approved by the appropriate chain of command—Technical Services Division's chief of operations— and coordinated with the area division.

Unbeknownst to me, I was asked to go because several other audio techs refused to go. Two of the techs had just returned from a TDY to Havana a few days earlier and had experienced physical and electronic surveillance. Both were glad to get out of there, but neither bothered to mention their experiences to me. Also, there were not any other techs available at the time. Although I spoke very little Spanish, I had spent a year in Central America in 1953, so I had the best credentials of the folks who were left. Dave picked himself, and Andy volunteered. Dave tried to enlist a specialist from another division, but he turned Dave down in no uncertain terms.

The wheels go in motion and I start the long hassle with paper-work, running here and there, getting signatures for travel orders, money advances, and so on. This is my first opportunity to meet Thornton (Andy) A., whom I had seen but never had a chance to really talk to. Andy was assigned to an engineering division whose office was located two floors away from mine. My only other encounter with him was at a headquarters meeting held a year or so earlier. To be truthful, I didn't think much of him at the time. He acted uninterested and aloof. Since the people I worked with were handling the meeting, Andy irritated me a little by his indif-ference. When I learned that he was coming on this trip, I was not exactly thrilled but I decided that it's always nice to have an extra body along to help out.

The time before we had to leave was only a matter of hours. I dashed over to one of the old temporary buildings to the Office of Central Cover to wrap up the last-minute details—getting money, tickets, my alias documentation, a cover story, and an address. Since Central Cover had no idea what to give me for a cover story, I decided to use the same story Dave was going to use. I had no idea who came up with Dave's story; he never mentioned it. The cover story was that Dave was an electrical engineer for an engineering consulting firm. I was hired as an electronics technician. What to use for a home address? This is a problem, since I'm not that famil-iar with New York City. Well, Syd's address should do. She was an old flame of mine. She was not affiliated with the agency, and thus there was no backstopping. She was a nurse that I'd met a year or two earlier in Florida and had dated ever since.

I left the tempo building and headed back to my office, which was about a fifteen-minute walk along Independence Avenue in downtown Washington DC. I met up with Dave and one of the officers responsible for the Latin American area, then known in agency jargon as WH (for Western Hemisphere). His organization hired the case officers, who were responsible for the overall operation, and for which we provided the technical input. He was a little nervous about our going on this trip because of the deteriorating situation in Cuba. Dave had halfway convinced him that there wouldn't be any problems. Dave had been there at least twice earlier—the second time during the past two weeks—and had experienced no problems. I was asked how I felt about going. My reply was that I should be able to lie my way around without too much trouble. We didn't try the cover stories out on each other to check them for inconsistencies.

The next day was more of a struggle than I could have anticipated. There was equipment (tape recorders, tools, test equipment) to be packed and lots of running around to get the logistics office to pack it and get it shipped. Somehow it all got done. In the process of getting everything packed and trying to think of any last-minute items I might need, a friend, Lou C., another tech from my office, comes in and offers the use of his multimeter. (Lou and another tech, Donald D., had returned from a TDY to Havana a day or two earlier. Lou and Donald felt they were lucky to get out of there alive, but never said a word about this to me. I learned of that several years after my release.) This gadget measures electrical parameters. Good deal! We need one and, at this late date, I could never get one in time to be included in this mail for Havana. On the outside of the case, Lou wrote, "Belongs to Lou C. Return." That little phrase gave me quite a jolt later on.

Wheels up

At long last, it's time to leave, so off Dave, Andy, and I go to National Airport. The weather bureau in Miami was watching a hurricane in the Caribbean and if we didn't get moving, we wouldn't make it.

We had warnings of the impending hurricane before we left Washington, so we rushed to get to Havana before flights were canceled. Andy had a reaction to the many shots (tetanus, typhoid, and several others I cannot recall) he had received and was in bad shape with a headache and a slight fever. Dave and a case officer sat in one section of the plane and Andy and I in another. This wasn't for any operational or cover reason, just luck of the draw because we had prearranged seat assignments.

We arrived in Miami and wandered around the lounge of the airport for awhile. We then retrieved our baggage and checked in with Pan American for the flight to Havana. This is where my new persona, Edmund K. Taransky, is born. Dave and I put our documents in one large envelope and mailed them back to Dave's home address in Bethesda. I do not remember what Andy did with his documents. We still had a few hours to kill before the plane left for Havana, so into the bar we go. We all had a beer and discussed our cover stories for the first time as a group. As I remember it, five minutes was all we spent.

The time comes to board the plane. Dave and I sit together in one section and Andy and the case officer sat together in another section. The ride is uneventful other than Dave saying he recognized a person, perhaps a Cuban, from another operation. I am of the impression that Dave was just playing Cloak and Dagger. We never did find out who this was. It was not mentioned in any counterintelligence report that I've seen.

Welcome to the Socialist Paradise

We arrive in Havana at about 5:00 p.m., where it is warm after the coolness of Boston and Washington. We went through the usual customs and immigration procedures at the airport, where our bags and visas were checked. One thing that struck me was that every Cuban in sight was carrying a gun—chrome-plated .45's with red plastic grips slung from the hip like they are trying to imitate John Wayne. I feel a little unnerved traveling under an alias. My concern is that I will not react to hearing my new name. Fortunately, our entry into Cuba was uneventful.

While going out the door of the terminal, Dave was stopped by a local photographer who snapped his picture getting off the plane. The photographer probably thought that Dave was a VIP and would be interested in buying the photo, but Dave was not interested.

We take off in a cab for the Foxa Building, a downtown Havana high-rise, the site of apartments and offices. I have no idea why we went there—Dave was making the decisions and I had to go along. On the half-hour ride into town from the airport, I saw that Havana, Cuba's urban area, was like that of all of the other Latin American countries I have been in (Guatemala, Honduras, Mexico)—there were new high-rise buildings standing next to corrugated tin shacks. The overall picture has that worn and rundown-around-the-edges look. I did not observe any people or activity, just the mix of buildings.

Our first stop was at the Foxa Building. We walked through the lobby and took the elevator to the fourteenth floor, got off, and pretended we were going into an apartment. We loitered for a few minutes in the hallway. It appeared that we were alone; no one else opened any doors or arrived on the elevator. We then went back down to the lobby, hailed another cab, and headed for the Crosby house; Ken Crosby served as the vice president of Merrill, Lynch, Pierce, Fenner, and Smith in Havana. Only Dave knew what this exercise was all about, and he did not keep me informed. This aspect was not mentioned during our discussions at the bar in Miami. We never returned to the Foxa Building. It seemed like a dumb sort of dodge to me (up with suitcases and back down a few minutes later). However, I'm not running the show, and there was nothing I could do alone. Where would I go, what would I do, and how would I meet up with Dave later? So I had no option but to go along with him at this point.

We got to the Crosby house. The case officer who had ridden on the flight with us had arranged for the three of us to stay here for the duration of the TDY. Mr. Crosby and his family had returned to the States permanently and had rented their house to the then chief of station. This case officer left shortly after we settled in, and I did not see him again. He had returned to the States before we were picked up. He was obviously in a hurry to get out of there.

I was very impressed with the house—a ranch-type home, all stone, beautifully done. It was apparent that a party of about thirty-five people was getting under way. I didn't recognize anyone. But after introductions, I realized they were all people from the embassy, including several marine guards. The one blonde gal was the center of attention, but I wasn't impressed. She just complained that things were so tough—no candy, no social dates, yadda, yadda. I thought this gal needed a tour in a place like Kabul, Phnom Penh, or, better yet, Vientiane.

Time passed and eventually the party was over, after which we went to the marine house. The only activity was a poker game in progress. I turned on the television because one of the marine guards mentioned there was nothing on TV except Fidel. I decided to check him out. Fidel was wearing his usual fatigues and was making one of his usual long speeches. I watched him for about an hour. He was well into his topic when I tuned him in and was going strong when I turned him off. At that time I could understand only every third or fourth word of Spanish, so I was not able to get the full impact for the entire hour. I don't know where he was or whom he was addressing.

During the next few days, we visited the Merrill Lynch office in downtown Havana. Our case officer made a crack about one of the buildings downtown that supposedly served as a prison, observing, "You don't want to go there."

We made two other trips to unpack seven huge boxes of equipment that had arrived. There was no storage space for these items, but the case officer, Bob N., promised to take care of it.

The Break-in

It is now Sunday, and it's time to get to work after waiting around for several days due to the hurricane. Since we were in town anyway, Bob N., the Far East Division case officer, decided to use our skills to enhance the work at an operational installation in Havana. At the time, this was viewed as one of the key intelligence collection operations against the communists in all of the Western Hemisphere. When—not if—the United States was thrown out of Cuba. the operation could be transferred to a friendly third-party government who would give us the tape.

So Bob grabs Andy and me and off we go to meet Mario, our local contact. Bob had made the arrangements beforehand with Mario for a meeting at a downtown coffee shop. On our arrival, we parked the car on a narrow side street and strolled to the coffee shop. We went in, sat at a booth, and Mario, having seen us arrive with Bob, left to go to the listening post. Bob pointed Mario out, but I could not identify whom he was talking about. So at this point, I had no idea what Mario looked like.

Some twenty minutes later, we left the coffee shop and went to the target, located in the Seguro Medico Building. The lobby had normal activity of some ten to fifteen people coming and going. There were two elevators located on each of two sides of the lobby, with a "starter" (a uniformed man with a clicker to indicate to the elevator operator that it was full and to close the door). The starter directed us to an empty elevator. We went straight to the eighteenth floor which, again, I thought was pretty stupid—anyone watching would have seen where we went. This time Bob was leading the group. I saw nothing that appeared to be surveillance on us.

We knocked on the apartment door. Mario opened the door and invited us in. There were no formal introductions. The apartment served as the listening post for the operation. After surveying the apartment and checking the current installation, we sat and talked with Mario for about an hour. All we discussed was the operation itself: were there any problems with it? No. We asked for Mario's comments and suggestions for improvements, and so on. Bob, Andy, and I then left to go to a hotel bar, leaving Mario in the apartment. We stopped by Sloppy Joe's, one of Ernest Hemingway's hangouts. We had the house special, a frozen daiquiri, and stayed about twenty minutes before leaving after noticing that we were the only customers. We then returned to the Crosby house.

The next day, Bob dropped us off at the Seguro Medico Building while he went off to another meeting. The doorman gave us the fish eye as we went through the lobby and into the elevator. Again, we didn't see any surveillance, and all other activities appeared to be normal. We took the elevator straight up to the eighteenth floor listening post above the target. We worked all day Tuesday, rerouting wires, drilling out 2-inch-by-6-inch cavities in cement walls to install additional equipment. As luck would have it, there were no cinder block walls, which would have made our work much easier. Bob and Mario came and went throughout the day, going out for supplies, bringing in food, and acting as gofers.

That evening, Dave had a meeting elsewhere and did not return until the next morning. Andy and Mario sat around talking about American appliances. Mario complained that the American companies sent all their reject products to Cuba. Andy took exception to that and said that this was not the case. Andy argued that when running a production line, all the items are identical—there are no good and bad ones. He was trying to make the case that there was no effort made to separate the rejects to send to Cuba and to keep the good ones in the States. I got tired of listening to this, so I went to bed. I wanted to be well rested and ready to go early the next morning.

On Wednesday morning, a meter reader stopped by. He did not need access to the apartment. Inside, Andy and I arose to continue our work. Mario made a pot of coffee. Dave returned about the same time, and we all worked like beavers installing the new equipment. The work was going smoothly and it appeared that we would be able to finish up on Thursday and leave. We stopped for supper, which Mario took great pride in preparing. After that, we sat around making small talk. I tuned the Zenith portable radio to the Voice of America program on WRUL to get the latest news and the position of the hurricane. Mario had been plotting its course on an Esso road map of the Caribbean. It was still well north of

Cuba at this point. There was not much new, so we went back to work for a few more hours.

Caught!

All of a sudden there was a hell of a pounding on the door. Andy was in the bathroom plastering the wall. He recalls that we had buried the power supplies and transmitters in the cavities beside the medicine cabinet. These are AC operated and that's where we had to pick up the power. The microphone wires went through the wall and down to the microphones. Right away I thought, That stupid case officer. When he gets inside I'll give him an education. Dave beat me to the door. There was a lot of thumping and crashing. The next thing I know, I'm looking down the barrel of a large .45 automatic. It could have been a .38 automatic, but at that point, it resembled more of a howitzer barrel. I could see the rifling down the barrel, with some rust in the grooves. The man holding the gun has a sneer on his face and my first thought was, What a crummy-looking jerk he is. He was unshaven and dirty. I could not tell if he was old or young, tall or short, skinny or fat. My mind just focused on the gun and his face.

The feeling that I had after the first few fleeting seconds is pretty hard to describe. It was a mixture of disbelief, fear, and the realization that we had been caught in the act, and how in the hell can this be happening to me?

We were spread-eagled against the wall in the kitchen/dining room, but Andy is still absorbed in what he is doing. I have to yell at him, "The man here wants to talk to you."

Our new friend motions us to move to the front room where we are then all lined up, facing a wall. No search was necessary since we were all in our shorts. The place was so hot we just couldn't work with clothes on. So literally and figuratively, we got caught with our pants down.

A voice from behind told us not to talk. After a while we are allowed to sit down, and even smoke, but still had to face the wall. We sat for quite a while and then were taken to a bedroom in the rear of the apartment. I don't remember whether they reiterated the order not to talk, but at that point nobody was in the mood for idle conversation.

The three of us sat in the bedroom on two double beds—for how long I don't have any idea. Time seemed to be standing still at this point. There was always a guy sitting in the doorway, in the corridor. There was a long corridor with all the rooms coming off it. He could look to his left up the corridor, and look straight ahead and see us.

The Cubans didn't interrogate us right away, apparently waiting to see who else might show up. They also started to search the apartment.

The next jolt was the bang of a pistol or automatic going off. I looked at Dave, whose eyes were showing terror—red and watery and ready to cry. The look on his face seems to indicate that he thinks we are next. Our friend in the door of the bedroom doesn't seem to be too excited. In fact, he still sits and motions with his hand for us three to stay put. The first thought that went through my mind was that somebody (probably Mario) in the next room gave one of the guards some lip and got shot.

After more sitting and waiting, Dave was called out of the room. I think, Well, here we go, boys. They'll take us one at a time. Bang! And that's it.

But it turned out that they are just asking questions, not shooting. At least, not yet. One of the Cubans had shot himself in the hand. Cubans are great for that. They play with guns, chamber rounds, and roll the cylinders. This guy was playing with his gun and bang! He shot himself in the hand.

Pretty soon, Dave came back. He tells us he passed along our cover story. To reiterate, our story was that Daniel (Dave) and I worked for Victor Vachuta Associates in New York City. Danny (Andy) worked for a mechanical engineering company in Baltimore. We were in Havana to help out Mr. N. with an electrical problem he had with some equipment.

Our cover stories didn't have much to back them up. We had driver's licenses, visas, credit cards, and our story. Dave was papered as Daniel L. Carswell, forty-two, electrical engineer, Eastchester, New York. Thornton A. was Eustace Dan-Brunt, thirty-four, a mechanical engineer from Baltimore, Maryland. I was Edmund K. Taransky, thirty, an electrical engineer from New York City. Andy remembers: "I have never dreamed that if we got wrapped up, we'd be any more than deported. I didn't think I would come that close to getting shot." This was his first assignment to a field operation; he'd previously been in engineering research and development. There was no doubt in my mind that if these guys figured out we were CIA, we were dead men. So, flimsy as it was, we stuck to the cover story.

That's about it for the rest of the night. Danny and I were not questioned, and after a while, we went to sleep. I do not know if Dave or Andy got any sleep that night, but I did.

Meanwhile . . .

Of course, when we did not return the next day, all hell broke loose. Bob went to check on our whereabouts, cruising past the apartment, but found only a phalanx of determined-looking police and intelligence types coming in and out of the building.

There was a rush to figure out what went wrong, and, as you can imagine, a flurry of memos were written at headquarters and the field assigning blame to everyone but those who deserved it. One memo, written on October 27, 1960, by the chief of operational services to the deputy director for plans, referred to this as "the operation which went wrong." No kidding. The memo noted that there were extenuating circumstances in deciding to go ahead with a much dicier operation than what we'd originally been sent to accomplish. It is important to recognize that the political situation in Cuba that existed at the time of this operation called for rapid action. The officers of the FE (the agency's Far East Division) felt great urgency in improving and expanding their audio coverage of high-priority targets in Cuba. One specific facility was rated by the FE as the number one target in the Western Hemisphere. A break in relations between Cuba and the United States was sufficiently possible that our colleagues had already started destroying files and strengthening stay-behind arrangements. The Audio Operations Branch of the TSD was very short of technicians (two were on vacation), so the chief of the branch, Mr. C., decided to handle the assignment personally with the assistance of two officers from other components of the TSD. On September 8, Hurricane Donna was approaching Florida and there was a good chance that air flights to Havana would be suspended.

That said, however, the memo noted that several things could have been done better:

1. Plans for this sensitive operation did not include coordinated details on emergency plans and story to be used in event of arrest and interrogation. Nor is there any evidence that the men who were arrested had received careful instruction on certain general rules of conduct and deportment, which might assist them under interrogation.

2. The tourist cover used by the technicians was very light. The cover could not be expected to hold up if the Cubans conducted a thorough inquiry and intensive interrogation.

3. Violations of operational security occurred in the travel and housing arrangements of the personnel on TDY in Havana.

4. Although officers of the FE Division went through the motions of coordinating with the WH Division (Western Hemisphere Division of the agency), they really did not provide WH with sufficient details to enable that division to discharge its responsibilities.

5. Control, supervision, and support of this operation was inadequate.

6. The failure to provide lookouts during the critical phase of the drilling was a serious lapse.

7. The operation that was blown certainly did not receive the careful analysis and thorough action that an activity of this

sensitivity requires. The whole question of sending the three technicians to Havana was considered . . . only incidental consideration was given to the more hazardous job in the (second facility).

The memo also jumped on Dave, saying,

> Mr. C. was probably the most knowledgeable officer in the Agency of world-wide audio operations. It is not evident that proper consideration was given to the hazards to Agency interests of exposing Mr. C. to arrest and hostile interrogation. Mr. C. was in Cuba under tourist cover during August. He returned to the U.S. on 30 August and traveled again to Havana as a tourist on 8 September despite having advised a fellow officer in TSD that he believed he had been under surveillance during the first trip. His second trip to Cuba, as a tourist at a time when few genuine tourists were traveling, was questionable, particularly in light of the suspected surveillance. In deciding to participate personally in the installation, Mr. C. showed commendable professional enthusiasm but questionable judgment.

First Days in Captivity

With the morning light, we got up with the sun. Our guard had been replaced with a small, skinny, young, friendly Latin fellow. Another young Cuban appears and asks if we want bacon and eggs. Everybody said no; we still didn't have much of an appetite with our stomachs in knots with the stress of captivity. However, we took him up on his offer of coffee. After a while the coffee comes. It's Cuban-style cafecito and very good. It came in a small demitasse and was very sweet. After sipping the coffee, I became hungry. I mentally kicked myself for not asking for the eggs.

After a short while, we go out to the living room and, lo and behold, all of the gear is spread out on the floor, plus what had been hidden under the sofa in the apartment, in a very neat arrangement. Actually, I was surprised to see so much equipment; I was unaware that so much gear from the previous op has been stashed in the apartment. Obviously they are going to take pictures. This is confirmed when they sit us on the sofa. Our coffee-making friend has an Exacta camera around his neck and is preparing to take some shots. When he started to take the pictures, I, like a jerk, tried to give the other guys more room on the sofa so they can be more comfortable. Andy, however, uses his head and stays where he is. As a result, he is indistinguishable in the background when the picture is published. The photos appeared in the Cuban newspapers under the headlines proclaiming the capture of American spies. The equipment was shown upside down. They obviously didn't know which side was right.

After more waiting around, the Cubans herd us into an elevator. The young, petite girl running it suspects something is up and gets a confirmation when one of our escorts reaches into his belt to move his pistol to a more comfortable position.

We're lead out through the lobby, getting the usual stare from the doorman. We start down the stairs to the outside, but the guards seem to be hanging back and there is some confusion. A small crowd is gathered around the steps. Suddenly, a mental light comes on: They're making movies of us. I don't see the cameraman, but I suspect that he's probably hiding in a car or across the street, armed with a telephoto lens.

We all pile into a car and off we go—ten of us in an eight-passenger Chevy sedan. The driver takes off and we zoom down the street at a great rate of speed. I'm sitting on the left rear seat; the only thing between the door and me is the guard. The door was not closed all the way. On impulse, I give it a shove, but it didn't fly all the way open, a tribute to American workmanship. The guard gave me a dirty look, pulled the door completely shut, and gave me an elbow in the ribs for my trouble.

I noticed that the oil warning light was on, but nobody seemed to pay attention. The radio was on full blast, playing some sort of military music, and the gas pedal was all the way to the floor. The Cubans must think that these are the only two items that you need in a car, the radio and the gas pedal. We're doing eighty miles per hour and the driver hasn't touched the brakes, although he is murdering the horn.

We arrived at what looked like a private home, but there were all sorts of people, both soldiers and civilians, milling around, so this must be some sort of police station. They took us inside and had us sit on benches in the main corridor. A dark-skinned black male soldier walked by carrying a Browning automatic rifle. Nobody paid us any attention, but we had no thoughts of escape; there were too many locals around.

An officer came out and took a long, hard look at us. Just the smile on his face and his attitude made me want to punch him right in the nose. He was holding an envelope and slapping it in the palm of his hand. It's obvious to me what was in the envelope—all the money that we had in our wallets when they picked us up.

He left and a young, blond girl was escorted in and seated diagonally opposite us. She introduced herself as an American named Marjorie Lennox, a secretary at the embassy. She kept protesting to anyone who would listen that she didn't know anything about what was happening. (Her apartment was to be used as a safe haven in the event that something went wrong. Her key was found in the listening post. She did not have a direct role in the operation.) Some men had come into her apartment in the middle of the night and told her she was under arrest. She hoped that the American consul would be able to get there to see her. What a break! The consul, Hugh Kessler, arrived and talked with her, and she sent him over to see us. Dave had a difficult time getting our plight through to him. I guess the term "bugging" was something new to the consul, but finally he jotted down our names, address, and Dave's embassy contact. By this time a soldier started making noises about our talking with the consul, so the conversation stopped. The consul did not protest that he was entitled to talk to us.

We are taken through a glass door into a room that looks like a library. There were about six other prisoners there. We were told to take seats apart from each other. On the raised dais at the front of the room there was a girl in her midtwenties going through some school books with a young boy who looked to be about eight years old. Her eyes showed that she was scared stiff, but the boy is going to get his studying done, come rain or shine. The boy looked bored by it all.

We stayed there for a couple of hours. It's now well past lunchtime, and everybody is getting hungry. Marjorie talks to one of the guards and he doesn't seem to know what to do about it. After much confusion and repeating the story to a few more guards, one of them volunteers to get a couple of ham sandwiches from the canteen. He disappears and after what seems like an hour later, comes back with some ham sandwiches and Cokes. The sandwich tastes like sawdust, but I get it down.

We were then taken upstairs to be fingerprinted and photographed. Everybody gave the impression that they were in no hurry to get anything done. Marjorie started making points with the chief of the fingerprint/photograph section, who spoke passable English. She wrapped him around her finger. It's like Gary Cooper in an old western when the heroine smiles at him. He kicks the dust with his toe and says, Aw, shucks. The chief does the same thing, but Latin style. He made an obvious effort to provide a comfortable chair and clean towel to remove the fingerprint ink. He also offered to get her a Coke or a glass of water.

After four hours or so, our fingerprinting and photograph session was completed. We were then taken downstairs to another room. There we found about a half-dozen Cuban prisoners. We waited around for the next step in this process. Food arrived, but it is not much—sweet potatoes and rice that doesn't appeal to me. But I nonetheless ate a small amount of it.

I looked out the window and saw Bob and Mario go by. It seems that the G2 (the Cuban intelligence agency, Dirección General de Inteligencia) had them, too. I learned later that they were arrested on September 15. Bob was promptly expelled. Mario was held for trial. His wife was deported, as was Marjorie Lennox, the U.S. embassy secretary implicated in the case because a key to her apartment was found in our possession.

It became obvious where we were headed. The group ahead of us in this room is stripped of belts, shoelaces, and so forth. They were escorted out of the room and that was the last we saw of them. At about five o'clock a guard came and asked for our watches, belts, and shoelaces, which gives you the clue that you're not leaving. Our belts and shoelaces were put into an envelope with our names on it. Then we were taken out into the courtyard and through a door.

We get our first taste of life behind bars in Cuba. Wow! Talk about a dungeon! We are greeted by yelling, hollering humanity on the other side of the bars. They look like animals. I can't figure out if we are going from the frying pan into the fire or vice versa. We're each placed into different cells. My eyes take a few moments to adjust to the dark and all I see is a bunch of men in their shorts. Naturally, they are all talking at once. Somebody explains that this is the Fifth Avenue G2 jail. Well, it's nice to know where you are. The room is about thirty feet square with a shower/toilet combination at one end and all the other available space taken up by three-decker GI beds. The Americans have been separated, each in a cell jammed with Cuban prisoners. Several people come up to me and ask if I am an American. I answer yes. There is much shouting and confusion. Everybody wants to know why I'm in there. For want of a better answer, I just say "tourist." You hear "What did you do?" "Nothing." "Well, I didn't do anything, either." So it goes. A lot of the fellows that I meet here I see later at La Cabana and the Isle of Pines.

A guard appears at the door to take orders for sandwiches and things from the canteen. My cellmates offer me all sorts of sandwiches and other food. Everybody seems to want to buy me some food, but I just settle for a Coke.

Later an American whose name I don't remember, a manager of an American company in Cuba, arrived and asked, "What's going on? Why are the Cubans putting us in jail? How can I get out?" The way he asks and the protestations of innocence gave me the idea that he was scared stiff and would see or do almost anything to get out. When I tell him I'm being held for espionage, he avoids me with determination. I just said this because he was a wimp who irritated me and I felt like pushing his button. I never again mentioned the word espionage; neither did the police. Later on that night he was taken from the cell. I assume he was released because I never saw him again.

Interrogation: Round 1

Later that same night I was called for the first interrogation. I was taken to a small room with a desk, two chairs, and three Cubans occupying the room: two sitting and one standing. One is very young and, from his dress and attitude, I would guess him to be a pimp. He was the standing Cuban, wearing baggy slacks and a Hawaiian-print sport shirt. One of the sitting Cubans, whom we nicknamed the Football Player, was a very large, muscular guy, probably there to keep you under control. For this first session, he just sat in a corner glaring at me. The last of the three Cubans was a young, blue-eyed man still sporting baby fat who wore his hair combed straight back. He had some very large cavities in his front teeth, so we nicknamed him Bad Teeth. However, he spoke excellent English, without any accent, and served as the interrogator. He started off with the usual questions—name, address, why are you in Cuba? I gave answers, which were my cover story—Edmund K. Taransky, address in West End Avenue, New York City, and so on, and I'm hoping that the address I give coincides with the one that he has. From where I'm sitting I can see that he has all my documents in front of him.

Of all the experiences that I would have during the next few years, this is the one that unnerves me the least. I never worried about what I would say at the interrogation sessions. When a question came up I would answer it as best I could.

Bad Teeth would ask me, "What are you doing here? Why are you here? Come on, Mr. Taransky, tell us. Why, you work for the CIA, don't you?" I'd reply, "Who, me? No, I don't work for them." The three of us stuck to the story that we were on vacation. A man from the U.S. embassy had asked the three of us to help him with some electrical equipment. We decided that we could help him out. CIA? FBI? No, nothing like that. (They usually asked A. about an FBI connection; I usually got the CIA questions.)

The interrogators warned us that if we didn't tell everything, we'd be shot. Questioning us separately, they'd say, "Well, we know all about this. Your buddies have told us the whole story, so why don't you tell us the whole story?" They were interested in knowing if there were more than just the three of us involved, and if the plot entailed more than just the bugging job.

All through this thirty-day interrogation period I remembered a comment made by an acquaintance while playing Scrabble. "Don't try to anticipate; don't embroider some new identity on the fly. Everything is the same except your name. Your mind gets cluttered and you tend to go off on a tangent. Then with your mind in a rut, the other person makes a move and you're caught by surprise."

A. believed that the Cubans had had us under surveillance and had spotted C. as the team leader. C., under interrogation, tried to shift the blame onto the man from the U.S. embassy, in the belief that he couldn't be harmed by the Cubans. He'd be taken back to the United States untouched.

So it goes for the next four days. We were permitted to sleep during the day, and were interrogated at night. There was no physical coercion. We were given regular meals three times a day, usually a blob of rice and a small amount of meat.

I Would Have Settled for Only Fifteen Minutes of Fame

About half a dozen local newspapers hit the cell the following day. After the guards finished with them, they gave them to us to keep and use as toilet paper. The headlines screamed captions such as, "ASI ACTUABAN LOS ESPIAS DETENIDOS" (Here are the actual spies in detention). Pictures of our equipment and of us were splashed all over the front pages. (The papers did not run faked confessions, or such details as our true names or agency affiliation.) The Cuban prisoners were elated; I received handshakes, winks, and thumping on the back. The prisoners thought we were heroes; the guard couldn't care less. I don't know how the story was handled in the electronic media—we had no access to radio or television.

Interrogation: Round 2

On the second day, I could hear a radio playing loudly from somewhere outside my cell, which I shared with up to thirty Cubans, all of whom spoke English to varying degrees. The announcer was talking about a landing of twelve to fourteen people on the coast of Oriente Province, of which two were Americans. They were trying to get to the hills in the Escambray. One of the Cubans stopped off to talk to his uncle in a small town along the way to let him know that he was a counterrevolutionary and was heading for the hills. The uncle was sympathetic to Fidel and called the authorities, who then captured the whole group. They were picked up that morning. Since Fidel was in New York visiting the United Nations at the time, his brother Raul attended the trial. The verdicts came down as thirty years in jail for the Cubans, and the *pelotón de ejecución* (the firing squad) for the two Americans. That same afternoon, Raul gave a speech and made a reference to the Americans in Havana. The crowd responded by yelling, "Pelotón, pelotón!" Stupid me, I thought it meant *perdón* (pardon) but one of my cellmates drew his finger across his throat. I got the picture.

That night, instead of the usual interrogation office, the guard took me to the second floor of the G2 headquarters building. Judging from the large plush chairs and the polished mahogany desks the size of ping-pong tables, it was obvious that this was where the senior officers worked.

Well, what have we here? A short fat Cuban appeared and took me into his office. He explained how the Cubans were very interested in new types of gadgets and asked me to explain how the equipment that we were caught with works. I did a little quick thinking and I decided that there was nothing to be gained by saying that I didn't know a thing about it. On the other hand, maybe, if I'm lucky, I can sabotage some of the equipment. He gave me some paper and told me to start writing. I asked for a typewriter; one was brought in. He was amazed to see that I could type. He then left the room. I started off with a running account of how a tape recorder works. The fat Cuban came back when I had half a page done and, in a very apologetic voice, told me I didn't get the idea. He tried to explain and I just sat. After an hour or so I'm taken back to my cell. Whatever he was thinking in Spanish, he was unable to explain to me in English.

After awhile I was called out again. I was taken back up to the second floor, where I was delivered to Fatty and another small, thin Cuban, whom I later learned was Ramiro Valdés, chief of G2. All Valdés said was, "Come." The two G2 officers and I left the room and went to a car in the parking lot adjacent to the building. We all got into the front seat, with yours truly in the middle. The drive was uneventful; nothing was said and it was a lot less harrowing than our first car experience.

We arrived at the listening post apartment and Fatty pounded on the door. This produced no answer, so Fatty pounded again. Valdés lets fly some choice words about the idiot who is supposed to be inside guarding the place. After they almost knock the door down, a sleepy-eyed individual opens it. When he sees who it is he straightens up and leaves in a big hurry.

So I am back at the scene of the crime. Now Fatty starts to be specific. He hands me a piece of equipment and asks how it works. With a blank look I say, "It's a receiver." He grabs another piece of equipment, "What is this?" "It's a drill." And so it goes for each piece of equipment on the floor. He'd pick it up and ask what it was, and I'd give a simple answer. This went on for about an hour. A photographer arrived and started taking pictures of me handling the equipment as directed by Fatty. This went on for four hours. The G2 officers were obviously impressed with the equipment, but equally obvious was the fact that they don't know much about electronics. They watched me like hawks sizing up a chicken for a meal, but I managed to leave some battery-operated equipment on and flexed a few printed circuit boards in the transmitters, hoping this would break the foil on the boards. Later we left the apartment, stopped at a coffee stand for a cup of Cuban coffee, and then went back to G2 and my cell.

Back in the G2 cell everybody wanted to know where I was taken and what had happened. Most of their interest centered on whether they had mistreated or manhandled me. I answered in the negative and everybody went back to sleep.

The next afternoon, Bad Teeth interviewed me again in the G2 building, but in a different room. The interrogation room had no windows, but this room had windows with curtains, a rug, and a large desk with an intercom that was on and probably connected to a tape recorder. This time he was looking for something different. After much beating around the bush, he says they want me to make a movie—in color, yet! At the same time I will be on television and radio. Big deal! When I tell him I'm not interested, he takes the other line—no cooperation, get shot. I think to myself that there can't be much cooperation between the higher echelons—Valdés and Fatty—and my friend, Bad Teeth, on the other side of the table. The previous night they used enough film to fill a couple of suitcases; what is this clown up to? Okay, I'll go along and see what happens. I'm brought back to the cell.

At 7:30 p.m. I'm called out again. Bad Teeth, a driver, and I got into a beat-up Buick. He gets a bottle of gasoline from under the front seat, pouring a little into the carburetor while the engine is being cranked and, after it starts, furiously pumps the gas pedal to keep it going. We went back to an apartment adjacent to the target.

Upon arrival, it looked like NBC setting up for a presidential press conference. One very smooth individual started questioning me and I got the impression that he was either a newspaper reporter or a radio announcer. We sparred verbally: "Hey, Mr. Taransky, are you a spy?" I said, "No, I am just a tourist trying to have a good time in Havana." When he asks me if I'm doing this of my own free will. I say no. I point to Bad Teeth and say, "He told me that if I didn't come here I would be shot." All sorts of confusion resulted. Bad Teeth raced over, pale-faced, and stuttered something to the effect that he never said that. I told him to go check his tape recorder. All the cameramen and crew packed their equipment and departed with much haste. I thought to myself, "Well, old buddy, you bought the farm this time."

But some minutes later, all was peaches and cream. Bad Teeth had regained his composure and we left. I was taken down to the floor below, to another apartment much the same as the one we had just left. It looked like somebody had been living there but left in a big hurry. The G2 folks were milling around. Bad Teeth asked, "Where is the installation here?" I played dumb and said, "I really don't know anything about it," even though I could see it. G2 brought in some muscle men who found the end of a microphone cord and started pulling on it. This brought no results, so they tore up the floor, following the mike cord. It ended up next to a power outlet on the wall. A lot of comments are passed in Spanish and everybody seems to be happy with themselves, except for yours truly. I guess a celebration was on because I was handed a bottle of beer. Although the day had left a bad taste in my mouth, the beer tasted pretty good.

Some minutes later we left the apartment. I got into the back seat while Bad Teeth and his two cronies got into the front seat. While it was possible for me to leave the car, I would have had no place to go, no money, and no identification documents. And so started a three-hour odyssey through Havana. We parked in front of a movie for about an hour. The movie let out and my three guards took off one at a time for reasons and destinations unknown. Eventually I'm alone. Escape again is possible, but I still have nowhere to go. After thirty minutes, they all returned and we drove off to another section of town. There's nothing much there when we arrive. As before, they took off one at a time and returned later. Maybe they're testing me, setting up the "shot while trying to escape" scenario. Then followed a lot of driving around town with no apparent purpose. Maybe they're conducting a surveillance detection run. It was almost as if they had forgotten about me sitting in the back seat. This was a wonderful opportunity to take off, but it could have been a trap. Besides, they still had the other guys in G2, as far as I knew.

There was a Texaco map I remember having in the apartment. At the time there was a hurricane coming through the Caribbean. We were plotting the path of the hurricane with Xs on this map. They wanted to know, "What's this map? All these Xs on here? What does that mean?" I told them, "They're not ships. That's where the hurricane is coming." Diversions such as this kept them from getting to the real truth.

Andy experienced some of the classic hot-and-cold treatment that interrogators are often taught to use in breaking down your resistance. After spending all day in a steaming holding cell crowded with sweaty Cuban prisoners, he'd be taken out for questioning. He don't know how much malice aforethought there was in this two o'clock in the morning business. He sat in that room freezing his butt off. They are asking all these questions, and he says, "Come on. Let's turn this air conditioner off." The interrogators didn't listen to him. They just kept on going.

Andy remembers facing the threat of death by thinking, "You're really caught with your guard down because you're not prepared for this. You have to have a talk with yourself and make peace with yourself. That's what I did. In that particular cell where I was at night there was nothing to do. The noise level was awful and the stench and the heat were awful. The interrogations were going on and this guy had me pretty well convinced that they were going to shoot me if I didn't cooperate with him and tell them what they wanted to know." He recalled the story of a marine colonel who was captured in Korea and confessed under duress. Andy said, "I kept thinking of my two sons. I just made up my mind that if I had to get shot that's where I was going to be and I wasn't going to do anything to disgrace my country. I didn't ever want to have any stigma passed on to my sons. I just became matter-of-fact about it—well, we'll see which way things go. I tried not to do anything stupid. But that's the way I felt. I'm going to beat the sons of bitches and I'm never going to give in to them no matter what they do. Until they shoot me, I'm going to outlast them. We were like marines crawling up the beach. We were in combat. We were expendable."

The interrogators didn't beat us or pistol-whip us, but we were a little leery of one very young guard who always was playing with his gun. On one occasion, I complained to the interrogator when the same guard was flipping the cylinder and pulling the trigger. "Tell him that men don't play with guns. Only kids do." When the interrogator passed the admonition on in Spanish, the kid shoved the gun back in his belt and sat there like the schoolmaster had scolded him.

Eventually the interrogations come to a close. Each of the four of us, during our twenty-nine days that we were held at G2, went through four or more middle-of-the-night interrogations. My sessions with Bad Teeth were really loose, not what you see in the movies. Bad Teeth kept referring to a guidebook on interrogation. He used to play with the pages. He would skip through it, go over the last page and pick a question, and then he would ask it. He would hit the middle and pick a question and ask it. That was the way he approached it. If he had started on page one and gone through it, we would have been dead meat.

One night all four of us, Dave, Andy, Mario, and I, were taken out of our cells, put into the library, and left to sit on a sofa outside the office for fourteen hours with no food or bathroom breaks. We were questioned one after the other. Two guards were practicing with an air pistol right next to us and ignored us.

For the next week and a half we were not called out for questioning. So we laid around reading magazines and pocket books that were brought by the American consul, although he was unable to visit us or send letters to our loved ones. The cells were so crowded there was no room to stand. The only hardship I suffered was the lack of exercise and the very unimaginative diet—plenty of it but pretty blah. It was mostly rice or potatoes and a chunk of something resembling meat.

One evening we were called out with a group of Cubans. Andy and I exchanged pleasantries, but we didn't dare say anything else. We were loaded into a truck and off we went. Dave was not with us; he was at Columbia Jail because his cell at G2 was being renovated with the installation of a ventilation fan. But no problem—we stopped to pick him up. The ride through the city was a pleasant change from the dreariness of the cell. The truck didn't have windows but we could see through the vents in the side.

The ride is a real thrill. This guard must have learned to drive at the same place as the first driver. He has a siren and leans on it. We have a couple of near misses but we manage to arrive in one piece. There is a lot of twisting and turning but finally we pull up to a gate, the truck backs up, and we are told to climb out. From the truck we go into what looks like a tunnel, except the inside is finished in wooden paneling and imitation granite. Welcome to La Cabaña, our new home for the next 101 days.

Life in La Cabaña

A. remembers that he hadn't heard of La Cabaña, but people had said, "Oh, my God, don't get sent there," as if we had any input in that decision.

All the prisoners found a place to sit. The front of the office was separated from the walkway by a set of bars. Behind these bars are the pro-Castro rebel soldiers who are in jail for petty crimes. They stare at us like we have two heads. This trait is nicknamed *sapo*. When the Cubans find somebody standing and staring at them, they usually tell the person, "No quiero sapos aqui," meaning, "I don't want any frogs here." Since frogs usually sit on a log staring, the connection is obvious.

The Chinese lieutenant in charge of the office is horsing around with the guards, all of whom are males—poking, grabbing, play boxing—just like recess in a schoolyard.

The guards fingerprint, then search, us. Our civilian clothes are taken away from us and we are given a set of khakis, but without the *P* (for prisoner, or *prisionero*) stenciled on the shirt or pants.

We are led out into the yard where there is a line of prisoners waiting to see the new arrivals. We are taken to Galera 12 (*galera* is Spanish for a galley or gallery) and there we meet Leslie (the Bum) Bradley. He was an American who came to Cuba with Chester Lacayo, who was trying to overthrow Anastasio Somoza, the dictator in Nicaragua. But something went wrong and Chester and Leslie ended up in jail.

My first impression of Leslie is pretty hard to describe. He seems to be the type of person that nothing can shake but, as they say, looks are often very misleading. We sit around listening to Leslie expound on the ways of prison life—whom to trust, whom not to trust.

One person he mentions in particular is the man across the aisle. His name is Pedro, and, according to our new guide, Pedro is not to be trusted. It turns out that Pedro is one of the nicest people that we ever met in prison. When Leslie first arrived in La Cabaña he was helped by Pedro, who gave him everything that he had. Pedro and his friend Louie, both of whom were well off, took Leslie in, fed him, took care of him, and showed him the routines. One day somebody mentioned that supper would be late. Leslie immediately put up a fuss, insisting on getting his meal on time. If this were not bad enough, at one point he met a Cuban girl who came to visit another prisoner on visiting day. She deposits ten pesos (the exchange rate was one peso to one U.S. dollar) to Leslie's account in the office. (This is a standard procedure in Latin American prisons. With this money you can buy cigarettes and miscellaneous items.) She probably felt sorry for him. Somebody finds out and asks Leslie about the money. He gets mad and quits the cooperative, calling everybody a bunch of no-good bums. (A cooperative is a loose configuration of prisoners formed to pick up the food and bring it back to the *galera*.)

Later at the Isle of Pines, Leslie sets a record by not taking a shower for a year. When he does go to the showers it's a cold dreary day, not many Cubans are inclined to shower, so Leslie's arrival in the shower causes a stir and a huge cheer.

At 9:00 p.m., the cannon goes off. Back in the days of Spanish rule, a cannon was fired every night at 9:00 p.m. to signify the closing of the harbor. The tradition has gone on for years and even today the cannon goes off every night at nine. The *galera* chief gets up and makes an announcement. There will be five minutes of silent prayer for the Americans who were shot in Oriente that day. This was the first landing in Cuba of Americans and Cubans. The story of how they were captured varies with the person telling the story, so I guess nobody will ever know the truth. But it made me think a little: here I am in a foreign country with a bunch of excitable, emotional people who will give you their last cigarette or put you in front of the firing squad, either without much thought. The firing squad doesn't bother me as much as it should, but it does seem a shame to get shot for such a piddling thing as bugging.

By 11:30 p.m., it's time to go to bed. Everybody is pretty exhausted and tired. The next problem is to find a bed. Dan gets the bed of Roberto Cruz, a Cuban who was shot the night before. Danny finds a top bunk almost across the aisle. Mario and I are at the front of the *galera*, directly opposite the toilets. Boy, oh boy, the smell is indescribable, and the beds and mattresses are just as crummy. Mario had enough foresight to bring his sheets, so we tear one in two and I get half. At least I can cover the mattress. There were no bedbugs, but the mattresses were very dirty. And so I go to sleep. I never did have any trouble sleeping in the whole two-and-one-half years I was in Cuban prisons. I even managed to earn the nickname Horizontal. Danny found it more difficult to sleep, fighting off the flies and the stink.

Morning comes and we find out about the routine at La Cabaña. The *galeras* are unlocked from 7:00 a.m. to 9:00 p.m. As everybody files out, guards on both sides count the prisoners. For the supposedly sick types, the guards come inside the *galeras* and count the ones still in their beds. This strikes me as pretty good service. You can stay in your bed if you want to sleep in and nobody will bother you. However, you have to make arrangements for somebody to bring you breakfast, which consists of warm milk, a piece of what looks like French bread, and strong demitasse coffee. Mixing the milk and the coffee makes a pretty good combination—a little on the sweet side but very tasty. We ate breakfast on the patio, and then had the freedom of the yard until 9:00 p.m.

The next thing to do is look around and see what it's like. My first impression is that the place is pretty dirty—piles of rubbish and garbage in the middle of the courtyard; trashcans are in use but they are overflowing, and nobody seems to be too interested or concerned. And there's the other item: flies—thousands upon thousands of them cover the patio like a black carpet. But this is just one of the things that you ignore after you get used to it.

There is a lot going on, but until you get used to the prison routine, everything looks like confusion on a grand scale. Actually, everything runs on a schedule. Another guy named Pedro, this one the laundryman, is out scrubbing the prisoners' khakis on one of the marble benches. In the afternoon he will press the clothes and, from this little business, he manages to keep a wife and three children fed, clothed, and housed. "Muscle Beach" is in operation— the boys are grunting and groaning lifting professional gym-class weights. A small dispensary is attending to the hypochondriacs— penicillin shots for colds, Merthiolate for ingrown toenails, sympathy for upset stomachs, advice on what is good and bad for the stomach, and so on. Cubans equate food, drink, and sex in terms of being good or bad for the stomach. You never eat two different types of melon late in the afternoon. It's bound to give you a knot in the stomach. So, obviously, melon in the afternoon is bad for the stomach. I always did wonder about the amounts of food these people eat—usually very heavy, a tremendous quantity, an unbalanced diet—"bad for the stomach."

The dining room is in use as a classroom. Classes are being taught in English, geography, and shorthand. Professor Carbell is moaning about his fate—being unjustly imprisoned. It seems that he is an astrologer and he predicted the fall of Fidel in his newspaper column. For that he was thrown in jail. Dr. Carbell apparently had been educated in the States and spoke with a cultured accent. He was a fat guy with bushy, curly gray hair and a very distinguished beard.

Some of the first friends that I made were the three Díaz Lanz brothers. After their older brother had fled to the States, the rest of the family was thrown into jail. Guillermo is the only one I remember, mostly because I knew him later at the Isle of Pines. He was a quiet artist who spent most of his time painting. I met the other two brothers, but remember them only vaguely.

Louis "Pop" Barreto, a black man who claimed he was in his eighties, was a thoroughly enjoyable person to talk with. Pop had spent quite a few years in New York City around 191st Street running a cigar store, so he was thoroughly acquainted with American customs and habits. We spent a lot of time talking about the USA before going to sleep since his bed was next to mine. Pop's biggest claim to fame was that he had been in every revolution in Cuba and had been a prisoner at the Isle of Pines. At one point during his life a drunk had given the old guy a hard time, so he shot and killed him. For this he had to spend a few years on the island. Pop was the only source of accurate information there was in the prison on what the conditions were at the island. Everybody else had a story, but it was always rumor and conjecture. Pop's wife, an American, was a wonderful person, scared to death about the events that were happening in Cuba, but a delightful person to talk with and, on visiting days, all of us spent some time with her.

After about a week at La Cabaña, the American consul, Hugh Kessler, was finally permitted to see us. I don't know how he heard about our whereabouts. He brought cigarettes and reading material and deposited money with the prison officials so we could buy the odds and ends we needed to make life more comfortable. Hugh was our one real confidant and friend all through our stay at La Cabaña and we were all very sad to find out that he had passed away during our imprisonment. He died while stationed in Brazil while we were at the Isle of Pines. He was with us until Cuba broke diplomatic relations with the United States.

The most celebrated character that we met in prison was William (Bill) Morgan. Typical of most Americans that went to Cuba to make a fast buck, Bill had a background that was, to say the least, pretty bad. It included a dishonorable discharge from the army, supposedly for a barroom fight in Japan where he allegedly killed someone; and in and out of trouble with various state and federal law enforcement agencies, and so on. I have no knowledge of his alleged crimes. Even with all this, Bill was a fascinating person to talk with and hear his side of his sagas in Pinar del Río. He was a good guy to know because everyone knew I was his friend and it is not nice to mess with Bill Morgan's friends. When any of us three Americans discussed anything with him, we felt Bill was always truthful with us. We never had reason to doubt him. With the Cubans, however, the stories were, I suspect, inflated just a bit. Most of the Cubans looked at Bill with a little bit of awe, seeing a revolutionary from the hills who actually participated in some fighting against the Batista soldiers. Bill was very good at barroom brawling. Several Cubans went groaning to the dispensary with aching kidneys after a horsing-around session with Bill.

The first ten days all four of us—Dave, Andy, Mario, and me—didn't do very much talking among ourselves. We were too busy meeting others.

Standing in line for food was always a chore. The workers, those with special diet needs, cooperatives, and the prisoners on death row all were allowed in line ahead of the rest of the prison population. We always ended up pretty close to the end of the line, and usually the portion of the line that had to stand in the sun waiting to get into the dining room.

At this point I had broken out in what is referred to locally as *fungo* (fungus)—white blotches where the pigment of the skin is eaten away by a fungus, a condition similar to athlete's foot fungus. The dispensary had been coating the affected areas on my shoulders and stomach with Sulfathiazol (grease), which naturally melts with heat. Standing in the sun roasting and feeling the little driblets of grease running down my back was one of the most uncomfortable feelings that I have had. This, coupled with the fact that we had no shoelaces or a belt, made me feel like a real bum. Here I was, standing around with a piece of rope holding up my pants, shoes flapping around and about to fall off, grease soaking through my shirt. I felt and looked very disagreeable at that point.

The food at La Cabaña was always good, a little on the greasy side but nevertheless sufficient. The greatest pleasure I remember, at this point, was a full cup of strong Cuban coffee and a cigarette (I quit cold turkey in late 1964). After lunch I would enjoy these out in the comparative quiet of the patio, since most of the prisoners had gone into the *galeras* to relax or take the afternoon *siesta*.

One of the most sacred institutions in Latin American jails is visiting day. Visitors are allowed in once a week, usually on Sunday. The morning of the visit, people are generally up at the crack of dawn shaving, pressing their clothes, borrowing a set of khakis, and so on. The thing that surprises me most is the time and effort that Cuban men put into combing their hair, applying deodorant, powder, and hair tonic. After a few hours the *galera* starts to smell like a perfume factory. The inmates are awaiting their visitors, and finally the hour comes and the families—women and children— arrive. Male visitors are also allowed at La Cabaña. Within a short time it looks more like a Sunday afternoon in the park—children are running back and forth and getting in everyone's way. The amount of food brought in is tremendous. Mario's maid brings enough food for all four of us on her visits. For the more well-to-do, two or three shopping bags come in filled with canned goods, smoked meat, and just about everything imaginable. For those that don't have much, sandwiches. But everybody has more than they can handle, and sharing is the order of the day. The prisoners tuck away whatever is left until the next visiting day.

Of course, the most important thing is the news. Everybody is getting filled in on who is doing what, when the invasion is coming, and what the latest news is from Miami. Most of it is hearsay and rumor, but it's always good news for the prisoners. Even during the discouraging days after the Bay of Pigs, I never heard any stories that you could call discouraging. We had access to all the Havana newspapers, but not to any American papers. We did not have to smuggle messages out because we could write letters or send cables. Better yet, we gave all our messages to Hugh Kessler. We learned of the Bay of Pigs through the concealed prisoner radio at the Isle of Pines.

The Bay of Pigs did affect our relationship with one of the Cuban prisoners, Jack Osorio, Fidel's personal interpreter and a very friendly schoolteacher type. He had lectured us often on how the United States had betrayed the Cubans. But after the Bay of Pigs failed, he would not talk to or acknowledge us.

Thanksgiving Day 1960 was a memorable one for all four of us. Rosa, Mario's maid, had learned that he was in La Cabaña and visited him several times. After a while we made arrangements through our lawyer, Fernando Colomar, for her to bring us food, which she did, by the shopping-bag full. (Colomar was a Cuban national who was employed for us by Kessler. We met with him usually once a week or when he had questions or had something to pass along to us. He was identified in John Martino's book under the alias Dr. Camargo.) We could usually count on seeing four bags crammed with all kinds of canned food, meat, roast chickens, and salads. Most of the items were impossible to find in Havana at that time and we received many comments from the Cubans about the type of food that we were getting although, when it came to quantity, the Cubans were doing much better than we were. Rosa was probably getting the food through the consul, who was getting it from Miami.

The Trial

We were doing very well by the time our trial came up on December 17, 1960. Everybody was on edge that Saturday morning. Our lawyer had stopped in the previous day to warn us that the trial was to take place the next day and to be ready for anything. So, bright and early, we were ready. By this time, we had received blue jeans and jackets so we wouldn't be going to trial in khakis. The current rumor in the prison was that anybody who wore khakis usually ended up with a pretty stiff sentence, since the tribunals were reminded by the khakis of the Batista regime. Everybody made an effort to wear something other than khakis, usually the blue denim jackets and pants of the common prisoner. So on a dull Saturday morning we paced around the patio, shivering. The temperature had taken a nosedive and the wind from the north was keeping things cool in Havana.

Our names were finally called to report to the office for trial. We were at the gate almost before they finished reading the announcements. After being taken inside, we were given copies of the statement of charges which, in effect, said that we were enemies of the state. The prosecutor was asking for thirty years. At least they weren't asking for the death sentence.

We milled around the office for a while before we were taken outside the prison compound and put into a truck. From the Fortress of La Cabaña we went to what looked like a deserted building on the military reservation. This was the courthouse. When the truck stopped and we got out I saw our lawyer, American consul Hugh Kessler, and two G2 officers that were among the men who arrested us. We were herded upstairs to the second floor. There were lots of people around—mostly Fidel's rebel soldiers (those that were with Fidel in the hills) and volunteer soldiers (*milicianos*), those who jumped on the bandwagon after Fidel came to power.

Presently the tribunal arrived and a scruffier lot I have never seen. The chief looked like something from hobo heaven—bearded, dirty, and wearing a rumpled uniform. The only person that looked like a professional military type was the naval officer on the tribunal. He alone was clean—with a presentable uniform.

As it was a military tribunal, they had representatives from, I guess, all the services that they had. The chief of the tribunal had a beard. It must have been a legal sort of trial. You went up and sat on a chair in front of the tribunal. They'd ask the questions in Spanish.

They would translate. Then you would answer. He would translate back to them.

There was nothing startling about the trial. The prosecutor rolled on and on about our crimes. (I can't offer many details, because my Spanish was not that good at the time.) Some of the questions I remember being asked were: How old are you? Are you married? Is this your first time in Cuba? Our lawyer gave a brilliant legal defense, according to Kessler. Basically, he said that we had not violated the sovereignty of Cuba and were well within the legal definitions of Fidel's declarations in the Sierra Maestra. The whole trial took about four hours.

I had a seat next to a window that was broken; a cold breeze was coming in and chilling me to the bone. I remember having a tremendous need to urinate during the whole trial. The urge to urinate is, as you know, greatest in cold water. Even though the trial was four hours long, it felt like a much longer time. When I did make it to the bathroom, I must have passed a gallon of water. None of this was attributable to worry; I just was very uncomfortable and I had a great urge to get to a bathroom; everything else was secondary. I did not feel threatened or anxious during the trial.

After the trial we went downstairs and sat on a green couch. Hugh Kessler bought us Cokes. He was elated. "You guys are great. Man, you're famous," he said. "Your answers were what you would expect from John Charles Daly." He thought we did a great job. He said, "Okay, we'll see you next visiting day." (That was the last we'd see of him, or any other U.S. official for more than two years. Right after that, they broke diplomatic relations.) Before he left, we shared a few short comments here and there, and the nervous guard, for something to do, told us to stop talking. A few minutes later we were escorted back to La Cabaña by two guards toting M1 rifles. Mario talked with the guards as we walked back. He was talking to them in Spanish, and, again, my Spanish was not good enough to know what was being said. They seemed to be pretty well at ease, laughing and wisecracking all the way back. While walking back to the fortress the thought occurred to me that it had been three months since we'd seen the outside. It was a strange feeling to see houses, fields, and people.

Back in the prison most people were surprised to hear that we had had our trial. Rosa, the maid, is there with the usual load of goodies, since this is a visiting day. Now all we can do is sit back and sweat it out. It's either the Isle of Pines or the quick trip back to the States. Somehow I just can't believe that we'll be getting back to the States. As Danny says, "It's too easy." And with our luck it will probably have to be done the hard way. We had never officially been told, but we were convicted of "activities against the security of the Cuban State." Two days later, the court sentenced us to ten years in prison. News of the sentence didn't get into U.S. newspapers until 1961, with our cover names intact (other than Dan-Brunt, which was a little frayed—it was variously misspelled as Dan Brunet, Danbrunt, and Van-Brunt.). Mario was convicted with us, but was later deported to the States.

It's now Christmas, 1960. Rosa has brought six shopping bags filled with food and presents from our families: electric frying pan, transistor radios—it's almost like home. Thankfully, we weren't dependent upon Cuban stations for the news; we listened to WKWF from Key West, Florida, in the morning and clear channel fifty-kilowatt stations at sundown and late at night. We have our little cooperative set up and, with a footlocker between the beds to store the food in and the electric frying pan to cook in, we are doing very well. It's obvious that the gifts are from home. Danny gets a couple of books that were on his night table. Daniel the same. The guards did not bother us or steal the stuff. Mario is a little confused by all the gifts we receive and by all the notes that are included in the books. He, being the wheeler dealer type and a little paranoid, is suspicious of the whole scenario. Who is pulling what on us? His eyes are wild with fear. I manage to gloss things over for a while. Then when he gets the fruitcake with a note from his wife, he is convinced that the articles came from home.

Little do we know that this is going to be the first of three Christmases in jail. Materially, this first Christmas, at La Cabaña, was the best one of all, although the others stand out for different reasons. Christmas at La Cabaña was pretty nice—we dressed in our clean, pressed khakis and had wine with our dinner. The wine was courtesy of the winemaker from Bacardi, but obviously not one of his finer vintages. It tasted more like vinegar than wine. The second Christmas, at the Isle of Pines, was much skimpier food wise. The last Christmas we watched the Bay of Pigs brigade leave for the States while we stayed behind and ate our watery soup.

That first Christmas comes and goes and things are getting just a little bit tight. Castro is doing a lot of name-calling and it is pretty clear that there is no love lost between the Cubans and the Americans. This is a great time to be in Havana's jails. The people start coming into La Cabaña by the carful.

The newest addition is John R. Gentile. The first time I see him I am startled—the resemblance between him and Jack Palance is amazing. During our stay at La Cabaña I saw John a few times. He moved into the *galera* with Bill Morgan. Morgan was one of Castro's commanders in Oriente Province who was jailed for plotting against Fidel. Gentile and Morgan stuck together, which was okay with all of us. All three of us were very leery of Gentile—why he was in jail and what his connection with Morgan was. He was a complete stranger to us. Was he really an American or an agent provocateur? In jail you don't trust anybody you don't know.

The next American we meet is John Martino, who would later write *I Was Castro's Prisoner*. John had many people buffaloed but, after talking with him for quite a while, I decided he had more baloney than three meat-packing plants. His stories were never the same—so many inconsistencies—and when these were pointed out he would just ignore them. Daniel, Danny, and I agreed that here was a first-class storyteller. I'm very flattered that John devotes a couple of pages in his book to Messrs. Taransky, Danbrunt, and Carswell, having deduced that we were just poor innocent types that had been suckered into going to Cuba. He believed our cover story.

And so it went, with more and more people coming in every day,

303

conditions getting worse and worse, and more dirt and noise. A natural resentment on the part of the old hands builds up because the newcomers force changes. Everybody had to give up space and things are not as comfortable as before. Pedro the laundryman finally has a trial after two years in the jug and is released. What a blow! The best laundryman is leaving. We take up a collection and send Pedro off with thirty pesos and best wishes.

Yet another prison—El Castillo del Príncipe castle in Havana—is emptied and all the prisoners held there are returned to La Cabaña. I don't know why they were with us, but they were held for about sixty days. Things are really tight, but old friends come back and it's a welcome break in the routine to catch up on the rumors from somewhere else.

1961: Year of Executions

New Year's Day 1961 comes and there is much shouting and hollering by the guard force. The prison commandant makes a midnight speech. He opens the *galeras* to let people out into the patio to welcome in the New Year, but everybody is so much in the dumps thinking about their families and what is going to happen to them that few people go out. Besides, who wants to get out of a warm bed and wander around in the cold?

The next person we meet is Dr. Julio Yberra, age twenty-eight, a graduate of the medical schools of Vienna, a pilot (he holds a stateside commercial ticket and instrument rating), skin diver, and linguist, proficient in French, German, Italian, English, and Spanish. He wins my nod of approval when he takes Mario down a few pegs by conversing with him in French and, when Mario falters, switching to Italian and giving Mario a run for his money. Julio was a man with a terrific brain and a very definite set of ideals: an anticommunist willing to die for his ideas. He did pay the supreme penalty and his death by the firing squad started the orgy of shootings that were heard by everybody in La Cabaña in January 1961. I never did hear shots, even though *La Pared* (The Wall) was only a few hundred feet from where I slept. The shooting sort of took the starch out of the Cubans' sails when they realized this could happen, and it could happen to them.

Our *galera* seemed to be the one where most of the people were being called for execution. Fellows that lived beside me and across the aisle were being called out for trial at four in the afternoon, the results of which were not apparent until the next morning. At 8:00 a.m. one or two, and sometimes none, of the men in the same trial would be back in the *galera*. The morbidly curious would be at the gates to the *galera* in the morning wanting to know who didn't come back from the trial. (I guess it's this same trait that makes people rush to see an accident.) The soldiers and *milicianos* can attend if they want and watch the victim get shot. Although I have never met a spectator, the stories seem to be consistent. It's just like a Roman circus—the spectators are laughing and joking and getting a big kick out of it. I'm sure the participants don't feel the same way.

A. has similar recollections about this experience:

You actually hear them getting shot. At two o'clock in the morning you hear them going off, and you see what eight M1s do to a person. There was a moat around this monument, which made it like a castle fortress. And they would stand them up there and shoot them. We were right around the corner and of course the sound is echoed right down this *galera*. They would bring in these young *milicianos*. They would all yell and hoot. Like the old days with hangings. And a couple of guys would resist, you know, and they would come and shoot you in the legs and break your bones and then lay you down on your knees and you couldn't get up, and then shoot you. They were doing that. Over the moat was a drawbridge. We were taken across that to our trial, and I could look down there and see where they were shooting. Red meat was still there.

We later learn that the Cuba and the United States have broken off relations. This news spreads like wildfire through La Cabaña the night that it is announced. Mario seems to be very shaken up by this turn of events. I don't think much of it one way or the other since I feel we are slated to be around for the long pull and we won't be getting any more visits by Kessler.

Our next big surprise is the day that Mario is deported, sometime in January 1961. At 10:00 a.m. his name is announced over the loudspeaker. He is ordered to come to the office with all of his possessions. I wait for the rest of the names—ours—to be read off. They don't come. Rats. That makes it official. We help Mario pack up all his belongings. He passes out a few things among the prisoners and off he goes. I'm not sure why he was freed, but I think he probably cut a deal with the G2. The one thing I thought was a little put on was the look of shock on his face and his actions. They just didn't look real. So Mario left La Cabaña with the three of us waving good-bye. He went back to the States and later managed the Naval Officers Club at Guantanamo. Well, that's it. Now we sit back and see what happens next.

We met five soldiers of fortune—Beck, Bean, Baker, Gibson, and Smith—who got involved with some Cuban exiles in Miami smuggling guns into Cuba. They were provided with a boat and a load of guns and set off for what they thought was Cuba. After some hours at sea, Baker, who was an older fellow, asked Gibson, the leader of the group, if they were going to Cuba. Gibson replied, "Yes." Baker replied, "If we are going south to Cuba, how come the sun is rising on our right?" (Rub-a-dub-dub . . .) They then returned to Miami and repeated the trip again the next night. This time they headed south. After some time they were intercepted by a Cuban patrol boat and taken to Havana. Beck was carrying a photo of himself with a Cuban exile (gangster), which undoubtedly was responsible for them being taken into custody. There were no guns in the boat when they were picked up; obviously, they were thrown overboard.

Island Hopping

January 22, 1961, arrives as a dreary, rainy Sunday that is spent inside the *galeras*. Everything is damp and wet and it's pretty miserable. I spend the day working on a model boat that came in via

Rosa, but my heart is not in the job. (These little handicrafts were later seized in the *requisa* [body search or shakedown] when we went to the Isle of Pines.) I hit the sack and it doesn't seem that I have been asleep for more than an hour when the loudspeaker is going off. I check my watch and it's 3:00 a.m. Well, that means a shipment to the Isle of Pines. The voice drones on and on; finally, it comes to our names and keeps on going. The number of names on the list amazes everybody. This is going to be a big *cordillera* (chain) of around 250 prisoners. We pack all our possessions and leave behind the things we know will be taken away from us, such as the frying pan, extra plates, knives and forks. We left our watches with John Martino to give to the lawyer to pass to the Swiss group who had taken the place of the U.S. embassy in Havana. In my case, I had a Rolex Oyster Perpetual that I had purchased in Japan for about $250. The Swiss later admitted to Danny that they had his and my watches, but they were never returned to us. Daniel kept his, which was a cheap Timex, and it kept on ticking until he was released from jail. I never saw mine again.

After packing we stand around and wait until 5:30 a.m., when we are taken out of the La Cabaña gate and lined up by twos to be taken to buses. The buses take us to Columbia, a military city. We are unloaded and marched to a spot on the taxi strip to wait for the airplanes.

A few of the prisoners are ready to give up, Oscar Tuya among them. He just collapses on the hardpan (ground), and from the look on his face, I'd say he has totally given up. Oscar was a courtly gentleman in his eighties, obviously a man with money, manners, and a very aristocratic bearing, who had probably been involved in several coups and revolutions, but never anything like this. This revolution was not something that he could handle. The rules had changed. Money and influence were ineffective. When people were sent to prison, they could not buy their way out. I felt sorry for Oscar and tried to cheer him up and convince him not to give up. He did snap back a little and tried to accept the situation. I also felt much better after having tried to lift his spirits. I also lifted my own.

The eagerness of most of the prisoners to get on the airplanes is amazing, but I guess most of them have never been on an airplane.

The day really drags. It's a good thing we brought something to eat. We open up some peaches and saltines, which suffices for lunch.

Things take an interesting turn. One of Mario's unnamed friends from La Cabaña is doing some plotting and a move is afoot to offer one of the pilots a bundle of money to fly to Miami instead of going to the Isle of Pines. The pitch is made and falls through. The guard who was approached reports it to somebody and the next thing we know a sergeant arrives and asks for all the Americans. Danny and I are put into one airplane and John Gentile and Daniel are put into the other. These were the last two planes of the day headed for the Isle of Pines.

We are the first to get into the planes and are told to sit in the back. The guards sit in the front. There were twenty-seven prisoners and six guards; there is no hope for any kind of maneuvering. In about forty-five minutes we arrive at the Isle of Pines. We are unloaded from the airplanes and put into trucks.

Welcome to the Isle of Pines

It is a desolate-looking place, to say the least. Mario was always commenting that this was a terrific spot for tourists, but I can't see it myself.

The model prison at the Isle of Pines was built in 1929–30 and, for its time, was a radically different type of prison. Castro kept six thousand political prisoners in circular structures designed to contain forty-five hundred. The four principal buildings (circulars) are round, approximately 155 feet in diameter, with six floors— five stories of cells surrounding a guard tower. The ground floor is called the *planta baja*, and the first floor is what Americans consider the second floor. There are ninety-three cells on each floor and each cell measures approximately four feet wide by nine feet deep. A projection in each cell supports a commode and a sink, but there is no running water. Water hours are from 5:00 to 7:30 a.m. and 3:00 to 5:00 p.m. on the *planta baja*. The sixth floor is different from the rest of the floors in that there are no walls. Circular 4 had just been painted light green; very different from what we expected. We expected a dreary, dark, dirty, dungeonlike building, but were pleasantly surprised. In the center of the building rises the guard tower. At any point in the building you can look right into the openings of the guard tower. The openings were designed to put guns in, although no guns were visible.

We arrive at the prison in the afternoon and are unloaded in front of the main building. A common prisoner takes our names and tells us to give up our money. After this is done we are double-timed up the stairs into the building and then down another flight of stairs to the *requisa* area.

This one is a pip. You strip to your shorts and socks, put your belongings on the counter, and wait. The guard goes through all my stuff and I manage to come through with blankets, underwear, a broken toothbrush, and cigarettes. Oh, well, the good old days are gone. Extra clothing, canned food, vitamins, and medicine are all taken away. We are given a new set of khakis with *P* stenciled on the back of the shirt and the pants (not even long pants, but riding breeches). When this is finished, we are marched out of the *requisa* room back up the stairs, turning left out of the building and under a guard tower, complete with a machine gun and light.

The first thing that hits you is the roar that is coming from the buildings. It sounds like a bunch of wild animals. When you walk between the buildings and hear the roar of the people, you don't know what you're getting into. Your first impression is, "My God, when I get in there, they're going to tear me apart limb from limb." Because they all sounded like crazies. They don't talk to each other; they yell. When a Cuban sees his buddy across the building, he yells at him and they continue the conversation.

Garbage and trash are piled underneath the windows. Evidently they just throw the stuff out the window. Dirty laundry is hanging out the windows. It's a crummy-looking spot, to put it mildly. There is a lot of hollering and shouting on the part of the guards. This is to subdue the prisoners, and it's certainly effective.

We march between Circulars 1 and 2, around the mess hall, to Circular 4. We stop, the guard opens the bars, and in we go. The door clangs shut. We look up and notice that everybody is staring at us. A lot of confusion follows; we are still lined up, but nobody seems to know what to do next. In the middle of the floor was a little table, where sat two prisoners with a notebook. We registered our names and the number of years (ten) of our sentences. Then followed much milling around.

A Cuban who identified himself as Manolo Bonza approached me and asked if I was an American. I said "yes," and he grabs all of my stuff and says to follow him upstairs. He didn't want another Cuban moving in with him. He tells us that they are dirty. They never wash. Get a nice clean American. Danny, Daniel, and John do likewise. I end up sharing a cell with Manolo; Danny and Daniel are next door. John is with another unnamed Cuban. Circular 4, cells 82 and 83, fifth floor, will be our home for some time to come and the location for lots of happenings.

Settling In: "Nothing Is for Sure"

Of course, we are all full of questions and Manolo is trying hard to answer them all. The one sage comment he makes that holds true for all the time we spent at the prison is "Nothing is for sure."

Inside Circular 4 there were individual cells but no bars, so we were free to roam through the whole building. The cells were about six feet wide by twelve feet deep. There was provision for two bunks in each cell, but most of them didn't have bunks. You could have from two to fifteen prisoners in a cell. If you had a lot of friends and they didn't have a place to sleep, then you could find a lot of people in your cell.

Beds are the first things on our minds. You either have one sent in by your family or you have money sent to you and you buy a bed from some other prisoner at a cost of thirty pesos. You could buy a bunk from somebody if you had the going price. If a guy had a bunk and he was hungry, he'd sell you the bed because he could then go to the prison store and buy cigarettes and extra goodies.

It's obvious where we will sleep for the time being—the terrazzo floor. Fortunately, it's not too dirty. Manolo keeps his cell fairly clean. Danny and Daniel are going to have it a little rougher since there is absolutely nothing in their cell—it's completely bare. A cold floor combined with the cool night breeze makes sleeping pretty uncomfortable.

We soon learn how a prisoner becomes hungry enough to sell his bunk. Our first meal at the Isle of Pines is really something. Breakfast was half milk, half coffee, and a piece of bread. The noon meal was rice and beans with a half cup of marmalade for dessert. Supper was a dish of beans. Most of the prisoners—at least the old-timers—are pretty happy about the arrangement—good food tonight. What must the bad days be like? At the time of my arrest, I was a lean 160 pounds; I wore down to 125 pounds or less on the island. A. claims it was less, and that you could see every bone in my body. A. weighed 170 pounds in September 1960. He weighed himself and calculated from kilograms to pounds and I think he was down to about 110 pounds. C. also lost weight.

Everyone wanders around finding out what is what. John has found Pedro, Lester Bradley's friend from La Cabaña, on another floor and he has invited us down to have tea later on. Some of the cells look like real dungeons. Small kerosene stoves in the cells have made the ceilings and walls sooty. The cells are full of boxes and various odds and ends, giving the impression of a junkyard with a nice greasy layer of soot.

For me it's been a pretty tiring day, so I go to the sack early. I spread out some paper on the floor, put down a sheet, fold the blanket so I can slip between it, and drop off to sleep. All during the night I wake up to shift positions. Boy, that floor was certainly hard and the cold breeze coming through the barred opening in the wall made for a mighty uncomfortable night.

Morning arrives and it must be pretty early. The sun is not up yet but people are moving around. I look around and it seems that breakfast is being served. I go down five floors to the *planta baja* where I get a cup of milk and a piece of bread, and that's it. No seconds. Nothing more until noon. Big difference from La Cabaña.

Surviving

Time is the prisoner's enemy. The days are certainly going to be long ones around here. Our first impression is that there is nothing to do, no sunshine, no patio to exercise in. There's just a big building to wander around in and stand around looking at the other prisoners or talking with them. It takes a little getting used to, but we do.

The first thing is to get busy with some projects. A few of the former Batista air force people are in the circular and one, Raúl López, takes us under his wing and volunteers to teach us Spanish. So every morning at nine we sit for a lesson with Raúl. Our progress is pretty good and after a few days we have a one-hundred-word vocabulary. Raúl also gives us our most valuable possession—a small wooden bench.

We carried that little bench around with us. Of course, we sat on it, but we also used it when we showered. It gave us a place to put our towels and clean clothes instead of putting them on a grungy, dirty floor. There were no hooks or a place to hang anything. The bench served as a handy portable shelf. We managed to keep it for eighteen months before it was taken away in a *requisa*.

I start to realize that so many things I took for granted and never thought about before are now unavailable luxuries. Running water, or just plain water, is a problem here. We don't have anything to store water in and it is a necessity. We brought a bucket from La Cabaña, which came through the *requisa*, and that is used for storing drinking water, which only comes every three days. The water from the tap in the *planta baja* is undrinkable but good enough for showers and washing dishes. Daniel swaps his Zippo lighter for a five-gallon can to store the drinking water in and we use the small bucket to store wash water. I never thought you could shave with a cup of water, but I learned to do it. That included a complete shave and rinsing the razor, too. It's amazing what you can do when you have to.

The first few days of getting used to the routine are punctuated by a little excitement. One afternoon, while things are pretty quiet, a fight breaks out on the fifth floor, accompanied by much hollering and yelling, buckets banging, bottles breaking, and a general roar in the building. The Mayor of the circular descends to the *planta baja*. (The Mayor, whose real name I never knew, was elected as such by the Batista army prisoners. Both the Batista army and the anti-Castro prisoners were coexisting at arm's length. The animosity was apparent from time to time.) The announcer for the circular, whose job it was to yell at the top of his lungs and act as a PA system for the circular, is shouting for everybody to stop, but things keep right on going. Finally the fight stops and the reason for the Grand Combat is that somebody called someone else an SOB. Fists swing, chains from beds are wielded—with very little accuracy—and, in general, a lot of hollering and yelling is going on. Occasionally a few good blows are struck. It breaks down that the Batista men are fighting the counterrevolutionaries. So it goes. There was a loose collection of groups—Batista army, anti-Castro, student activists, and anti-American radicals. There were no common criminals mixed in with the political prisoners, except for one. He had been given a life sentence and was caught aiding the political prisoners, so his designation was changed from common criminal to political prisoner.

The next bit of excitement is when Circular 3 is having a *requisa* and some brave soul hollers out of the window at the guards, calling them and their mothers various names. This incenses the guards, naturally, and they come storming over to the circular. During this, all the brave types are yelling over the rail and out the windows. However, when the guard sticks his pistol through the door and sends a shot through the roof, things quiet down considerably. Many of the loud mouths are observed hitting the floor and diving for the safety of their cells. The guards enter the circular and proceed to do some yelling of their own, waving their guns around with an invitation for anyone to come downstairs. Nobody accepts the invitation. The guards leave and things are quiet. The sergeant that came in is called Pingita (the Spanish diminutive for the male organ) because of his size. In all the time I spent at the Island, he was the only one of the guards who seemed to take an interest in his appearance, with his olive drab uniform, which was always pressed and clean. He presented a 180-degree difference from his compatriots, who took no interest in how they looked. They were unshaven, dirty, and generally sloppy in their appearance.

Ten days have passed since we have come to the Island and, at this point, it's obvious that we are in bad shape if the lawyer doesn't send money or arrange for somebody to send things from the outside. We have sent collect telegrams to Rosa, Mario's maid, to get to the lawyer and send us money, beds, and arrange for a canteen service. For those that can afford it, restaurants and private individuals on the island prepare food and put it into metal containers that are delivered to the prison. The prison administration, in turn, delivers these containers to each building. With this supplement to the prison diet, a person can get along very well. So far we have had nothing extra in the way of food. John manages to scrounge a can of condensed milk from somewhere, and we save some of our white rice and pour the condensed milk over it. It makes for the best-tasting rice pudding I've ever had. Somebody finds some cinnamon and, even though there is not enough to taste beyond one mouthful, the whole concoction tastes very good.

Tomorrow makes two weeks that we have spent at the Island and it's been interesting so far, but I'm ready to have a substantial meal and a bed to sleep in. It's afternoon and we're all looking over the rail at the packages coming in, and our expectations are raised. There are a lot of cots being delivered. Maybe we will luck out today. We do—three of the folding beds are for us—whoopee! We waste no time getting these up to the fifth floor. Our luck is holding out. A lot of the beds that have come have had the mattress cut open with a bayonet, but ours don't have a mark on them.

After we get them to the fifth floor, it's time to try them out. So into the sack I go. Boy, what comfort I get from sleeping on something soft for a change instead of a hard floor!

Monday rolls around and our names are called to come and get our packages. Our lawyer has contacted a family on the island and has come through with canteens. Boy, am I ready! We carry them upstairs and look inside, where we discover French fries, lettuce-and-tomato salad, and steak! Boy, I'm ready to tear in and so is everybody else. But we decide that we should wait until supper time. So meanwhile, we try the bread and butter that came with the canteen. The first slice of bread tastes just like rich pound cake, like the kind you see on TV commercials. I never knew that plain old bread could taste like that. Putting butter on it just makes it even better. Ever hear of gourmet bread? That was it!

So for a month, we eat very well. But like everything else, good things have to come to an end, and they do. One month to the day later, the quality of the canteen changes radically—chicken necks, noodles—good food for somebody that is starving, but for people that have been spoiled on steak, it's a step down the ladder. So off goes a telegram to our lawyer, but things never get back to what they were before. I guess the lawyer thought it was getting too expensive. He didn't know if he was going to get paid. As the months wore on, the food became worse: watery soup with no meat or vegetables; no protein to speak of. The standard fare consisted of one of either cabbage, macaroni, or fish soup. The macaroni was horrible.

At the Isle of Pines, in general, we found an abundance of disease, filth, bedbugs, lice, and rats in an environment with a shortage of medical care, sanitation, food, and water. (As an indication of how Cubans assess their own prison conditions, in late 1987 at federal detention centers in Louisiana and Georgia, Cuban detainees, fearing a return to Cuba, rioted and took hostages.) The water piped to the ground floor of the circular had the smell of dead fish and was only good for showering or washing clothes. Drinking water was trucked in and dumped into a cistern. A. remembers:

We would go down with our little bucket and get our gallon or two of water, take it up to the cell, put it on the floor and put something over it to keep out the flies. And that's what you drank from. We never got dysentery because we were very particular. We washed our dishes. The average Cuban, when he would finish his rice and beans, would throw the bowl on the floor and let it sit there until it hardened up and there was a crust all over it. Flies had been down in the crap room and were all over the bowl. Then they wondered why they got dysentery.

Getting a pail was tricky, but Dave obtained one by swapping his Zippo lighter. We carried the brackish water up five flights in five-gallon cans to flush the toilets. A. thinks that's how he got his hernia.

Andy also blames the wrong type of food eaten on custom. "The problem was the damn Spaniards came into Cuba and gave them the wrong diet for the climate. Rice and beans are the worst things you could eat in that climate."

Keeping occupied between the struggle to get fed was difficult. How do you occupy your mind? We made a Monopoly board from memory; the game fascinated the Cubans. A. made a slide rule from a cigar box, working out logarithms from an old engineering book that somehow had remained in the circular. Andy said, "The slide rule served its purpose. It enabled me to do these little problems, and Dave was an engineer, too. I remember we got into descriptive geometry."

We also made a radio. An earpiece had been smuggled in, and we scrounged up Russian transistors and pieces of tubing used for intravenous feeding. To make a battery, we obtained zinc from a pail, copper from a wire, and copper sulfate from the sparse medical supplies. The radio worked like an overgrown crystal set. We sometimes picked up broadcasts from a fifty-thousand-watt New Orleans station.

Religion played a quiet part in our lives, although we rarely spoke of it. Dave C. was a Lutheran, A. was an Episcopalian, and I was lapsed Catholic. I suppose our faith in ourselves came from our fundamental faith in God.

The training we got during our military service—C. and I had been in the army; A. was a former marine—was a big advantage. Andy says, "We were used to discipline and used to improvising if we had to." Many of our fellow inmates, such as the political prisoners from the professional and wealthier layers of Cuban society, lacked that advantage. "A lot of these Cubans had been waited on by nannies all their lives. They had never picked up anything. They were used to having someone else do it. And if they didn't have someone to help them, I don't think they could survive. They had no preparation for life except to be waited on."

Depressed, disoriented, and defeated, some of the Cubans became suicidal. A. recalls, "Usually, they would jump off about the fifth floor and hit the concrete, and that was it. They would carry them down to the hospital. The doctor explained that the liver and kidneys would break like a balloon."

However, we were able to prevent one suicide. We were standing on our little railing one day and Dave looked over and saw Professor Carbell, our acquaintance from La Cabaña, the astrologer and journalist who had predicted Fidel's fall from power and so was serving two years. The Cubans all stepped back because they were afraid of him. Andy and I ran as fast and as hard as we could and grabbed him and pulled him back. Dr. Carbell was filthy as hell. Andy said, "I was almost afraid to put my hands on him. He was so filthy and slimy. The first thing I did when I got back to our cell was to wash my hands."

An American soldier of fortune, Richard Allen Pecoraro, was in a similar condition of absolute filth and had gone mad. He would get into a fetal position and hide in a corner, which is what he was doing when we ran into him. The Cubans would go into his cell and poke him with a stick. He would push them away and they would poke him some more. Finally he would growl. He would rant at them. They would run away. Then they would come back and poke at him again for amusement, like kids poking at a dog. Andy felt that we as Americans could not let this happen to a fellow American. So we befriended him, brought him to our cell, cleaned him up, fed him, and had one of the imprisoned Cuban psychiatrists talk to him through an interpreter. It always amazed me that you could psychoanalyze someone through an interpreter and determine that valium might help. Eventually, we got some of the drug for him.

During this time we have our first *comisario* (commissary) purchase. There are a lot of things to buy, but we are somewhat limited by lack of money. The money sent to us has not been posted to our account, so we can buy only a limited number of items. Nevertheless, we are fat with cigarettes, canned meat, and large cans of pears made by Swift and Company. How many we had escapes me, but I remember that the four of us polished off one gallon-sized can. It was so good we had another gallon. The results of eating that much fruit when you haven't had any for a while are pretty disastrous—terrific gas pains and many quick trips to the toilet. But it was worth it. After eating a bland diet for so long, anything that has a little seasoning tastes wonderful and you tend to gorge yourself.

During this time, we met some of the old hands in Circular 4. All of them served in Batista's army, air force, or rural guard. Two of the most outstanding characters were Carlos and Roberto, two real friends who were anxious to do anything they could to help us out and categorically refused anything in return. Roberto, whose last name I never knew, took it upon himself to keep us off any work details that were taken out of the circulars. When Batista was in power, Roberto had been sent to Panama to the U.S. Army Ordinance School. During his time off, he went to every American cowboy movie he could find. His hobby was learning cowboy slang.

Common practice was that each floor went to the *comisario* in turn, starting with floor number one. By the time the fifth floor's turn came around, there was no guarantee that what you wanted or needed would be available. Roberto's cellmate, Carlos—I never learned his last name—was a buyer for the third floor. He was a very quiet, private person, but very helpful to us. Carlos would take the orders of the people and go to the *comisario*, pick up everything, bring it back, and distribute it. He insisted on getting our purchases at the commissary too. We didn't think it was right to pull a sneak like this, buying with another floor, but he insisted. We later found out that this was a common practice and the old story of having a friend fix things for you held true even in prison.

Another ex-Batista army chap was Raúl Capote, the image of what a Cuban gentleman should be: suave, debonair, and an operator. When people were racing around to get clothes pressed for visiting day, Raúl took us in hand and had our khakis pressed, shoes shined, and so on, all gratis. He was a real gentleman's gentleman. Every time I went by his cell he would invite me in to have coffee, an offer I always accepted.

Other interesting folks included Dario Prohias, the brother of the cartoonist who created *El Hombre Siniestro*, a syndicated comic strip that appeared in Latin American papers in the mid-1960s.

One night, as I was sitting in the window of my cell looking out at the back of the mess hall, I noticed two common prisoners walking along the road. One had his arm over the other's shoulder and it looked like they were the best of friends. When they got almost to the front of the circular, they paused for a minute. Then the man with his arm over the shoulders of the other turned abruptly and started walking the other way. The second man stopped for a moment and then fell to the ground. Shortly afterward, a guard came out of the entrance of the circular and went up to the man. He talked to him but the man did not move. Much confusion followed and finally the jeep patrol arrived and the man was loaded into the back and taken to the hospital. After the jeep left I could see a large, dark spot on the road where the man had lain. Obviously it was blood. I had seen a knifing and didn't realize what had happened until it was all over. The next day, in the afternoon, the bugle sounded "Taps" and the hearse rolled by. One minute of silence in the circular, really eerie—you could hear the proverbial pin drop. Another common prisoner went to a grave in Nueva Gerona.

Even though everyone was expecting an invasion momentarily, the security of the prison was very poor in the early days. The guards slept at the front door, lighting around the buildings was very poor, trash piles were everywhere, and the grass had grown up around the buildings to a height of three and four feet. This made excellent cover for getting newspapers, bottles of rum, and other contraband into the prison.

However, you needed a contact on the outside. There was another political prisoner in our circular with contacts among the common criminals. He had been a common prisoner at one time but, because of some offense he committed while in prison, his status had been changed to political. Every night at about 8:30 p.m. two prisoners would be walking by the circular, each in a different direction. This is so they could check if anyone was behind the other man. In intelligence tradecraft parlance, this is known as countersurveillance. It's simple, but it gets the job done. When the contact man was directly opposite the right cell, he would give the signal and a match box propelled by a slingshot crossbow arrangement would come flying out and land at his feet. The man would stoop down, tie his shoelace, untie the matchbox, tie a newspaper—or whatever the people were asking for—on the end of the line, and leave. After he left, the newspaper would start its trip through the grass, up the side of the building, and into the circular. This went on for quite a while, and several times a guard would happen along at just the wrong time. But the contacts were lucky and never got caught.

The Bay of Pigs and Its Aftermath

This same routine continued for almost three months, the longest three months that I have ever spent waiting for anything. But things got interesting after that.

Dave had been briefed on plans for an invasion of Cuba before he left Washington for Havana in September 1960; Andy and I had not. Rumors of an imminent uprising flew among Cuban prisoners in La Cabaña during the winter of 1960–61, and the rumors bounced around the Isle of Pines circulars through the spring.

But so did a lot of other rumors in a prison society where rumor is a major form of entertainment.

I remember going to bed one Sunday night with the thought that Monday was always a quiet day and nothing would be happening tomorrow. So I dropped off to sleep and the next thing I realized was that I was awake. It was daylight but there was something else bothering me. Finally it penetrated. Shooting—and lots of it. A .50-caliber machine gun emplacement up on this hill by the prison was drumming away at something; the tracers were going right past the building. They reminded me of Fourth of July fireworks. Right over the top of the circular a B-26 flew in.

The place went into an uproar. Guys were running around screaming, "The invasion! The invasion!" My cellmate says, "What you think, gringo?" "Keep your head down," I said.

John Gentile came running by the cell, hollering that a plane was strafing a boat in the bay and had managed to sink it. I got up and went to the sixth floor to look out a window, and sure enough there was the plane strafing the boat, which was keeled over in the water, but not yet sunk. There were very small windows up there on the sixth floor, and you could see out to the ocean and the patrol boat. I caught the last sweep of the B-26. He just popped out of the clouds and made a pass. The patrol boat went down. The .50-caliber stopped shooting. The guards outside were panicked and running in all directions. They were hollering at the prisoners and shooting at the buildings. More shooting followed and this time it sounded pretty close, so I ran back down to the cell and hit the deck until it was over.

Back in the cell, Manolo and I are on the floor, and the shooting is still going on. Manolo wants to know if it's an invasion of the island. I comment that he better keep his head down, and, if it is, we will find out in due course. Somebody comes running by with the information from Circular 3 that all the stateside radio stations are talking about the invasion, which is in progress. Well, it sure sounds like things are getting active. Eventually things quiet down, there is no more shooting, and it looks like the planes have left. The circular is super quiet; everybody is talking in whispers.

The next item on the agenda comes when the *milicianos* drive up to the circulars and wave their guns to keep the prisoners away from the windows. It's pretty obvious that what they are bringing in to the circulars is not for our health and comfort. The boxes of whatever it is goes into the utility tunnel under Circulars 3 and 4. Immediately everybody is talking about what it could be and, although everybody has been talking about dynamite, nobody seems inclined to believe that this is what was brought into the circulars. A few months later, though, when the cardboard boxes are taken out, the bottom falls out of one, scattering sticks of dynamite all around the entrance to the circular.

Of course, all meals were canceled for three days. The uproar also continued for three days, with the guards yelling at the prisoners to stay away from the windows. Anybody who gets close to the windows would get shot.

On the fourth day the turmoil continued but we did get a late lunch of watery soup. Of course there are no packages, but the optimists are expecting them anyway. Days go by and it is getting clearer that something is wrong. Finally one day the news comes from Circular 3 that the invaders have been captured. This news hits the circulars, but nobody wants to believe it. As each day goes by it is apparent that the invasion we were all waiting for has come and flopped. It's quite a horrible feeling to know that you are on the losing team. The thing that makes it harder to take is the stories that are drifting around—that it's not over, something else is coming. Of course, everybody plus you knows there is nothing else. It has failed and that's that. I could never understand the habit of the Cubans of kidding each other. It's back to the drawing boards for the next try.

At about the third day, the guys over in Circular 3 were listening to Miami on their radio. The story started to get a little bit funny. And right away, you know. Oh, there's something wrong here.

The stories and rumors are as thick as flies. There were so many that it's hard to remember them all. Although at the time the truth was in among the other stories, there was no way of finding it. The radio reports from Circular 3, plus rumors and the tacking on to the news by the Cubans, really created a mess. Some rumors had the invaders marching toward Havana; two or three provinces were in rebellion; Castro had left for places unknown. The clincher, of course, was the day a newspaper came into the circular detailing the battle of Cocoon Bay. Well, it's official—we are going to be around for quite a while.

Things are getting pretty tight as far as food goes. We've had watery soup for a month and everybody has just about used up what they had tucked away. But lo and behold, one month after the invasion, packages start coming in again. But our bad luck holds and we don't receive any. Visiting is announced for the circular. The big day will be the first of June. We get busy and send off a telegram asking for water buckets, extra clothes, a one-burner kerosene stove, and other odds and ends. The day before visiting, the goodies arrive. We can now store water without having the cans rust out on us. The new stove is terrific—now we can get rid of old smokey.

Tomorrow is the big day. The circular is up most of the night pressing clothes, shaving to and fiddling around, taking care of last-minute items. It's 4:00 a.m. and people are getting up, ready to take a shower, yelling for their friends. Well, might as well get up, I won't be able sleep with all of this racket.

I should have stayed in bed. We wait around until almost 10:30 a.m., when we are called out. What a sensation it is to go out of the circular after months of being inside! The only thing that I notice is that the sun is hot and I'm thirsty. I hope the lawyer brought something to drink. Alas, he didn't bring anything except himself, so we have to scrounge a little water for *him* to drink. There is not much to talk about. He tells us that our lawyer in the States has made a pitch for us, but nothing has come of it. The best news is that he has made arrangements with a woman in Nueva Gerona to send us packages. What the content of the packages will be is not too clear, but something is better than nothing. The lawyer departs and we spend the rest of the allotted time for visiting seeing other people's visitors. Time is up and the visitors leave the *corral* (a fenced-in area). The prisoners line up and go back to the circulars. After being out for a few hours, it's really discouraging to go back into the building. It smells, it's littered, it's dirty. But it's home.

Back inside I notice for the first time that I have a splitting headache. I'm tired and the only thing on my mind is to hit the sack to rest up. Even though the physical exercise was little in comparison with what we do in the course of a normal day, everyone is all pooped out. After a while *cubre* (count) is held and everybody is in place in front of his cell while the guard checks to make sure nobody slipped out with the visitors. Most of the guys are gorging themselves on the loot brought by the visitors. This, plus catching up on the latest news and rumors, sure doesn't make things look good from our side.

A few days later, Daniel and I are sitting in the cell talking about nothing in particular when suddenly there is a yell, and then the sound of something like a watermelon splatting on the floor. From the noise, and then the sudden hush, it's not hard to figure out that somebody jumped over the rail to the cement below. It's a sickening sound when you realize all that it implies. Going to the rail, we see for ourselves that somebody is lying on the concrete below. The building is in turmoil; people are running to get downstairs to help. Half a dozen men pick up the body and start to lug it toward the gate, hollering about hospitals and such. To me this is a little foolish—the people that picked up the body probably did as much damage to lungs and intestines as did the fall. Hope is pretty slim for any chance of recovery, and the next day we heard the news that so-and-so died. That afternoon, the old Ford hearse goes by and one more prisoner leaves.

Things are pretty slow for the next few months, and with each day that goes by it is quite apparent that nobody is thinking about the prisoners at the Isle of Pines—except the prisoners. Things pick up a little when the water system is finally completed and there is sufficient water for laundry, bathing, and so on. But, like everything else, days go by when there is barely a trickle of water, and then other days you can fill all the cans and buckets you have and there is still an abundance.

An Escape Attempt Brings a *Requisa*

The next bit of excitement comes when there is an attempted escape. It's August and just about every night there is a terrific thunderstorm. It's on one of these nights that three prisoners cut some bars and, under the cover of rain, leave the circular. Unfortunately for the escapees, a common prisoner picks that same night to commit suicide in the hospital. With this, all the guards go running to the hospital. The rain ceases, and the escapees are pinned down and can't move. A guard happens by and they are caught.

This means that things will be pretty hairy the next morning for everyone else. So people are hiding knives, files, *pinchos* (an extra-long knife), and all sorts of contraband. I decide that the best thing to do is resume sleeping, which I do.

Comes the dawn and there is a lot of shouting and hollering at the gate. Of course, all the prisoners are up and keeping very quiet. The guards come roaring in, armed to the teeth. The director of the prison, Julio Tarrau, has honored us by his presence. He makes a statement to the effect that the first person to move will pay with his life.

Nobody takes him up on the offer. The orders are to strip completely and start coming down. Daniel is looking a little green around the gills at this point and almost passes out. He collapses to the floor and Danny and I help him up. We go to the *planta baja* and stand around in our birthday suits, pushed together, while the soldiers tear up the cells looking for what I don't know, and I'm sure they don't, either. The word is passed to keep heads down. I guess the guards are shy about the prisoners looking at them.

But as always, one person doesn't get the word. John Gentile is standing next to me looking around at the goings on, when he is rapped on the head by a soldier's rifle stock. He is pulled out of the line and I figure he will be a guest of a punishment cell (solitary confinement) for quite a while.

Hours go by. It's a little uncomfortable standing with your chin on your chest and no place to put your hands. Pockets are a real handy item to have when you're standing around doing nothing.

Finally the *requisa* is over and the guards leave. The prisoners start running up the stairs to get back to their cells and to straighten out the mess. John is still with us. He spent his time lying on the floor in urine, slop, and whatever else, while we were standing up.

Back up the stairs we go to see what the damage is. At first sight, things are all over the place and there seems to be more vandalism than searching. Toothpaste tubes are squashed on clean clothes, grease for cooking has been dumped on beds, but very little is missing. Our knife comes through the *requisa*. I guess a garbage bucket is a handy place to put things. In checking around I found that nobody has suffered with the *requisa*. A lot of knives and swords (three-foot-long knives, made out of reinforcing bars pulled out of cement) have been taken, but nobody is missing a significant amount of anything else.

So the first *requisa* has come and gone, and we are still alive to tell about it. From the comments of the other prisoners, especially the old hands, we gather that this is being vocally shrugged off as nothing at all, but it's obvious that they are impressed with the toughness of this one. The newer types are pretty happy with themselves that they made it through one of the tougher searches with no problem.

As the months drag by, a rare Red Cross package might arrive. We could tell from the way it is wrapped that it came from our friends in the Technical Services Division back at headquarters. We got powdered orange juice in hermetically sealed plastic containers along with pipe tobacco, Mixture 79.

But whatever items we had created or acquired were at constant risk because of the *requisas*. Some squealer would tell the authorities of the existence of a radio, or weapons, or other contraband.

Another *requisa* was the way to find the stuff, and also a way to terrorize the prisoners. So at, say, 7:30 in the morning, they ring the building with soldiers. "Down the stairs!" they yell. "Everyone down the stairs!" They get everyone lined up against the wall while the soldiers search the prison, throwing all your stuff out. You're facing the wall. You're not allowed to look. The first guy to turn around is going to get it. And there you stand. They usually set up a couple of machine guns behind the prisoners. Snap! Clack, clack, click! They're loading the rifles, snapping the bolts, putting the heavy ammo in the machine guns. One of these *requisas* lasted fifteen hours, into darkness. The lights went out, and the jittery soldiers began snapping the gun bolts behind the prisoners. The Cubans all squatted; some of them defecated in their pants. We remained standing, feeling that if we were going to get it in the back, we would at least take it standing up. It apparently impressed our fellow prisoners, who were also aware that the gringos had great technical expertise.

Unwelcome Visitors

One of the things that we were always conscious of during our stay in jail were *las cucarachas* and *los chinches* (cockroaches and bedbegs). During our time in Circular 4, we never had much of a problem with the little bugs. Danny always insisted on a weekly scrubbing of his and Daniel's cell since we stored most of our food there, and it also served as a kitchen. My cell, number 84, was no problem since the hard items were stored there and the cell was not used as much as number 83. But occasionally someone visiting would bring in a couple of bugs. The *chinches* pick the most unusual hiding places—inside the springs of a cot, holes in the wall, and so on. Our first indication of bedbugs came one day when some Cubans came in to shoot the breeze. One of them, Reno Puig, leaned against Daniel's folded bed that had a paper suitcase sitting on top. Immediately he backed up and started swearing in Spanish. When asked what was wrong, he said, "There are the little animals here." Lo and behold, across his belt line on his stomach red welts appeared. This is the symbol of *chinches* bites. We immediately started to search, but to no avail. Later on we found where the little visitors were hiding—in the creases of the paper suitcase. The only reason that we kept looking was that Danny would be in bed at night and see them going up the wall. Come morning and we would have a *chinche* count.

Another hiding place for bedbugs is in the crease of a belt, just behind the belt buckle. I found *chinches* there several times. For a short while it was a mystery how I would be getting the bites. You cannot feel them when they crawl over you, but when they bite and draw blood they tend to go off the deep end and run around in circles. You can generally find them and kill them before you get another bite. The worst bites seem to come from the smaller ones. These rascals are really ravenous. They look like a piece of red fuzz from a blanket, thinner than a pencil line and about a sixty-fourth of an inch long. The larger bedbugs are triangular in shape and quite large. There is no problem finding these. When you see one, start looking and you will find a nest of them somewhere close by.

As for remedies, there were none available, but the best bedbug killer seemed to be plain old kerosene or creosote. This would kill them immediately. DDT, although it would also kill them, was not as fast acting. Soap and water would rid your cot or bed of the bugs for a while but, unless you washed your bed canvas and frame, besides keeping your linen clean, you could expect that you would have them back in a short time. Circular 4 was pretty good in that a treatment for *chinches* would last three to four months. In Circular 1, where we later went, the treatment was good for a few days only. Circular 1 was dirtier—it housed more people for a longer period of time. Circular 4 was the last one to fill up.

The cockroaches were gigantic and very numerous, mostly because the locals didn't know how to keep their cells clean. In cells where cooperatives were set up, cockroaches were abundant, mainly because the cooks were sloppy and nobody felt like cleaning the cell out once in a while. The only way to get rid of roaches was to move everything out of the cell at least once a week, scrub everything down with soap and water, and put it all back. This was the only sure cure we had for roaches. The Cuban who lived next to me was always amazed that we never had roaches like he did. And he was one of the neater types in the circular. But nobody could convince him that when you heated rice and stirred it you shouldn't slop it over the stove and surrounding area, or, if you did, then sure as little green apples you will have visitors.

But no matter how well you attempted to take care of yourself, eventually some malady would strike you. Some of our Cuban friends helped us greatly in such circumstances. In one instance, Dr. Emilio Sorrondo, a medical doctor, treated me at La Cabaña for fungal infections and boils. When I was standing in line for the dispensary, he came and took me by the arm past all the waiting Cubans. Some of them complained loudly, but Dr. Sorrondo told them to be quiet or he would give them a healthy dose of salts.

If They Hand You a Lemon, Make Lemonade

Things have changed around the prison since it becomes apparent to the administration that they and the prisoners will be around for a while. Things are beginning to shape up. The huge piles of trash and garbage outside the circulars are removed, and work details are being called from the circulars each day to clean up around the prison. C., A., and Gentile make it out on a couple of work details, but I luck out and never get called. But one fine day the three of us find ourselves being called downstairs by the guard to clean out the passageway where the guards spend all of their time. It's a matter of sloshing water around and sweeping it out, we thought. But the guard that called us down decides he is going to get his money's worth. We have to load the garbage on the garbage wagon. This involves fifty-five-gallon drums as crummy on the outside as they are on the inside. Then you sweep and pick up trash and papers around the circular. At first I don't think much of the idea, but it's amazing how much you can pick up on the outside of the building that can come in handy—nails, discarded lengths of plastic tubing, pencils, and all sorts of little goodies. Besides all this, being in the worker status, we can put in a request for new khakis. The ones that we have and others that we acquired by swapping cigarettes are not the best, so what started out as a pain in the neck ends up being a gold mine.

Our friends next door—Smith, Beck, Baker, Bean, and Gibson—in Circular 3 razz us from the windows, and we find out later that they had made the suggestion to the guards next door to get the three Americans in Circular 4 out to work. Little did they know the terrific favor they were doing us. It was a little ironic in that they volunteered to work but never managed to get a thing for their labors, whereas we on the other hand had been forced into it and did pretty well.

Another Failed Escape Attempt

I guess it was only a matter of time before somebody with a little bit of smarts started to think about escaping again and did a little planning ahead of time. One person who did was Pedro Luis Boitel, a professional student at the University of Havana. Pedro spent most of his time playing politics instead of studying but, nevertheless, when it came to playing politics, Pedro was unmatched in his field. (For what it's worth, a terrorist group claimed credit for several bombings in the late 1960s in his name.) Physically, Pedro was five feet, nine inches and weighed ninety pounds soaking wet. He made up for his size with his thinking ability. Among his confederates was Ulysses Silva, whom we had met in La Cabaña. He was the most unlikely candidate for an escape attempt. The guy was a nervous wreck, and I never would have pictured that he would do it. But he proved to have the guts when it came down to the wire. Another was Armando Valladares, a very aloof, private sort of individual. He always ignored us and walked by with his nose in the air. The last was Julio Ybarra, a doctor and student activist nicknamed Marinero, which is the word for a person who is a sailor. I never met the man, and if I ever saw him I did not know who he was.

Acquiring a cell on the second floor, Pedro started to work on the escape plan. German hairs, or *pelo alemán*, as the Cubans call the metal-coping saw blades, were in the circular, having been smuggled in to Boitel. They were perfect for sawing your way through the bars of your cell.

The next move was to manufacture some clothing similar to what the guards wore. The hats were American-style fatigue caps, but painted white with a painted emblem on the front. Duplicating these was no problem. Dying the prison uniforms with green ink easily made guard clothing.

The plan was to cut through the bars just before escape time, then the prisoners would climb out the window and shinny down a rope ladder to the ground. This would happen just after the evening count and before dark, when the jeep patrol would be in action in the prison compound. Then it would be a simple matter to walk away from the circular to the guards' *cuartel* (living quarters or barracks), the only opening in the fence around the compound. In the rear of the *cuartel* was a ditch under the fence. From there it was walking distance to a river where Boitel and his confederates hoped to steal a boat, which was supposed to come from Havana and go to Grand Caiman Island.

On October 22, 1961, all went off as smooth as clockwork. Pedro and his three friends went out just before dark. It was almost half an hour before the circular in general found out that there had been a *fuga* (escape). The first reaction was that all the noise in the circular stopped. The black prisoners, who gathered every night and made Lumumba music using homemade drums and pots, fell silent when the word hit. All conversation came to an abrupt halt. Some of Boitel's friends attempted to take up the music making, but they just didn't have the rhythm and were not loud enough, and the sound was not the same.

The guards never suspected a thing and the escape was not discovered until the next morning. There was much excitement among the guards, with the new chief of interior order running around and not quite knowing which direction to go. The circular was expecting a *requisa* but it never came. The administration was too busy trying to locate the escapees. Three days went by and the current rumor was that the boys had made it to Grand Caiman. I wasn't convinced.

On the evening of the third day just before evening count, lo and behold, between the circulars on the way to the punishment cells comes Pedro Boitel, leaning on a guard for support. The prison is quiet, and a few types yell to Pedro as he goes by. The next one is Ulysses Silva. Then came Marinero, the sailor. The fourth member, Armando Valladares, was driven to the punishment cells because he broke an ankle during the escape.

Spirits in the circulars plummeted to zero. Up to this time, everyone had been hoping that the boys had made it but now they were back. So when William Galvis, the governor of the island, came strolling by, it was the catalyst to start a riot. Immediately a great roar went up, with everyone yelling out the window words to the effect that Galvis's mother had a very unsavory reputation. Fortunately, the man had a head on his shoulders and, instead of sending a few rounds into the circular, he walked away. The prisoners vented their frustration by throwing bottles and anything else they could lay their hands on at the tower inside the building. It's an interesting sight to see a mob in action, and that night was the night to see it. After the bottle episode, everyone started banging on the rails with anything they could make noise with. In about an hour, the noise subsided, and the roaring lions had become meek pussy cats worrying about what reprisals the prison administration would take against them.

Morning comes and still the feeling that something is going to happen prevails in the prison. The talking is done in whispers and people are pretty quiet. The cleaning crew is sweeping up some of the glass prior to *cubre*. Everybody is wide awake and waiting for something, just what they don't know.

Finally, the fateful moment arrives. Pomponio (named after a Cuban comic strip character), whose real name is Bernardo Gonzales and who is the chief of interior order, arrives with a couple of guards and they commence to count heads. This morning there is a lot less of the usual goofing off. Everybody is out of the sack. The only ones still in bed are those that are really sick. *Cubre* is finished and the guards and the Mayor of the circular have a few words. Then the guards leave. Well, will surprises never end; no *requisa*, no anything. The atmosphere has changed; why, we don't know.

Time passes slowly, but it does go by. Thanksgiving arrives and we have managed to save a few items from what we purchased at the prison store. So we plan a big dinner. No turkey or cranberry sauce, but considering the fact that this is prison, we fare pretty well with stuffed green peppers that John has conjured up out of something, plus beans and crackers, some of Daniel's chocolate pudding made with *gofio de trigo* (a finely ground wheat flour), and a couple of bottles of Malta. To top it off, some wine from Gallego, the wine maker, makes Thanksgiving a memorable occasion. Plus we did dress for dinner; we put on our clean shirts!

Explosive Operations

The next thing that comes along is something everybody will remember for quite a while. One fine day in November 1961, an air compressor is wheeled up outside of Circular 3. From my window I can see all the preparation to set it up. Something is afoot, but specifically what I'm not too sure, although I have a pretty good idea. The compressor is started up and for a month it's the same old story. Starting at 8:00 a.m. until about 4:00 p.m., with a break for lunch, the guards have the compressor running and something is being drilled out in Circular 3. Watching from our circular, we can see an occasional chunk of concrete knocked out when the drillers get too close to the outside wall of the building. After a while another compressor is wheeled up to Circular 4 and they start on our building.

That makes it pretty certain, but there is still a sliver of doubt until C. and A. are called one day to go down and clean out the guards' passageway. Then it's confirmed. The soldiers are drilling each of the columns in the building, both top and bottom, and

333

from the size of the holes it's pretty obvious what is going to be put into the holes: TNT!

They started cutting holes in the support pillars of our building. All the way around it. They'd work with a jackhammer. They'd start that at nine in the morning and go until five in the afternoon. It took them about three weeks to get all the holes dug. And then one night lots of trucks pulled up to the circular. They were plugging in the TNT in boxes. There is a prisoner inside the circular who is in charge of bringing packages in for the prisoners. About ten-thirty or eleven o'clock at night this guy hollers up, "Hey, Sanchez, you've got packages downstairs." A little bit of gallows humor.

The lines to the explosives were threaded through plastic tubing, buried, and running from the circular to a little wooden building about one mile beyond the perimeter fence.

There are still people that don't want to believe that this is what is going to be put into the holes. Many of the more intelligent people are talking about a mess hall, or beds for the *milicianos*. Even the day when they carry in boxes marked *mecha explosiva* (explosive fuse or primer cord), people are still deluding themselves.

Well, life doesn't change too much in the prison. The routine remains the same, although everybody has something new to think about. A few people want to make sure that this is not just psychological warfare going on, so attempts are made to fish blocks through the holes on the inside wall, but with negative results. It's a sort of half-hearted gesture and it finally stops.

The thing that really starts some action is when, late one night, after the order for silence has been sounded, trucks are moving around in the prison compound. They pull up to the buildings and *milicianos* start unloading boxes. Everybody is guessing, nobody is sure of anything, but it's not candy bars for the prisoners that they are bringing in. There is much running around and excited talk, but nothing happens. Finally everybody settles down and goes to bed.

The next morning everything is confirmed when the boxes are unloaded in the utility tunnel and the empty boxes are thrown right outside the entrance to the circulars. In big black stenciled letters on each box is TNT. They contain approximately fifty pounds to a box and, from the number of boxes they brought in, we can tell we are sitting on approximately five tons of the stuff. It sure looks like "the Beard" (Castro) is going to keep his promise that if the island is invaded, all they will find is a lot of dead prisoners. Of course, this makes any potential invader think twice about it if he knows that the prisoners are ready to go sky high.

Defusing the Explosives

Some of the Cubans got more confirming information from the guard. Videl Guillermo Morales was given black plastic rings with white numbers: 27560, his prison number. He and his colleagues were warned to wear the rings so that bodies could be identified if the prison was blown up. Others were tattooed, some for the same reason, some for the reason that prisoners in other settings get tattooed. My prison number was 26821; Andy's was 26655; I don't recall Dave's. We weren't tattooed nor did we receive the rings.

We all worried about the guards' intentions with all of these explosives. Even if they never use the stuff, it behooves us to come up with something to make sure they never do. Danny has been talking with a fellow prisoner, Captain Miro, a B-26 pilot, on the first floor who has a good head on his shoulders and uses it. The political intrigue that goes on in the prison is enough to foul up any attempts at stopping the people who want to get to the TNT and do something about it. But Miro is smart enough to do enough talking in the right places and, although he does not want the job, he ends up being the man in charge of stopping the TNT from going off.

Miro represented a group of Cubans who had found a small access hole that went from the first-floor toilets down into the utility tunnel on the ground floor where the explosives were being installed. He asked us to take charge of the operation to thwart the explosives operations of the authorities. We knew that we should protect our cover and not draw attention to ourselves, and we also knew that every one of the eleven hundred prisoners in the circular would be aware of our participation within a few days. We decide that the lives of the eleven hundred men have to be protected and that we, as Americans, have a special responsibility in the matter.

There are many self-proclaimed explosives experts in the circular, and it's not hard to figure out who the baloney artists are. After talking with these "experts" it comes out that they, at some time or another, once saw a box of dynamite or carried a stick of it in Havana, or something else about on that order. So by default, Danny is the one that ends up giving the advice to Miro who, in turn, passes it on. But it looks like the people that are handling the whole thing don't know what they are doing and are in it just for the glory. After much fooling around and buck passing, the whole job gets back to Miro, period.

So what to do now? Biscayino (he looked like Richard Conti, the movie star) and Manolo (not the one I shared a cell with, but a good copy of the Michelin Tire cartoon ad) start things off by making a hole through five inches of concrete in the toilet on the first floor. Swinging hammers, they enlarge the hole in the ground floor to the tunnel where the explosives are. The theory is that in any *requisa*, the guards are not going to look around too carefully in the smelly, dirty toilet, so the chances of discovery are pretty small. After a lot of sweating and pounding, they finally get an enlarged hole through. To me it seems miraculous that they even managed to make a dent in the concrete, much less put a hole in it. What they actually did was enlarge a hole that drain pipes went through so that a small person could slip through the opening into the utility tunnel.

With the hole completed, it's time to find somebody willing to go down into the utility tunnel and see exactly what is what. Captain Miro approached the smallest person in the circular and, at first, he turned the job down flat. Days later, after being assured the *americanos* are masterminding the job, Luis Lemus, a small, fair-haired street-smart Cuban kid, about five feet, five inches tall and weighing no more than 120 pounds, finally consents to do the job. Appropriately, he is nicknamed Americano because he looks so much like one with his blond hair and blue eyes.

The big day arrives. Manolo and Biscayino have been checking on the movement of the people that work in the tunnel, and they feel the noon hour would be the best time for Americano to take a look-see. Lookouts are posted and the operation is all set to go. We tell him to bring back samples of everything he could find. Nothing to do now except wait and see what our friend comes back with.

For what seems like an eternity, he is in the tunnel, but finally he comes up. Americano doesn't need to crawl anywhere—the tunnel is eight feet wide and six feet high. However, he does get stuck coming up through the enlarged opening on the floor in the first-floor toilet. He never mentioned hearing anything other than the normal noise made by the prisoners. Danny takes off for Miro's cell to get the latest. The news Americano brings back is that these people are not fooling—they have a dual-channel system. There is an electrical line for detonating and also a primer-cord line. So if one system fails, there is a back up.

Now it's up to us to think of a way to sabotage the system without having it discovered. If they find out we have tampered with the system, they will go over it with a fine-tooth comb and then make sure we don't have the ability to get at it again.

Danny asks for and gets samples of the primer cord and blasting caps, which Americano steals. At one point, Americano brings up several two-kilogram blocks of TNT and some of the wire. Dave confirms that it is TNT. Andy looks at the primer cord and deems it good stuff. It is the real thing. So then we have to figure out how we would stop it. One day Americano brings up a fifteen-pound block of TNT. After a hasty look we manage to get it back to Miro, who tells our friend to put it back. He is a little disappointed that we don't want it as a souvenir.

How do you stop primer cord from shooting? You put a gap in it. We have essentially zero to work with. We have no tools, no files, no saws, nothing like that. The only things we have are razor blades, knives, and sewing kits. Using a spool from a sewing kit, we figure out a way to put a gap in the primer cord without leaving obvious evidence that it has been tampered with. To disarm the dual electrical system, we slice through the insulation, twist the wires to short the connection, and let the insulation slip back into place.

After much talking, drawing, and thinking, we devise a technique for shorting the electrical blasting line and interrupting the primer-cord line so it won't be detectable. For four nights, when almost everyone is asleep, we bring Americano into our quarters and brief him in the technique, making him do it blindfolded under a blanket with his hands outside. There is very little light in the tunnel and we want to be sure there are no slip-ups. It's our necks if we goof. We teach him to attach a spool with pins to one end of a severed primer cord and shove the spool through the plastic tubing until the pins catch and the cord cannot be drawn back. We put him through the wire cut-and-twist exercise until we think he is ready.

Finally the day and time arrives for Americano to go down into the tunnel to do the job. The soldiers and *milicianos* have completed most of their work, and they come around only during the morning to work on the TNT installation. So in the afternoon approximately an hour before *cubre*, Americano has to do the job and be back in the circular before the whistle blows. If he is not, there will be all kinds of excitement with one man missing.

So down he goes armed with all the little gadgets we made for him. They include the modified sewing thread spool, the handful of straight pins, and a small, sharp knife. Danny and I are sweating the whole time Americano is gone. I've never been so uptight in my life waiting for something to happen! It seems like years that he is down in that tunnel.

Finally he comes up and the whistle goes off for *cubre*. We all heave a sigh of relief.

After dinner and later, when it's dark, Danny goes down to Miro's cell and gets the details of the job. Much later Danny gives us the details. Americano did an excellent job and there is very little chance of the sabotage being discovered. A guard tugging at the primer cord would not be able to tell that it had been cut. The electrical circuit could still pass a galvanometer test. The whole system will have to be torn out to find the trouble. We all breathe a second sigh of relief upon hearing this.

Unfortunately, an operation like this couldn't be kept secret in the prison. Within that week, a visitor to the prison ran up to us and thanked us for stopping the TNT and mentioned that all of Havana knew that the Americans had disabled the TNT. However, we never found any evidence of an attempt to repair the sabotaged connections. And we were never punished, which would have meant isolation in the pavilion—a place of no beds and no food other than slop thrown in once a day, where prisoners were kept naked for the swarming mosquitoes, and where many prisoners went mad after thirty days.

To many of the prisoners, the mining was even more frightening than the October 1962 missile crisis, which had simply meant alerts and blackouts, but not TNT rigged to blow up under our feet.

During this period, the TNT project was not the only thing being pursued in the circular. Since it looked like things would soon be coming to a head, and we would have nothing to fight back with, people were coming up with all sorts of ideas for weapons, one of which was a flame thrower. An old kerosene stove was cannibalized for the pressure tank and valves, and I spent four days seating (grinding and polishing the valve so it sits in its seat and provides a seal) brass valves with toothpaste and marble dust. The best squirt we could manage was approximately ten feet, and this was not too effective. Pressure in the tank would bleed off and, after the valve portion of the stove got warm, the rascal would start acting just like a stove. So the project was abandoned.

But someone else came up with the brilliant idea of making alcohol. Oranges, grapefruit, mangos, watermelon and anything that would ferment were put into glass jars with water and sugar and set in the sun for a few days. This product was then cooked in a pressure cooker that someone had sent in at one time or another. From the pressure cooker the vapor went through plastic intravenous tubing (tubing from intravenous feeding bottles, which we obtained from the medic) and was submerged in a thirty-gallon water can. The output of this still was some pretty potent alcohol. After running the distillate through two or three times, the chemical engineer of the crowd ventured to say that it was at least 170 proof alcohol—very fine stuff for Molotov cocktails.

Another project was the making of fuses. Four or five people were put to work cutting the heads off matches. After several pounds of match heads were accumulated, they were very carefully (after the first time, when a pound or so went up in smoke and one intrepid individual lost eyebrows and hair) ground up and rolled in a short length of plastic tubing. This was then tied with string to keep everything together. When this fuse was lighted and dropped from the fifth floor to the concrete, it would still keep burning. This was a method of using the nonelectric blasting caps.

With the availability of nonelectrical blasting caps in the utility tunnel, and all the TNT we could possibly use, hand grenades would be no problem. Fortunately, we never had to use any of the homemade hand grenades. These were old condensed-milk cans that were partially filled with rocks, bolts, nails, glass, and so on. The TNT that had been melted in a double boiler was poured in. A small wooden dowel or pencil inserted in the top provided the space for the blasting cap and the fuse. How many of these were made is anybody's guess, but I would venture to say that there are several of these still in the rafters of Circular 4.

Welcome to Your New Home

After the meeting of foreign ministers at Punta del Este in Uruguay, when it was obvious that there was going to be no invasion or intervention in Cuba, the atmosphere relaxed quite a bit. The meeting did not end the invasion scare, however. The meeting fell apart because the foreign ministers of the Organization of American States could not agree on what to do about Fidel. Thus, there were no sanctions imposed and no invasion was mounted. This is when everybody looked around and realized that nothing was going to change for them. Again, we saw the old Cuban prisoner refusal to accept the fact that no sanctions or invasion was coming. So it went for about a month or so.

Then one morning our old friend Pomponio, the chief of interior order, puts in an appearance in the circular armed with a list. After a short conversation with the Mayor, the announcement is made that everyone whose name is read is to be ready to leave with all of their belongings. What now? Just in case we get called, we scramble around getting all of our possessions together. It's surprising how much one can accumulate in a year, even in prison. But Danny has been thinking about what to take and what not to take if something like this ever came up. So we are organized and all set to travel in about an hour. But it's the same old story. Hurry up and wait.

The time finally comes and our names are called. We say goodbye to a lot of old friends, then go out the door carrying all our bedding, clothes, and other items. There are all sorts of rumors floating around, and the best one is that we are being transferred to the mainland to cut sugar cane. Phooey! If this is so, why are they letting us take our beds and other gear? To the *corral* next to Circular 1 where we meet are the other Americans: James Bean, George Beck, Thomas Baker, and Leonard Schmidt. Al Gibson was in the hospital, so he did not get transferred. It is the first get-together for the American contingent in more than a year, so we swap stories back and forth.

A few hours pass, and it becomes clear that we are headed for Circular 2. The thing to do is try to get to the front of the line and get inside and quickly get a cell before they are all taken. We get inside the circular, but it's no cell for us. We go to the sixth floor. Many of our friends from La Cabaña are here and, as usual, everything is confusion. Daniel gets a spot to bed down with Tony Martinez, a Cabaña acquaintance. Danny and I are pretty much out in the cold until Chester Lacayo comes along and installs us in the dispensary on the sixth floor. You will recall that Chester was a Nicaraguan who was trying to organize an overthrow of Somoza from Havana, but got tripped up and thrown into jail by Fidel.

Looks like these people are a little better organized than we were in the previous circular—they have an operating table, surgery lamp, antibiotics, clamps, forceps, and other equipment. They are crude but when you have nothing, anything will do. There were also jugs of sterile water, bandages, one bottle of an antiseptic, and saline solution, all made by the prisoners. To say the least, we're impressed.

Confusion is still rampant and, with all the routines thrown out, it's just about every man for himself. After supper we try to get organized. I set up my mattress on the operating table. It's not too bad except for the hole in the middle and the fact that it's very narrow. Still, it's better than sleeping on the floor, which would be very dirty and uncomfortable.

We meet many new faces. We finally get to meet the legend of the Cubans, Austin Young, and his sidekick, Peter Lambton. Austin is a man in his early forties, although prison has taken its toll and he certainly looks much older. Peter is in his late twenties and is a hero worshiper. Although he tries to give the impression of a blasé soldier of fortune, Peter is somewhat lacking in this respect. Austin usually plays the lead, and the straight man is Peter. At times, it's pretty amusing to watch Peter ask Austin, "Well, when you were in the RAF, how did they do it?" And so it went. They had been picked up in one of the provinces, trying to fly guns to the counterrevolutionaries.

Life in general is a little inconvenient at this point—we had no cell and not much prospect of getting one. All of our water cans, stove, and other gear made the move with us but with no space that we can call our own, we have to set up our housekeeping routine all over again.

Dealing with Mental Illness

One day I hear about the crazy American on the third floor, Richard Pecoraro. It's apparent that we have to do something to help Richard since we know no one else will. So we get all the Americans together in Austin's cell to see what we can come up with.

We have to get him out of his cell and living with one or all of the Americans if we can swing it. A few are ready to cooperate, but I'm sorry to say that most are not interested in having anything to do with this problem, the feeling being that he got himself into this mess, now let him get himself out.

We soon realize that the job of taking care of Richard is going to fall to us, so we accept it by default. Danny, in his usual hard-charging manner, gets hold of Chester Lacayo to get some of the people out of the area next to the dispensary. This is quite an exercise, but he finally manages to get everybody out. Richard by this time has pretty much accepted that he is going to move up to the sixth floor with us. But each time we got him up there, he would decide he wanted to go back to his cell. This happened several times. Finally, we convinced him to stay on our floor, and we got ourselves established. We are pretty well off with the amount of space we have. We have the room of three cells with none of the walls. However, there is only one window and that is much smaller (two feet by three feet) than what we have had (three feet by five feet). But you can't have everything.

Finally, after we get Richard to move in with us, life starts to take on the regularity we knew in Circular 4. This is my first experience with someone who is mentally ill, and I can say that it is a really trying experience. There are times when Richard is just like any other person, but then the slow grayness seems to creep over him and the subtle change is suddenly there. He is hard to get along with—he doesn't listen, he becomes argumentative over nothing, and reasoning with him is out of the question regarding taking a shower and any personal hygiene, going for food, and so on. In general, he becomes very good at ticking you off instantly. It seems that no amount of talking will make him change his behavior. I guess to us it seems foolish, but a little insignificant item to us is of major importance to him. He sits in a corner tying knots in a little piece of string, staring at the blank wall. Danny has talked with one of the more qualified doctors in the circular. The only real hope for Richard is proper diet, drugs, and medical help. We can't provide the diet, but we send a cable to our lawyer in Washington, Mr. Murphy, to send tranquilizers to the Swiss, who will eventually get them to us. The reply that came back was a typical staff cable: "Please indicate height, weight, and description of subject." Lots of guffaws from the three of us, who recognize the writing style. But nobody seemed to pay any attention to the cable that we sent, which gave them all the information that they asked for. So we essentially resend the first cable, and about a month later, the medication arrives. In the meantime, Andy has the prison psychiatrist talk to Richard, through an interpreter, to plot a course of treatment.

Welcome Visitors

Things are pretty well organized at this point. Then one day we get a surprise. Names are being called out to get downstairs and get ready to go to the administration building, but no indication of what's up. Only the names of the Americans in the circular are being called. Something is up. We change to our less crummy uniforms, comb what little hair we have, and off we go to the front office—all twenty-one of us. After we arrive, we find out it's the Swiss that have come to visit us and, since it's lunchtime, they have gone back to town to get some lunch. So we sit around and wait for their return.

Upon their return, we have our interview, but it's not really much. One member of the Swiss delegation doesn't understand English very well, and it's pretty hard to put anything across to him. It is like talking to a blank wall—no reaction on the part of the Swiss, not even a smile or a simple greeting of hello. We did get a few very welcome American cigarettes (not packs, which were never allowed in). In addition, some of the details are straightened out regarding Richard's tranquilizer pills, and we ask for various other items (vitamin pills and injectable medicines to keep our shots current), which the Swiss promise they will send.

Back in the circular we are the focus of attention. Everyone wants to know what happened. Fernando Pruna comes over and, by the look on his face, I can see that he is dying to get all the details. Fernando is a Cuban in his midtwenties, a ladies' man, who spent a lot of time in New York City and was more American than Cuban. But when I tell him that it was just a visit, he is a little deflated. The only other bit of news is that Al Gibson has been transferred from Circular 3 to Circular 1. So now all the known Americans are in Circular 1; the others that have not acknowledged being Americans are in other circulars.

During this period (April 1962), we were in good shape with medicine, food, and clothes. Our packages had been arriving regularly from Benilde, Raúl Gomez de Molina's mother, who was a close friend of the Cuban lawyer who made arrangements for her to send us packages and, at the same time, take care of her son. The package of American pipe tobacco and vitamin pills really kept up our spirits and general health. The other item that was really enjoyed was the tremendous amount of fresh fruit that we received. The grapefruits were almost the size of basketballs and not tart, but deliciously sweet. Mangoes, oranges, and bananas were also superb.

So the summer of '62 passed, with the hot afternoons on the sixth floor where the radiant heat from the asbestos ceiling made life pretty uncomfortable from noon to sunset. But with a little luck, somebody would be out of their cell on the cool side of the circular and I would spend the afternoon just sitting and enjoying the cool breeze. The height of luxury was when Ricardo Rodríguez, one of the pilots who fought against the Batista army in the hills, would vacate his cell for the afternoon. Details of Ricardo's actual combat missions were alluded to, but were never talked about, probably because of the rebel soldiers who were in the circular with us and who were not interested in meeting the pilots who had been shooting at them. Then I could sit in a real lawn chair and read one of the pocket books that was circulating around the circular. *A Biography of Benjamin Franklin* was one of my favorites.

Hunger Strikes

It all came to an end with the hunger strikes. The first one by the prisoners was for the lack of food, and it caught the administration off guard. They submitted to the demands of the prisoners, giving us two items for each meal. This amounted to corn meal and sweet potatoes, whereas we used to get cornmeal only. But for quite a few of the people this was all there was, since they had no packages coming from the outside. Occasionally they could get an orange or mango from a friend who was receiving packages.

With the winning of the first hunger strike, the prisoners started to feel a little cocky. I'm sure the administration sensed this, but they were only biding their time until they had a good excuse to shake the prisoners up.

Their chance came when Circular 2 was having a *requisa*. When the last of the prisoners was going back to the circular, something happened. Reports said it was a guard hitting a prisoner, or vice versa. In any case, the yelling started pouring out the windows of the circular. Since most of the guards were of mixed race, they were called apes and a few other choice names. This started the guards shooting at the circulars. For a while the shooting got hot and heavy. Everybody was on the floor, and this is when we found out that the walls on the sixth floor were not poured concrete but bricks with a stucco finish. Two or three bullets hit our area and knocked out plaster on the inside, showering everybody. One individual that I remember quite vividly came up the stairs just as the bullets hit. He hit the floor and, without any apparent moving of arms or legs, went across the floor like a snake, headed for the other end of the building.

With this incident, the prisoners started another hunger strike. I should clarify that a hunger strike at the Isle of Pines consisted of not accepting the food the prison was sending in. Instead, everybody lived on what was cached in the building from the packages that were received during the week. So nobody suffered any hardship. The hunger strike went on all day Sunday and Monday morning before the reckoning came. With the dawn, everybody was more or less prepared for another dull day of waiting, but the prison officials had other ideas. Armored personnel carriers, a few tanks, and hundreds of *milicianos* arrived at the circulars. Everybody was ordered downstairs in their shorts, with no exceptions. After everybody arrived in the *planta baja*, the *milicianos* lined up across the floor and a guard appeared in the tower. Then followed a little milling around, with the prisoners still feeling frisky. Somebody made a comment and, naturally, everyone surged forward to see what is going on. This was the signal for the sergeant in charge to tell the *milicianos* to charge with fixed bayonets. The crowd beat a hasty retreat. I was just moved bodily backward as the rush started to get out of the way of the bayonets. Nobody was hurt, but it proved who was running the show. Then came the biggest surprise of all. The *milicianos* started entering each cell and throwing out everything, including beds. It took a little while for the prisoners to catch on, but they did. This was going to be a real *requisa*.

So it goes, hour after hour. The troops go from one floor to another, methodically cleaning everything out. It's amazing how much is being thrown out, but out it goes. I have a feeling of detachment about the whole affair until they get to where we live, and then it hits home. There goes the stove, the tabletop, suitcases, water buckets, everything. My cot is folded up along the rail and I'm waiting for it to come sailing down, since cots from other floors have come down. But through some oversight of the soldiers, it stays. Things are getting weary for both the prisoners, who have been standing through most of the *requisa*, and the soldiers, who have had to lug out the piles of junk on the first floor.

Now comes the next surprise. Everybody on the first floor is told to go to their cells, collect all their belongings, and move to the same cells on the second floor. Oh, boy, if they are going to move everybody around, it will be a real mess. The sun has gone down and the lights on the tower are on—it certainly looks gloomy. We are treated to a speech from Pomponio, the chief of interior order, who extols the virtues of communism. Then comes another speech from the chief of the guard force, which actually made a lot of sense, declaring that the prisoners brought this on themselves. If they had behaved themselves, they would be a lot better off than they are now. But just wait for the future, when things are going to get a lot tougher.

The lights go out and there is a moment of panic, but the sergeant of the guard keeps everything under control. The soldiers are snapping the bolts of their rifles. This makes quite an impression on the prisoners, who move back. A few are crying because they think the end is coming, but the lights come on and all is normal again.

Now comes another talk from Pomponio and the offer "Do you want to eat?" For all that do, the food is there. For those that don't, fine. The yell goes up, "No, no!" Somebody tells Pomponio that it should not be a voice vote. Let the ones that want to eat go ahead, and those that don't can go hungry. With this, the hunger strike is effectively broken. There is a mad rush for the food pots. The soldiers leave. It's been quite a day—eighteen hours of standing around with nothing to eat and some salty water to drink. One idiot managed to get some water but laced it with salt before passing it out. Good for the stomach, I suppose.

The three of us—me, C., and A.—dash upstairs to survey what is left. We see that there is darn little left. We still have our beds, but everything else is gone. What is left has been trampled on the floor. After picking up most of the stuff, I go downstairs to get some of the fish soup, and we talk for a while before going to bed. Tomorrow is another day and that will be time enough for cleanup.

Dawn comes and the circular is much quieter than usual. Everybody is tired from yesterday's adventure and, after opening your eyes and taking one quick look, the inclination is to close them and go back to sleep. What a gigantic mess! The only way to clean it up is to get busy, and so we start. Things are still pretty well confused, with people running here and there trying to find their belongings and get settled. Some have ended up without a cup, so there are problems. Food comes at different times. All the routines are broken up. With nothing to store water in, you have to get your food, eat in a hurry, and wash the plate before the water goes off.

Time goes on and on, and life is just a little uncomfortable.

That's probably because there is no chance to goof off during and after mealtime. The routine is getting the food, eating, washing the plate, then, for me, a short nap before the water comes on, and down to the showers before the crowd hits. As time goes on and the food stays tight and not very good, little things like an orange or candied fruit that have been sent in by Benilde make a real difference. But everybody is still hungry. It gets to the point where dissolving four or five tablespoons of brown sugar in water tastes terrible but kills the hunger pains until you can fall asleep. The days drift by, but the radio the prisoners had built and concealed in the circular still hasn't been found, although the prison administration is still looking for it.

A month or so after the big shakedown, we have another search. Everybody out. Before going back in everybody is stripped to their birthday suit. The clothes end up in a pile along with all the shoes. I go through the line and am walking into the circular when all of a sudden, Bang! I get swatted on the rump with the flat of a bayonet. It raises a fine red welt on the left cheek. Immediately the Cuban prisoners come to give me their sympathy. I have finally made the grade—the Purple Heart for injury at the Isle of Pines. Luckily, we have some extra clothes, so it's no problem waiting until the clothes are sorted out, which takes three days. The pattern is repeated about every two weeks, but without the clothes ending up in a pile.

Negotiations and Disappointments

While in prison, the world was treated to such milestones as Roger Maris hitting home run number sixty-one to break Babe Ruth's record, John Glenn becoming the first American to orbit the earth in space, the Beatles releasing records. None of these things meant anything to us, since they did not change our situation. We had heard about all of them through the prisoners' newspaper. It was published every morning after the prisoner listening to the radio wrote notes that were copied and distributed in the circular.

One morning the news arrives that negotiations for the Brigade (in the States, the people that were picked up in the Bay of Pigs were called the Brigade; in prison, they were called the Invaders) are in full swing and things are looking good. Spirits go up, but the three of us are pessimistic about everything. With our luck, anything could happen. Things drag on—negotiations are still going on, but slowly.

The next big item to come along is the missile crisis in October. Somehow we miss the importance of it all. About a year ago, there was a mobilization and this one doesn't seem to be much different. Except for the blackouts at 8:00 p.m. every night and Castro's speeches about an imminent invasion or sanctions, nobody seems to be very excited about it. The *milicianos* are checking the TNT in the tunnel, but nobody seems to be paying much attention to it. Almost two weeks pass and things go back to normal.

More news arrives that prisoner negotiations are on again. Things are getting encouraging. Thanksgiving comes and goes and, as usual, we dress for dinner. But as I remember, it was not an outstanding meal. In fact, it was the worst meal we'd ever had—watery soup and nothing else. At this point, we had not tasted meat for a year. Everybody is looking forward to Christmas and the packages that will be coming with the meat sandwiches and other things.

Christmas season comes and the prisoner exchange is viewed as a sure thing for the Brigade. We get the confirming news from the radio—the only source of news we trusted—that the deal has been concluded and the boys are off. In the morning we see the airplane coming in over the island and one brave hotrod pilot makes a pass past the prison and hot rods it in to the landing field. Relatives of the Invaders are being called from the circulars and everybody is pressing their faces against the bars, sticking their arms out, waving to the fellows as they go by. We are among some of the noses pushed against the bars and we see some familiar faces going by. We hope against hope that we are going to be called, too. But no American names are called. It's extremely disappointing to say the least, to be leaning against the rail and hear the announcer call out the names and yours is not among them. But that's the way it goes.

As the days pass, everybody is still talking and thinking about the exchange, but no one talks about it with the Americans because it looks like we have missed the boat. My old friend Colonel Díaz, the former chief of the air force under Batista, still sits in his cell sketching and not saying much. He is sort of asking, "Well, Edmund what do you think now?" I reply that we have pretty well had it. The colonel says philosophically, "It's not right that the Invaders go and the Americans stay, but patience, something will work out."

One afternoon, I remember distinctly, we had just come up the stairs from the first floor after we had collected our ration of soup. I was just getting ready to tear into it when it happens. The announcer of the circular bellows for silence and starts reading names. I didn't really hear the names that are being read off, but there was that sudden jump in noise level as if something is happening. The buzz of the circular goes up to a new height. Suddenly somebody is hollering and yelling that they are reading our names off! Sitting the soup down on the floor with a clatter and running over to the railing to lean over the edge and listen, I hear the names: Austin Young, Peter Lambton, Richard Pecoraro. The feeling and exultation is tremendous and you know automatically what it is. Nobody has to tell you. It's almost indescribable that you finally know that "this is really it."

But that old pessimism still persists. Danny and I still have the feeling that it is great, but there is still something missing, something that's still not right.

Everything is all confusion. Hundreds of well-wishers are crowding around and wanting to say good-bye, shake hands, thump us on the back, and the vultures are around to pick up what items they can get—the beds we are leaving behind, some of our eating utensils, and just the junk that you don't want to take with you. It's a real struggle to get from the fifth floor down to the first floor. The stairs are jammed. Everybody is hollering, "Hurray for the Americans."

Finally we end up on the ground floor and it's a sight that's really something to see: looking up at a thousand faces and realizing that you know them all, some well, some not too well, some are friends, some are not friends, but you are saying good-bye to all of them.

We are lined up and taken out of the circular through the massive bars into the little *rastrillo* (passage). Papers are shuffled, names are called out, heads are counted. Finally we line up on the outside and there is our little friend we have seen from the windows so many times, with his galvanometer that he used for checking the blasting lines in each circular. Everybody is looking at us because, after all, we are the celebrities.

The word is given to march straight ahead. What now? The office and checkout are to the right. Straight ahead leads to the road around the mess hall, but not to freedom. So we are off. Dario Prohias mumbles something about changing clothes, getting rid of uniforms at the warehouse.

Well, marching we go around the mess hall, and it's apparent that we are not headed for the warehouse to change uniforms. We are going between Circulars 3 and 4 and it's amazing how crummy and disreputable they look from the outside. The hum and noise of a thousand human beings inside each one suddenly rises when a few discover that something is happening outside and rush to the windows to look out. The rest do pretty much the same. The noise rises to bedlam, with prisoners shouting at friends among the Americans. At this point Danny and I look at each other and mumble about sleeping on marble floors again. Our wonderful luck seems to be holding up. As we pass Circulars 3 and 4 it's pretty obvious where we are going—to the *pabellón* (pavilion). This and the hospital are the only places that we have missed during our stay at the island. We are marched up to the door and there is banging and hollering as the guard yells for the sentry inside. He opens the door and we are told to go inside. Everything is quiet; you can hear a pin drop. The apprehension and suspense are tremendous. What sort of filthy hole are we going to end up in? The guard goes to the right, unlocks the lock, opens the door, and motions us inside. A room thirty-five to forty feet long and twenty feet wide with steel cots and mattresses is what we see. In the excitement and tension we almost miss the fellow that is already there, but the Bobbsey Five—Bean, Baker, Beck, Smith, and Gibson—know our new group member, John Pedro Koop. He was a Cuban American imprisoned in Circular 3, a farmer-landowner whose family has extensive land holdings in one of the provinces.

Freedom

On March 16, 1963, we are visited by James B. Donovan, the New York attorney who a year earlier had arranged for the exchange of U-2 pilot Francis Gary Powers for Soviet spy William August Fisher (real name, Colonel Rudolf Ivanovich Abel) and bartered the release of the Cuban exiles captured at the Bay of Pigs. He told us that we'd be coming out in another prisoner exchange. A. told Donovan that he would rather stay in prison than be part of any deal that would embarrass the U.S. government.

The Cubans moved us from Circular 1 to the pavilion, not to the punishment cells, but to the less uncomfortable quarters. Our food improved, and we were permitted to see the sunshine.

We left the Isle of Pines on a ferryboat for the main island, and returned to La Cabaña. Sitting on the poop deck of the ferry headed for Cuba and watching the Isle of Pines get smaller in the distance, it was the most significantly emotional time of the whole ordeal. It was a feeling I cannot put into words. I was elated at leaving and depressed for those left behind.

On April 21, 1963, with eighteen other Americans, including the mentally ill Pecoraro, whom Castro swapped for four of his followers imprisoned in New York, we were flown to the United States. Donovan said six others declined to return to the States. Three of them were native-born Americans who chose to fly to South America. The other three were Cuban Americans who chose to stay in Cuba with their families. Donovan did not publicly identify the men who went to South America.

Our release was followed by the dismissal of a sabotage con-
spiracy indictment against two Cubans and a Cuban American in
New York. A federal district judge dropped the charges after the
Justice Department said it would be "in the national interest." So
twenty-one Americans were swapped for four Cubans.

The soldier-of-fortune types were the first off the plane and into
the lights of the news media's cameras. Security officers hustled
us out of camera range to a safe house, then to an aircraft for the
flight back to DC. During the flight I was told that my mother had
died. That was a tremendous shock to me. I thought the news
would be that my dad had passed away since he was in bad health
A. sat down and cried with me. After arrival in Washington, they
brought in A.'s wife and mother, and Dave's mother, wife, and
brother. The next day they let the wives stay there. The following day, the women got out of the house and we were treated to
a series of sessions with shrinks, medics, and whatnot. Then all
of a sudden our release was leaked. Security folks said that the
White House—Kennedy—had leaked that we were CIA officers.
Our cover had lasted for 949 days in Cuba, and only three days at
home. (But our cover names, albeit misspelled, still held!)

Castro did not release Cuban-born Miami resident Rafael Del
Pino, whose wife and three-year-old daughter came to Home-
stead Air Force Base expecting to find him among us. He had
been shot down while trying to land a light plane near Havana in
July 1960. She said that she had been informed that he would be
among our group.

I went to Boston to see my father, while Dave C. and Andy saw
their children again. Andy's youngest son didn't know him; his
older boy barely remembered him. Gail A. had moved the boys
from their northern Virginia home to Florida. Living her husband's
cover, she had found it increasingly difficult as Christmases came
and went to explain to the neighbors why he could never get home
leave from his "overseas assignment." In Florida, the woman who
moved in with two small boys and no sign of a husband was encoun-

tering raised eyebrows and wagging tongues. Andy observed, "You pay a price for cover."

Epilogue

You would think that after our release, things would have been roses for us. But we returned to an atmosphere that could at best be called bureaucratic indifference and at worst filled with counterintelligence suspicions. Upon arrival in the Free World, we were not met at the airport by our division chief, but by his deputy. After thorough debriefing for several days, we were put "on ice" (no work, just administrative leave) for several months while the counterintelligence boys attempted to figure out whether we had been "turned" by the Cubans and sent back into the CIA as Castro's moles. Fat chance after the less than luxurious treatment in jail.

Once the counterintelligence folks and polygraphers had been satisfied, we went through extended debriefings, medical and psychological evaluations, and a host of other chats. When we were all deemed clean, we returned to work. We had thought that the director of central intelligence might call us for an attaboy and pat on the head, but we were taken instead to the executive director.

We had a great time swapping stories with our colleagues back in headquarters, trying to determine whether our mutual attempts to get messages to each other had succeeded. They were surprised that we hadn't picked up on their attempts to get messages to us. But early in our incarceration, the consul, after he'd chatted with our colleagues in the United States and found out that we were CIA officers, told us that our orders were to attempt nothing operational, such as sending secret writing messages, collecting intelligence, or fomenting disturbances among the prisoners. We were to live our cover—we were just tourists who'd been asked to do a favor for some embassy guy. But two years into our captivity, we received a batch of photographs of folks from headquarters. There were a few photos of people at an office picnic. In one of them, the head of our secret writing team was lifting one of the secretaries while wading through a stream. We thought it was rather odd, and that it might be an attempt to get a message to us. Our headquarters friends told us, "The photo of the water was telling you that you should dip the photo in water. The secret writing message would destroy the emulsion of the photo, and the hidden message would be revealed." Oh, well.

On the other hand, headquarters didn't get the message all the time, either. During the period when the Cubans were mining the area surrounding the circulars, we painstakingly created a map of the whole operation on onionskin paper. After folding it until it was smaller than a postage stamp, we managed to smuggle the map out of the prison via a female Cuban activist visitor. She in turn passed the vellum on to one of the groups in Havana who sent it to Miami where it got into the hands of people who forwarded it to headquarters. Headquarters put it into one of their multitudinous Cuban files. After my release when I was visiting the Western Hemisphere Division, a case officer brought the map out and asked what I knew about it. (The headquarters attitude was that Cubans tended to create a story where there is none.) I replied that I had helped to draw it. He replied, "Oh, that's nice," and put it back in the safe. "We could never be sure whether it was bogus, so we ignored it."

We also learned that cover can backfire when well-meaning friends try to pry. Stephanie Coffey Krupinsky Cooper, whose roommate I had dated in 1957 when we met during a Florida vacation, almost exposed us. Stephanie and I had hit it off immediately—we were both from the Boston area. She was dating an FBI agent from their New York field office, whom she later married. During the next two years, my relationship with her roommate ended, but my friendship with Stephanie and her husband continued. When I took the Far East assignment, they were transferred to Chicago. We kept in touch on a regular basis. In April 1960, their first daughter was born, and I told them that I would be coming back to the States, probably in the late summer or early fall, and would stop by in Chicago to see the three of them. But the FBI moved them again, this time to Washington DC in late August. After getting settled into their new apartment, Stephanie reminded her husband that they should tell me that they had moved. She eventually got exasperated with her husband for not getting in touch with me by September. He said, "You can call the CIA's number yourself; it's in the phone book!" She said, "Wow! CIA's in the phone book! Okay, I'll call them." After repeated calls to various offices in an attempt to track down Wally Szuminski and getting the "no such person" response, an authoritative voice came on the line and twenty-questioned her. Now he wanted her husband's name and phone number. About an hour later, Stephanie's husband called her, fit to be tied, telling her to stand down. "You got me in trouble. I'll tell you about it when I get home. Have the martinis ready." And there, but for a great deal of luck, our cover could have been blown.

Through it all, Dave C. would say as loudly and as often as he could that his two compadres were heroes (true to form, he never attempted to cloak himself in glory) and called for us to receive medals as the victims of a mismanaged operation and the heroes of the aftermath. C. sent a memorandum on July 7, 1964, to the deputy director of central intelligence and the director of personnel, recalling some of our experiences. He was putting us in for a special commendation, so he wrote about us rather than himself. But all of what he says applies to him, too.

> The Isles of Pines Prison . . . was the one most dreaded by all Cubans. For months on end they felt no sunlight, only the dank filthiness inside the circulars. Food was incredibly bad. No facilities for literature. Long months of prison . . . living in a strange country with different languages, thinking, and personal habits, with longing and concern for the loved ones at home, more than a year with no word of any kind from home, and then sporadic, closely censored mail—all these things and worse were the . . . routine.
>
> Added to this were unusually violent and trying pressures—threats and intimidation because they were Americans, frequent bloody riots, emotional breakdown and suicides. Then there were

the *requisas* or searches, the attempted escapes, the turbulent period of the April 1961 Bay of Pigs invasion and the October 1962 confrontation. Frequently the guards sent shots ricocheting through the building. For an entire year they lived in circulars mined with 6,000 pounds of TNT; the severe lightning storms during these nights did not encourage sleep. For at least a year they were on the death list of one of the anti-American groups. There was practically no time during which they could really expect to get out of this situation alive.

In retrospect, it is truly remarkable the manner in which they retained morale and complete emotional stability. They always maintained high standards of personal cleanliness and decency— their cells and personal effects were always the cleanest in the circular. They shared their food, medications, and personal possessions with the Cubans and other Americans. They encouraged and stabilized the "soldier of fortune"-type Americans, some of whom were considering entering the communist rehabilitation program. They adopted the mentally ill American who on occasion became criminally insane. They circulated through the prison community making friends and giving encouragement. They were always leaned on for moral support when the news was bad. They interpreted and explained the news in support of President Kennedy and the United States government. They studied Spanish and taught English. They gave lectures on the Constitution, capitalism, our legal and law enforcement system, elections, and other aspects of American democratic life. They spoke on such subjects as the U.S. development of nuclear electric power and the conversion of salt water for improving the underdeveloped areas of the world. In essence, they forgot their own problems by concerning themselves with those of others.

Ultimately, in 1979, DCI Stansfield Turner arranged for the three of us to receive the Distinguished Intelligence Cross, which is given to agency employees "for a voluntary act or acts of exceptional heroism involving the acceptance of existing dangers with conspicuous fortitude and exemplary courage."

Dave C. continued his professional life at the recently formed

Directorate of Science and Technology to create and populate new divisions and complete a highly successful career. Upon his retirement in 1970, he was awarded the Intelligence Medal of Merit. After retirement, he founded an electronics research-and-development firm. He died of cancer on December 9, 1985. He is buried in Arlington Cemetery.

Andy and I returned to Technical Services Division for additional operational adventures, such as having our light aircraft hit by ground fire as we flew over Laos in 1968. We came through that and other narrow scrapes unscathed. However, during a tour in the Far East in 1975, Andy's youngest son was killed in a train-car accident. Andy retired in 1979. He and Gail live in a splendid house with a swimming pool in Longwood, Florida.

A couple of years after we were freed, I began dating Elsie C., the branch's secretary. We got married in May 1965. We and our two children live in Fairfax, Virginia.

I retired from the CIA in 1980 and have worked off and on with the agency in a contractual capacity ever since. In September 1997, in celebration of the fiftieth anniversary of the founding of the agency, I was chosen to lay a wreath at the Memorial Pond, which is a monument to all individuals—staffers, contract hires, agents, and anyone else—who have died in service to the country and the agency.

It has been an honor to serve my country and be affiliated with the agency. I wouldn't have missed it for the world.

The Isle of Pines circulars were later converted into a museum. So I guess all's well that ends well.

A Word from Our Predecessors

30

Operation Oshima

JOHN BEHLING

After the December 7, 1941, Japanese attack on Pearl Harbor, President Franklin Roosevelt directed then Colonel William Donovan, his coordinator for information, to create a wartime Office of Strategic Services. The OSS, forerunner of the CIA, conducted intelligence collection, propaganda, and paramilitary operations. A memorial to the OSS officers who died in service to our country provides the backdrop to the Donovan statue in the lobby of the CIA's Original Headquarters Building.

After Berlin fell and Germany surrendered in May 1945, I was working with the OSS in Linz, Austria.

One day my commanding officer (CO) called me into his office in Salzburg and told me that apparently I was uniquely qualified for a special job. It seemed that I was the only intelligence specialist or agent in his command that had any background whatsoever in the Japanese language and maritime facilities. Before the war I had worked for a sugar import firm and had to deal with documentation and Japanese shipping lines. Since they did not speak English, in self-defense I had learned basic Japanese.

The job, as the CO explained to me, was very delicate in nature. All the Japanese diplomats and attachés in Germany had been rounded up and were now interned in Bad Gastein, Austria, in a luxury ski resort hotel. Two burning questions existed: Would the German submarine fleet travel east and join up with the Japanese? And would Japan consider surrendering, now that Germany had?

The difficult problem, as he explained further, was that all the interned Japanese had diplomatic immunity and could not be questioned. We had also to remember that they held Americans as prisoners. Under no circumstances could I let it be known or found out that I worked for an intelligence agency.

"Fine," I said. "What will be my cover then?" He suggested hotel staff employee. "No," I said. "Gastein is a small town, all employees will be townspeople. They all know each other. I would stand out like a sore thumb." The same was true for a repairman sent to fix something. Finally I asked, "Who's keeping the Japanese interned? Who is on guard duty?" U.S. Army Third Division, I was told. Good, then transfer me to the Third Division as a new, freshly arrived replacement. Only the officer in charge of guard detail will know my identity, and tell him that I will pick my guard post and time. Can do, the CO replied, and then added, "While you're there, try to search their rooms and see if you find anything."

So, after two years in North Africa and Europe, I was now a freshly minted soldier, green as grass. The Third's veterans were uncommonly kind and helpful to the new rookie. I picked the evening shift and the dining-room post. I figured everyone would be down for dinner and I could survey the scene and make some kind of a plan.

I soon noticed that the Japanese were constantly talking to the hotel staff in German. Why not? They had been there around ten years and spoke it quite well, albeit with a typical Japanese accent. That gave me an idea. I, too, started speaking to the help in German. As I expected, soon the Japanese noticed the American soldier who was fluent in German. The Japanese ambassador, Baron Oshima, approached me and asked how it was that a typical one-language American could converse in a foreign language.

That gave me my opening. "I'm not really American," I lied. "I was born in Germany. My father was a professor on an educational exchange in the U.S. when Hitler declared war. I was interned for the duration, and when the war ended, they drafted me to pay them back for my upkeep, and here I am."

Now I was a fellow intern, I was one of them, a compadre, so to speak. They were almost eager to talk to me, and all I had to do was channel the conversation to get the two sets of answers. Forget the submarines, I was told; they couldn't get past the British navy, and even if they did, they would be of no use. We don't have fuel for our own U-boats. On the question of surrender, I got an explanation of how the government would be saving face. The existing government couldn't surrender; it would require the suicide of its officials. The solution would be to hand the government over to a less rigid regime, which probably still couldn't surrender and lose face, but which could give way to another set of officials who could ask to surrender. The whole process, they thought, would take about three months. Unknown to any of us, Hiroshima and Nagasaki were about three months away.

All that was left was to search a few rooms. To do that, one needed a passkey. Who always has a passkey? The chambermaids. Fortunately, all German men were in military service or otherwise absent, and German women were starved for male companionship. I expressed the usual American interest in getting some kind of "souvenir" and soon had a passkey. But the rooms were sterile, nothing but clothing and a bit of candy.

I now had the information I needed, and had preserved cover and security, so I told the Third Army to transfer me out, and I returned to the OSS.

The denouement, however, came when I was debriefed. The debriefing officer was a new arrival, an artillery captain with no background in intelligence. When I gave him the information, he looked at me incredulously, and said, "Did Oshima tell you all that?" Absolutely, I replied. The captain looked at me for a moment, said, "I don't believe it," and turned on his heel and walked away. I don't believe he ever turned in a report, and I have often wondered whether if that information had gone to higher headquarters it might have made a difference in our decision to use the atomic bomb.

And from the Next Generation

31

The Other Side of the CIA

My Life as a CIA Analyst

SCOTT SCHLIMMER

Quick—name your favorite movie about a CIA analyst. Having trouble naming one? Hollywood loves its CIA spy movies, but movies about analysts are few and far between. Is intelligence analysis boring, not worthy of the silver screen? You won't see a movie shadowing a day in the life of Scott Schlimmer anytime soon, but the job can be surprisingly exciting at times . . . and surprisingly mundane at other times.

If you've ever wanted the excitement of the CIA with the lifestyle of a nine-to-five desk job, then a career as an analyst might be what you're looking for. This article describes the life of a CIA analyst, sparing neither the boring nor the exciting, since the job is a mix of both.

The Workplace—Langley

It all starts with the security clearance process, which can take several months or even years. The process is rigorous because all CIA analysts have Top Secret clearance with access to extremely sensitive information from human sources, telephone intercepts, and satellite imagery. After a polygraph, a physical exam, drug tests, and a background investigation that includes interviews with friends and former neighbors, I was deemed free of exploitable vulnerabilities and fit to be trusted with classified information. The process took thirteen months.

Once cleared, you show up at Langley, Virginia, where intelligence analysis takes place. You might expect a hidden compound, but instead you'll find road signs (which even include the CIA abbreviation) directing you to the George Bush Center for Intelligence. Not the most secretive introduction. But then you'll be greeted by many guards with extremely large guns, which feels more like something you'd see in the movies. The feeling doesn't last long when you reach the parking lots. A lot of people work at Langley, which makes parking spots difficult to find and usually far from the building. If you arrive at 8:30 a.m., expect a ten-minute walk to get into the building.

Walking through Langley the first time, I was struck by how similar the compound felt to a college campus. It was vibrant, full of people strolling about. I expected a stuffy atmosphere and black suits, but a surprising number of analysts often don't wear ties. Most people wear jeans—and even Hawaiian shirts—on Friday, which is a casual day. Of course, suits are required when interacting with people outside of the agency, so there is an interesting mix of people who are dressed extremely well and those who look more casual.

Overall, you don't get the sense that you're in a building full of spooks. Everybody looks like standard, normal people.

What Is Intelligence Analysis?

Most analysts begin their day by firing up their computers, checking their emails, and then reading through the new intelligence cables. These cables are the key to analysis work.

You've probably seen plenty of CIA spy movies, but those movies don't show what the CIA really does. The CIA is in the business of information. The CIA "spies" are actually called case officers or operations officers. Their job is to recruit real spies—non-Americans who are willing to provide information on their country. The spy gives information to the case officer, who then writes the information into a cable that is sent to Langley. The cables usually include specific information on an event. For an older instance, this could include where the Soviets were hiding their missiles. Or perhaps, long ago, General Secretary Khrushchev's plans and intentions in Cuba.

That's where the analyst comes in. The analyst connects policymakers with the intelligence. Our main customer is the president and his executive agencies—especially the National Security Council, the Department of Defense, and the State Department. We also write often for Congress. I've had my papers read by everybody from working-level analysts to ambassadors to the president!

While case officers are good at coaxing information from spies and ensuring everybody's safety, analysts are the substantive experts. Analysts read many cables containing information from many spies over time, then put the information into context and search for trends and patterns.

Here is an example. Keep in mind that this is an old example from the Soviet days to keep this article unclassified. If I used a more current example, this whole section might be covered with a black box!

An analyst might receive a cable from a reliable source saying that Khrushchev wants to move SS-21 missiles into Cuba to attack Washington. Emergency?! Call up the president and warn him? Absolutely not. The Soviet missile analyst knows the range of an SS-21 and realizes that such a missile could never reach Washington. Many people would overreact to the news, but that wouldn't be helpful to policymakers. The expert analyst puts the information into perspective.

The next week, the analyst gets a cable from a questionable source saying that Khrushchev wants to move R-12 missiles into Cuba to attack Washington. The analyst knows that the R-12 could plausibly strike Washington from Cuba. Time to sound the alarms? It's not entirely clear. Could the source be lying? Could the Soviets be feeding us bad information through the source intentionally? Could the source think he's telling the truth but be mistaken? Even if the source is correct, how does the analyst know whether Khrushchev will follow through on his intentions or change his mind? Analysts have to make just such judgments about complex situations based on limited information that is often vague and contradictory.

Two weeks later, the analyst might get a report from imagery analysts indicating that something that looks like a disguised missile was being moved into Cuba. (Yes, analysts get to see the actual imagery photos, but it's hard for the untrained eye to make any sense of them. I rely on the imagery analyst's report.)

Now is it time to warn the president? It just might be. Perhaps the analyst will spend the day writing a paper for the President's Daily Brief (PDB) the next morning.

Is Khrushchev Moving Long-Range Missiles to Cuba?

Analysis of imagery indicates that missiles are being moved into Cuba. We lack reporting to determine the type of missiles being moved, but reporting suggests that the missiles could include Soviet long-range ballistic missiles intended to strike Washington.

> Analysis indicates that probable missiles were transported, most likely by ship, to Cuba. General Secretary Khrushchev intends to move R-12 missiles into Cuba to attack Washington.

The above is one paragraph of a PDB. The paper usually will include another paragraph or two. One might outline why Khrushchev might be moving the missiles or what he hopes to achieve. Another could lay out options or ideas for the president to address the situation.

DI Style

This theoretical/notional paper, or President's Daily Brief, is written in DI style. The Directorate of Intelligence (DI), the analysis branch of the CIA, has a distinct writing style designed to be unmistakably clear about what we think and why we think it. The main paragraph states our analytic judgment—what we think, why we think it, and how confident we are in the judgment. The following bullets then share details about the information we used to form our judgments and the sources that information came from.

The DI uses an inverted pyramid style, which means the main

point goes in the first sentence—the bottom line is up front (we even give it an acronym: BLUF)—and then you expand on the main point. This differs from other styles of writing, like academic writing, where you might use your evidence to build your way to a bottom line. The idea is that the president or other policymakers might be too busy to read every word of the paper. If that's the case, they can read just the title or the first sentence and still get the main point of the paper. Alternatively, they can also get more depth or more details, if they choose, simply by reading on. No matter how somebody reads a properly written DI product, they should get the same message.

Also unlike academic papers, a DI paper does not include all of the evidence that supports its main point. DI papers are designed to be exemplary, not exhaustive. Only the one, two, or three best pieces of evidence are included.

DI papers are also supposed to be concise. The language is terse and needless words are omitted. This doesn't always play out in reality. I haven't found DI papers to be nearly as concise as advertised. In fact, they often try to pack in as much information into a small space as is humanly possible. This isn't surprising, since DI analysts often care deeply about and know a great deal about the topics they write about.

Café

Has all that analysis worked up an appetite? Usually you'll have lunch in the café. Some people go to restaurants at lunch, but the Langley compound is pretty isolated. It's almost impossible eat lunch in a restaurant and make it back during your thirty-minute lunch break, so you'd probably have to work later to make up for it.

The café is large and pretty nice. There's a traditional cafeteria, with two or three entrée selections, soup choices, salad bar, sandwiches, and a griller. The food is usually fairly good, healthy, and there are tons of selections to choose from. However, portion sizes tend to be small and it's hard to find a good value.

There's also a fast-food section, with Sbarros, Subway, Burger

King, Chinese food, a barbecue place, Dunkin Donuts, and Starbucks. You can get more food here for less money, but it's not the healthiest.

Most analysts eat lunch at their desks. However, plenty of people eat in the café's large seating areas. When the weather is nice, you can also eat in the courtyard. When you open the door, you'll see a sign reminding you not to bring classified material outside into the courtyard. Presumably, satellites from foreign intelligence services are pointed toward the courtyard and might be able to read the classified material.

The courtyard is quite nice. It's full of trees, has a fountain, and an odd sculpture called Kryptos to remind you where you are. Kryptos is a sculpture in code. Three-fourths of Kryptos has been cracked, but one section remains unsolved.

Briefing

After lunch, perhaps you'll have a briefing scheduled. Analysts' key products are papers, like the President's Daily Brief, but we also communicate our judgments and observations through other types of briefings. Briefings are essentially oral presentations to policymakers. Most of us never get to brief the president, but we often brief senior officials like ambassadors and generals.

Early on, I was struck by the DI's culture, which manifests itself clearly through briefings. The DI values expertise over seniority. That is, when a policymaker requests a briefing on a topic, the DI will send the substantive expert on the topic, regardless of their experience. During my first year, I was amazed to be briefing colonels with twenty years of experience. I was only twenty-six years old! But this is common in the DI.

Training

Fortunately, even first-year analysts are trained very well. Everybody in the DI—analysts as well as graphic designers and cartographers—go through the Career Analyst Program (CAP), a training program designed to teach intelligence writing, briefing, and analytic thinking. The CAP also includes an interim assignment, essentially an internship with a policymaking organization or another component of the agency. The interim is a great experience for seeing intelligence from a different perspective. I served my interim with a policymaking customer, the White House Office of National Drug Control Policy. There I learned firsthand how policymakers use the papers and briefings we produce. It's important to note that the CIA pays your salary during the CAP and your interim but gets no actual productivity from you. The agency definitely values training.

Perk: No Work at Home

Don't like to take your work home with you? You're in luck. The CIA won't let you.

Almost all of our work involves classified information, so it has to be done in a sensitive compartmented information facility (SCIF), which is essentially a safe or a vault. Work has to stay in the SCIF in Langley.

Usually it's nice to keep work and home separate. At home you never are burdened with the thought that you could be doing work. However, it can be burdensome if you're at home but you need to know something on the classified computers. On Sunday, you might want to check your calendar for Monday, but you'll have drive to Langley to do so.

Downside: Where do you Work?

If you work at the CIA, eventually you'll dread the common small-talk question, "Where do you work?"

Covert employees are under cover and cannot acknowledge their affiliation with the CIA. Most analysts, though, are overt, which means they openly work for the agency. We even get tax forms at the end of the year that say "CIA" on them! Overt employees technically can admit they work for the CIA. We have great access to classified information, and foreign intelligence services might target a known CIA analyst to spy against the United States. However, overt employees aren't given a cover story.

So when asked, "Where do you work?" different people handle the question differently. Some are very secretive—one overt employee told me she had not told her parents where she worked—while others will respond truthfully. Both, however, dread the question.

Is Hollywood Ready for CIA Analysts?

After reading this chapter, are there any takers on making a movie, perhaps *The Mighty Pen: The Scott Schlimmer Story*? I understand if Hollywood isn't interested in the life of an analyst, but as you can see it's a unique, interesting way to make a living. Analysts get a taste of the CIA without having to swallow all of it.

Overall, I've enjoyed working as an analyst with the CIA. I get a lot of responsibility and great training for that responsibility, pretty early in my career. My papers get read by senior policymakers who are very interested in what I have to say. Any good ideas I come up with have a good shot at becoming a reality.

I've also met a lot of smart, interesting people at the agency. We have fewer "happy hours" than people who work downtown in DC, which is probably because we're a little isolated in Virginia. Perhaps also because the security clearance process weeds out the heavy drinkers! However, I've interacted socially with lots of agency coworkers in the many intramural sports leagues we have. A surprising number of people even met their spouses at the agency!

I'm not sure where my career will take me in the next ten years. The CIA is a great place to spend an entire career. Plenty of people spend twenty to thirty years there and there are lots of different career fields to jump around to. However, many also leave the agency to try their hand at something else, well-prepared for work in other agencies or fields. For me, the CIA has definitely been a once-in-a-lifetime kind of experience.

APPENDIX

The Vision, Mission, and Values Statement of the Central Intelligence Agency

Vision

We will provide knowledge and take action to ensure the national security of the United States and the preservation of American life and ideals.

Mission

We are the eyes and ears of the nation and at times its hidden hand. We accomplish this mission by

collecting intelligence that matters;

providing relevant, timely, and objective all-source analysis; and

conducting covert action at the direction of the president to preempt threats or achieve United States policy objectives.

Values

In pursuit of our country's interests, we put nation before agency, agency before unit, and all before self. What we do matters.

Our success depends on our ability to act with total discretion and an ability to protect sources and methods.

We provide objective, unbiased information and analysis.

Our mission requires complete personal integrity and personal courage, physical and intellectual.

We accomplish things others cannot, often at great risk. When the stakes are highest and the dangers greatest, we are there and there first.

We stand by one another and behind one another. Service, sacrifice, flexibility, teamwork, and quiet patriotism are our hallmarks.

SUGGESTED READING

Andrew, Christopher. *For the President's Eyes Only: Secret Intelligence and the American Presidency from Washington to Bush*. New York: Harper Perennial, 1996.

Carland, Maria Pinto, and Candace Faber, eds. *Careers in International Affairs*. 8th ed. Washington DC: Georgetown University School of Foreign Service, Georgetown University Press, 2008.

George, Roger Z., and James B. Bruce. *Analyzing Intelligence: Origins, Obstacles, and Innovations*. Washington DC: Georgetown University Press, 2008.

Firth, Noel E., and James H. Noren. *Soviet Defense Spending: A History of CIA Estimates, 1950-1990*. Williams-Ford Texas A&M University Military History Series. College Station: Texas A&M University Press, 1998.

Gates, Robert M. *From the Shadows: The Ultimate Insider's Story of Five Presidents and How They Won the Cold War*. New York: Simon and Schuster, 2007.

Helgerson, John. *Getting to Know the President: CIA Briefings of Presidential Candidates, 1952-1992*. Washington DC: Center for the Study of Intelligence, Central Intelligence Agency, 1996.

Heuer, Richards J., Jr. *Psychology of Intelligence Analysis*. Reston VA: Pherson Associates, 2007.

Jones, Morgan. *The Thinker's Toolkit: 14 Powerful Techniques for Problem Solving*. New York: Three Rivers Press, 1998.

Latell, Brian. *After Fidel: Raul Castro and the Future of Cuba's Revolution*. New York: Palgrave Macmillan, 2007.

Lowenthal, Mark M. *Intelligence: From Secrets to Policy*. 4th ed. Washington DC: CQ Press, 2008.

Smith, Russell Jack. *The Unknown CIA: My Three Decades with the Agency*. New York: Pergamon-Brassey's, 1989.

Westerfield, H. Bradford, ed. *Inside CIA's Private World: Declassified Articles from the Agency's Internal Journal, 1955-1992*. New Haven CT: Yale University Press, 1995.

And just in case, after reading these memoirs, you'd like to compare these officers' experiences with officers from the Directorate of Operations (now called the National Clandestine Service), here is a small sample of the literature by operations officers, including those memoirs mentioned in the introduction.

Baer, Robert. *See No Evil: The True Story of a Ground Soldier in the CIA's War on Terrorism*. New York: Three Rivers Press, 2003.

Bearden, Milton, and James Risen. *The Main Enemy: The Inside Story of the CIA's Final Showdown with the KGB*. New York: Presidio Press, 2004.

Berntsen, Gary, and Ralph Pezzullo. *Jawbreaker: The Attack on Bin Laden and Al-Qaeda: A Personal Account by the CIA's Key Field Commander*. New York: Three Rivers Press, 2006.

Clarridge, Duane, and Digby Diehl. *A Spy for All Seasons: My Life in the CIA*. New York: Scribner, 2002.

Colby, William, and Peter Forbath. *Honorable Men: My Life in the CIA*. New York: Simon and Schuster, 1978.

Dulles, Allen W. *The Craft of Intelligence: America's Legendary Spy Master on the Fundamentals of Intelligence Gathering for a Free World*. New York: Lyons, 2006.

Helms, Richard, with William Hood. *A Look Over My Shoulder: A Life in the Central Intelligence Agency*. New York: Presidio, 2004.

Holm, Richard. *The American Agent: My Life in the CIA*. Boston: Little, Brown, 2004.

Olson, James M. *Fair Play: The Moral Dilemmas of Spying*. Bethesda MD: Potomac Books, 2007.

Paseman, Floyd. *A Spy's Journey: A CIA Memoir*. Minneapolis: Zenith, 2005.

Phillips, David Atlee. *The Night Watch: 25 Years of Peculiar Service*. New York: Ballantine, 1987.

Schroen, Gary. *First In: An Insider's Account of How the CIA Spearheaded the War on Terror in Afghanistan*. New York: Presidio, 2007.

Shackley, Ted, with Richard Finney. *Spymaster: My Life in the CIA*. Bethesda MD: Potomac Books, 2006.

Waters, T. J. *Class 11: My Story Inside the CIA's First Post-9/11 Spy Class*. New York: Plume, 2007.

CONTRIBUTORS

MERRILY BAIRD is the author of *Symbols of Japan: Thematic Motifs in Art and Design* (2001) and the chapter on North Korean strategic thinking in the Air War College's *Know Thy Enemy* (2002). Based in Atlanta, she today spends the majority of her time as a docent at Emory University's antiquities museum, as a student of French, and as a lecturer on the art and cultures of East Asia.

JOHN BEHLING worked in Linz, Austria, during World War II for the Office of Strategic Services (Company B, 2677th Regiment), the predecessor organization of the Central Intelligence Agency. He now resides in the northeastern United States.

ROBERT BLACKWELL spent thirty enjoyable years as a Directorate of Intelligence analyst and supervisor, including as an office director and National Intelligence Officer on the Soviet Union. In retirement, he traveled extensively and was active in the Alzheimer's Association's Early-Stage Advisory Group.

JERI DiGIULIO is one of the very few CIA retirees who moved to the Midwest, not the Sunbelt. She taught English as a second language, toured architectural wonders in Illinois and Wisconsin, and has come to admire prairie grass.

MICHAEL D. FLINT served his country his entire working career. He started his career in the U.S. Army from 1967 to 1969. After a tour in Vietnam he left the army and became an analyst with the Defense Intelligence Agency until 1975, when he transferred to the Central Intelligence Agency. As an analyst both in the DIA and CIA, Michael authored many intelligence articles and published several classified books on Soviet military topics. After federal retirement in 1995, he became a contractor working for the National Geospatial Intelligence Agency where he supported strategic planning for future intelligence systems. Michael retired a second time in 2004 and now lives in California.

ANNE CAMPBELL GRUNER, after obtaining a law degree from Georgetown University, was a law clerk in Fairfax County Circuit Court and practiced family law for five years. She is Vice President of Gruner Associates, a consultancy specializing in global business intelligence, international and domestic investigations, due diligence, litigation support, asset and person searches, risk assessment and management, and international problem solving. She is a member of the Board of Visitors of George Mason University.

HAZEL HARRISON retired from the CIA in 1989 after thirty-two years of service in the Office of Logistics, Supply Division. Following retirement, she received her BGS degree from Longwood University, Farmville, Virginia. She and her husband, George, now live at a senior home, The Summit, in Lynchburg, Virginia.

JOHN HOLLISTER HEDLEY retired as Chairman of the CIA's Publications Review Board, which determines if writings by current or former CIA officers can be published (including the original manuscript that became the Academy Award–winning movie *Argo*). During more than thirty years at CIA, he also edited the President's Daily Brief, the nation's most sensitive current intelligence publication, and regularly briefed its contents at the White House to the National Security Adviser, to the Vice President, and the Secretary of Defense. Dr. Hedley has been an adjunct professor at Georgetown University, is on the editorial board of the *International Journal of Intelligence and Counterintelligence*, and is the author of *Harry S. Truman: The "Little" Man from Missouri*, chapters in five other books, and several journal articles on intelligence.

JOHN HELGERSON had a sterling career in the intelligence community, serving in a wide variety of senior positions, including Deputy Director for Intelligence, Chairman of the National Intelligence Council, Deputy Director of the National Imagery and Mapping Agency, and Inspector General of the CIA. His pioneering *Getting to Know the President: CIA Briefings of Presidential Candidates, 1952–1992* (1996) served as the basis for his presentation to the CIA Retirees' Association, which graciously permitted its reprint here.

RICHARD IRWIN retired from the CIA in 2005 and began as Vice President of Alutiiq's Homeland Security Division the next day. He continued in this capacity through January 2010 when he joined MELE Associates as their Vice President of Homeland Security. In 2011, he joined SNVC as the Chief Operating Officer/Senior Vice President for National Security, serving in this capacity until June 2013, when he formed his own security consulting company, Cead Mile Failte Consulting LLC, as the President and Chief Executive Officer.

DAN KING served as Support Officer for the CIA from 1964 to 1994, eight years of which were served abroad. Although an engineer by education, he developed a fascination with intelligence operations and foreign affairs and entered the agency through the Junior Officer Training program. During his career he headed several support offices including the Offices of Logistics, Communications, and Finance and served for a short period as the Associate Deputy Director for Administration and a Chief of Station abroad. Following retirement from the agency, he worked nine years as a program manager for a large information technology firm. In retirement he enjoys family, community service, and furniture making.

ROBERT E. LEGGETT, since retiring from the CIA, has worked for Booz Allen Hamilton and SAIC as a program manager on contracts with the intelligence community, principally focusing on analyst training, mentoring, and evaluation of analytic products.

EDWARD MICKOLUS, after a thirty-three-year career with all four CIA directorates and the DCI area of the CIA, teaches at several intelligence community agencies, serves as President of Vinyard Software, Inc., and is the author of several dozen scholarly journal articles and twenty-four books, with several others in process. Book topics include international terrorism, intelligence studies, teaching, contemporary history, international organizations, and humor.

ALAN MORE retired from the CIA in 2005 after thirty-two years in a variety of positions and assignments at other federal agencies. The agency awarded him the Career Intelligence Medal upon his retirement. Since retiring, he has been an Adjunct Professor at George Mason University, where he teaches in the Intelligence Analysis and the Bachelor of Individualized Programs. He also serves as the Employer in Residence for U.S. government programs in the university's Career Services Center. He teaches writing, leadership, and national security at the federal Management Development Centers and serves as an informal consultant to a number of spy thriller writers.

ROBERT A. MORGAN JR. in 1984 established and incorporated a travel agency in Virginia with his wife. He retired from the CIA in 1988, working in the travel agency as the Vice President. The couple sold the firm in 2006 and moved to a West Virginia retirement community. He found his agency service to be "interesting, rewarding, challenging, and fulfilling because I served my country."

JON NOWICK since 2006 has been instructing U.S. government personnel in counterterrorism, collaboration, and intelligence support. Before that he served for thirty years as an analyst, manager, and staff chief in the CIA's Directorate of Intelligence. Nowick is also a Senior Fellow at George Washington University's Homeland Security Policy Institute.

MARTIN PETERSEN rose through the analytic ranks of the CIA, serving as an analyst before becoming an Office Director, Associate Deputy Director of Intelligence, and Executive Director, the third-ranking officer within the agency. He was one of the first people that rookie analysts met in their orientation courses.

HUGH S. PETTIS retired in 1977 from the CIA, where he was responsible for the career management and development of the agency's telecommunications specialists and electronic technicians, including their hiring, assignment, evaluation, and advancement. He went on to become a research assistant and publications editor for the Smithsonian Institution for a decade, was a thesis and dissertation editor and undergraduate writing tutor and consultant at the University of Maryland at College Park, and an Adjunct Instructor in Literature and Language at Eastern Mennonite University. During his second try at retirement, he is augmenting his collections in intelligence, cryptanalysis, British railroad engineering, and radio communications history.

WILL ROGERS served in the CIA as an analyst from 1963 to 1992, with rotational assignments to the Office of Personnel and Training and as a recruiter. From 1992 to 2013, he was an independent contractor with the intelligence community.

VOLKO F. RUHNKE, a 1986 graduate of the Master of Science in Foreign Service Program at Georgetown University, teaches at the Sherman Kent School of CIA University. He has also served as the Deputy National Intelligence Officer for Science and Technology and as a Deputy Group Chief in the CIA's Counterterrorism Center.

FRANK RYAN, after retiring from the CIA after twenty-five years of service, came back on contract for two more years. He then established his own company, Rytec, Inc., a tech security firm. He later joined USATREX, Inc., and was Vice President and part owner of the company.

SCOTT SCHLIMMER is an intelligence analyst in the CIA's Directorate of Intelligence. He holds a bachelor's degree in political science and a master's degree in public policy. Gregor prides himself on keeping America safe and does not drink coffee.

TOM SHERIDAN, after college and eight years in the U.S. Navy, entered the CIA's Career Trainee Program in 1972. Tom's almost thirty-year career was in the Directorate of Intelligence. His focus was on the use of secret, government satellite imagery—and later commercial imagery and GIS—in combination with other secret and open-source information for the analysis of military issues in the Middle East and South Asia. Much of his work was on paramilitary and counternarcotics projects.

NICHOLAS STARR had a distinguished career in the CIA, rising to senior positions in the Directorate of Intelligence, Directorate of Operations, and the intelligence community. He entered on duty in 1961. His career ended tragically when terrorism came to the agency's doorstep on January 25, 1993. He retired in 1994. He has published a book of doggerel verse, *Paradise Mislaid*. His courage remains an inspiration to all of us who know him.

BOYD SUTTON, after retiring from the CIA in the late 1990s, moved to northwestern Wisconsin with his wife, Carmen, settling on her family's farm by a large lake. Boyd became active as a writer, producing a regular column for the local newspaper and publishing short stories, essays, and articles in magazines and newspapers. He produced the *Wisconsin Writers' Journal* from 2005 to 2010, was a member of the Wisconsin Writers' Association's board of directors from 2006 to 2011, and was the association's executive director from 2010 to 2011. He "retired" from those positions and is back to focusing on his writing. He has won prizes for humor, short stories, articles, essays, and juvenile short fiction.

WALTER E. SZUMINSKI entered on duty with the CIA in 1950 and retired in 1980. He received the Distinguished Intelligence Cross. He worked as a contractor for several different agency offices for the next decade. He also worked for ABC Auto Auction in Chantilly, Virginia. His hobbies have included flying, ham radio, and woodwork. He was active in his community's work shop until 2009.

Tony Williams retired from the CIA in August 2005 and assumed the Francis W. De Serio Chair of Strategic Intelligence at the U.S. Army War College, which he surrendered in May 2013. In 2005 Tony was also appointed Visiting Professor of Security Studies at Dickinson College, which position he currently holds. Since his retirement from the CIA Tony has also kept busy serving on the boards of various public service organizations in Central Pennsylvania and has led many battlefield tours of Gettysburg and Antietam for various church and social groups.